Becoming a Midwife:
A Complete Career Guide

Becoming a Midwife: A Complete Career Guide

Megan Jackson

STATES
ACADEMIC PRESS
www.statesacademicpress.com

Becoming a Midwife: A Complete Career Guide
Megan Jackson
ISBN: 978-1-63989-069-9 (Hardback)

Published by States Academic Press,
109 South 5th Street,
Brooklyn, NY 11249, USA

Cataloging-in-Publication Data

Becoming a midwife : a complete career guide / Megan Jackson.
    p. cm.
Includes bibliographical references and index.
ISBN 978-1-63989-069-9
1. Midwives--Vocational guidance. 2. Midwifery--Vocational guidance. I. Jackson, Megan.
RG950 .B43 2022
618.2--dc23

For more information regarding States Academic Press and its products, please visit the publisher's website www.statesacademicpress.com

Table of Contents

Permissions

Index

Preface

Midwifery is a health care profession that specializes in pregnancy, childbirth and the health of newborn infants. This area comes under the medical field of gynecology and obstetrics. Midwives provide support to women during childbirth and the postpartum period. They are responsible for the process of labor as well as the care for newborn infants. Midwives may work at a birthing center or at home. They can also direct clients to gynecologists and obstetricians if complications arise during childbirth. The topics covered in this extensive book deal with the core aspects of midwifery. It will serve as a reference to a broad spectrum of readers.

To facilitate a deeper understanding of the contents of this book a short introduction of every chapter is written below:

Chapter 1- Midwifery is the health profession that deals with childbirth and women's reproductive health. Midwives also provide care for newborn infants. This is an introductory chapter which will introduce briefly all the significant aspects of midwifery.

Chapter 2- Midwives provide prenatal care to pregnant women. Vaginal bleeding, fatigue and back pain are some issues that may arise during pregnancy. Diet and exercise are also provided by midwives. The topics elaborated in this chapter will help in gaining a better perspective about professional midwifery.

Chapter 3- Midwives provide care to reduce pain during childbirth. The woman's body goes through physiological changes that midwives monitor and assess. The aspects elucidated in this chapter are of vital importance and provide a better understanding of labor assistant in midwifery.

Chapter 4- The postpartum stage begins after childbirth and it is a period when the body is recovering. Complications may arise during this stage such as depression and hemorrhage. Midwives provide care for the mother as well as the baby during this period. Postpartum conditions dealt by midwives are best understood in confluence with the major topics listed in the following chapter.

Finally, I would like to thank the entire team involved in the inception of this book for their valuable time and contribution. This book would not have been possible without their efforts. I would also like to thank my friends and family for their constant support.

Megan Jackson

Midwifery: A Comprehensive Overview

Midwifery is the health profession that deals with childbirth and women's reproductive health. Midwives also provide care for newborn infants. This is an introductory chapter which will introduce briefly all the significant aspects of midwifery.

Midwifery

Midwifery, as known as obstetrics, is a health science and health profession that deals with pregnancy, childbirth, and the postpartum period (including care of the newborn), besides sexual and reproductive health of women throughout their lives. In many countries, midwifery is a medical profession (special for its independent and direct specialized education; should not be confused with a medical specialty, which depends on a previous general training). A professional in midwifery is known as a midwife.

A 2013 Cochrane review concluded that "most women should be offered midwifery-led continuity models of care and women should be encouraged to ask for this option although caution should be exercised in applying this advice to women with substantial medical or obstetric complications." The review found that midwifery-led care was associated with a reduction in the use of epidurals, with fewer episiotomies or instrumental births, and a decreased risk of losing the baby before 24 weeks' gestation. However, midwifery-led care was also associated with a longer mean length of labor as measured in hours.

Main Areas of Midwifery

Pregnancy-First Trimester

Trimester	Month	Week
1st	Month 1	1-4
	Month 2	5-8
	Month 3	9-13
2nd	Month 4	14-17
	Month 5	18-21
	Month 6	22-26
3rd	Month 7	27-30
	Month 8	31-35
	Month 9	36-40

This image shows the progression of pregnancy over the three trimesters.

Trimester means "3 months." A normal pregnancy lasts about 9 months and has 3 trimesters.

First trimester screening varies by country. Women are typically offered a Pap smear and urine analysis (UA), and blood tests including a complete blood count (CBC), blood typing (including Rh screen), syphilis, hepatitis, HIV, and rubella testing. Additionally, women may have chlamydia testing via a urine sample, and women considered at high risk are screened for Sickle Cell disease and Thalassemia. Women must consent to all tests before they are carried out. The woman's blood pressure, height and weight are measured. Her past pregnancies and family, social, and medical history are discussed. Women may have an ultrasound scan during the first trimester which may be used to help find the estimated due date. Some women may have genetic testing, such as screening for Down's Syndrome. Diet, exercise, and discomforts such as morning sickness are discussed.

Second Trimester

The mother visits the midwife monthly or more often during the second trimester. The mother's partner and/or the labor coach may accompany her. The midwife will discuss pregnancy issues such as fatigue, heartburn, varicose veins, and other common problems such as back pain. Blood pressure and weight are monitored and the midwife measures the mother's abdomen to see if the baby is growing as expected. Lab tests such as a UA, CBC, and glucose tolerance test are done if the midwife feels they are necessary.

Third Trimester

In the third trimester the midwife will see the mother every two weeks until week 36 and every week after that. Weight, blood pressure, and abdominal measurements will continue to be done. Lab tests such as a CDC and UA may be done with additional testing done for at-risk pregnancies. The midwife palpates the woman's abdomen to establish the lie, presentation and position of the fetus and later, the engagement. A pelvic exam may be done to see if the mother's cervix is dilating. The midwife and the mother discuss birthing options and write a birth care plan.

Childbirth

Labor and Delivery

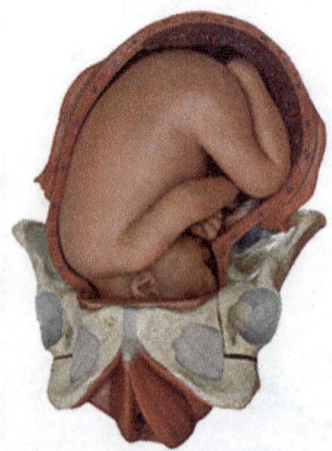

An illustration of normal head-first presentation. The membranes have ruptured and the cervix is fully dilated.

Midwives are qualified to assist with a normal vaginal delivery while more complicated deliveries are handled by a health care provider who has had further training. Childbirth is divided into four stages.

First stage of labor The first stage of labour involves the opening of the cervix. In the early parts of this stage the cervix will become soft and thin thus preparing for the delivery of the baby. The first stage of labour is complete when the cervix has dilated the full 10cm. During the first stage of labor the mother begins to feel strong and regular contractions that come every 5 to 20 minutes and last 30 to 60 seconds. Contractions gradually become stronger, more frequent, and longer lasting.

Second stage of labor During the second stage the baby begins to move down the birth canal. As the baby moves to the opening of the vagina it "crowns", meaning the top of the head can be seen at the vaginal entrance. At one time an "episiotomy", (an incision in the tissue at the opening of the vagina) was done routinely because it was believed that it prevented excessive tearing and healed more readily than a natural tear. However, more recent research shows that a surgical incision may be more extensive than a natural tear, and is more likely to contribute to later incontinence and pain during sex than a natural tear would have.

The midwife assists the baby as needed and when fully emerged, cuts the umbilical cord. If desired, the baby's father may cut the cord. In the past the cord was cut shortly after birth, but there is growing evidence that delayed cord-cutting may benefit the infant.

Third stage of labor The third stage of labour is where the mother must deliver the placenta. In order for the mother to do this they may need to push. Just like the contractions in the first stage of labour they may experience one or two of these. The midwife may assist the mother in delivering the placenta by gently pulling on the umbilical cord.

Fourth stage of labor The fourth stage of labor is the period beginning immediately after the birth and extending for about six weeks. The World Health Organization describes this period as the most critical and yet the most neglected phase in the lives of mothers and babies. Until recently babies were routinely removed from their mothers following birth, however beginning around 2000, some authorities began to suggest that early skin-to-skin contact (placing the naked baby on the mother's chest) is of benefit to both mother and infant. As of 2014, early skin-to-skin contact is endorsed by all major organizations that are responsible for the well-being of infants. Thus, to help establish bonding and successful breastfeeding, the midwife carries out immediate mother and infant assessments as the infant lies on the mother's chest and removes the infant for further observations only after they have had their first breastfeed.

Following the birth, if the mother had an episiotomy or a tearing of the perineum, it is stitched. The midwife does regular assessments for uterine contraction, fundal height, and vaginal bleeding. Throughout labor and delivery the mother's vital signs (temperature, blood pressure, and pulse) are closely monitored and her fluid intake and output are measured. The midwife also monitors the baby's pulse rate, palpates the mother's abdomen to monitor the baby's position, and does vaginal checks as needed. If the birth deviates from the norm at any stage, the midwife requests assist from a more highly trained health care provider.

Birthing Positions

Until the last century most women have used both the upright position and alternative positions to give birth. The lithotomy position was not used until the advent of forceps in the seventeenth century and since then childbirth has progressively moved from a woman supported experience in the home to a medical intervention within the hospital. There are significant advantages to assuming an upright position in labor and birth, such as stronger and more efficient uterine contractions aiding cervical dilatation, increased pelvic inlet and outlet diameters and improved uterine contractility. Upright positions in the second stage include sitting, squatting, kneeling, and being on hands and knees.

Postpartum Period

For women who have a hospital birth, the minimum hospital stay is six hours. Women who leave before this do so against medical advice. Women may choose when to leave the hospital. Full postnatal assessments are conducted daily whilst inpatient, or more frequently if needed. A postnatal assessment includes the woman's observations, general well being, breasts (either a discussion and assistance with breastfeeding or a discussion about lactation suppression), abdominal palpation (if she has not had a caesarean section) to check for involution of the uterus, or a check of her caesarean wound (the dressing doesn't need to be removed for this), a check of her perineum, particularly if she tore or had stitches, reviewing her lochia, ensuring she has passed urine and had her bowels open and checking for signs and symptoms of a DVT. The baby is also checked for jaundice, signs of adequate feeding, or other concerns. The baby has a nursery exam between six and seventy two hours of birth to check for conditions such as heart defects, hip problems, or eye problems.

In the community, the community midwife sees the woman at least until day ten. This does not mean she sees the woman and baby daily, but she cannot discharge them from her care until day ten at the earliest. Postnatal checks include neonatal screening test (NST, or heel prick test) around day five. The baby is weighed and the midwife plans visits according to the health and needs of mother and baby. They are discharged to the care of the health visitor.

Care of the Newborn

At birth, the baby receives an Apgar score at, at the least, one minute and five minutes of age. This is a score out of 10 that assesses the baby on five different areas—each worth between 0 and 2 points. These areas are: colour, respiratory effort, tone, heart rate, and response to stimuli. The midwife checks the baby for any obvious problems, weighs the baby, and measure head circumference. The midwife ensures the cord has been clamped securely and the baby has the appropriate name tags on (if in hospital). Babies lengths are not routinely measured. The midwife performs these checks as close to the mother as possible and returns the baby to the mother quickly. Skin-to-skin is encouraged, as this regulates the baby's heart rate, breathing, oxygen saturation, and temperature—and promotes bonding and breastfeeding.

In some countries, such as Chile, the midwife is the professional who can direct neonatal intensive care units. This is an advantage for these professionals, because this professionals can use the knowledge in perinatology to bring a high quality care of the newborn, with medical or surgical conditions.

Midwifery-led Continuity of Care

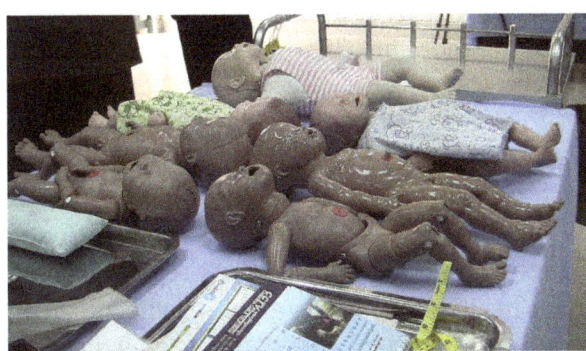

"Babies" for student practice

Midwifery-led continuity of care is where one or more midwives have the primary responsibility for the continuity of care for childbearing women, with a multidisciplinary network of consultation and referral with other health care providers. This is different from "medical-led care" where an obstetrician or family physician is primarily responsible. In "shared-care" models, responsibility may be shared between a midwife, an obstetrician and/or a family physician.

According to a Cochrane review of public health systems in Australia, Canada, Ireland, New Zealand and the United Kingdom, "most women should be offered midwifery-led continuity models of care and women should be encouraged to ask for this option although caution should be exercised in applying this advice to women with substantial medical or obstetric complications." Midwifery-led care has effects including the following:

- a reduction in the use of epidurals, with fewer episiotomies or instrumental births.

- a longer mean length of labour as measured in hours

- increased chances of being cared for in labour by a midwife known by the childbearing woman

- increased chances of having a spontaneous vaginal birth

- decreased risk of preterm birth

- decreased risk of losing the baby before 24 weeks' gestation, although there appears to be no differences in the risk of losing the baby after 24 weeks or overall

There was no difference in the number of Caesarean sections. All trials in the Cochrane review included licensed midwives, and none included lay or traditional midwives. Also, no trial included out of hospital birth.

Emotional Stress on Midwives

Midwives are rostered to work long hours, this not only results in physical exhaustion but also emotional exhaustion. The most stressful situations that occur for a midwife are during their routine work. The most stressful part of their routines is when it comes down to life or death situations with mother or baby. These events may be sudden and unpredictable which puts a large amount of stress on the attending midwives. When these situations occur midwives general have a lack of control and can become quickly stressed. Due to the update in technology the many common complications that can occur during childbirth are now easily prevented or easily attended to. Although on rare occasions midwives cannot do anything more but their best and sometimes that is not enough.

Midwife

A midwife is a professional in midwifery, specializing in pregnancy, childbirth, postpartum, women's sexual and reproductive health (including annual gynecological exams, family planning, menopausal care and others), and newborn care. They are also educated and trained to recognise the variations of normal progress of labor, and understand how to deal with deviations from normal. They may intervene in high risk situations such as breech births, twin births and births where the baby is in a posterior position, using non-invasive techniques. When a pregnant woman requires care beyond the midwife's scope of practice, they refer women to obstetricians or perinatologists who are medical specialists in complications related to pregnancy and birth, including surgical and instrumental deliveries. In many parts of the world, these professions work in tandem to provide care to childbearing women. In others, only the midwife is available to provide care, and in yet other countries many women elect to utilize obstetricians primarily over midwives.

Many developing countries are investing money and training for midwives as these services are needed all over the world. Some primary care services are currently lacking due to the shortage of money being funded for these resources.

A study performed by Melissa Cheyney and colleagues followed approximately 17,000 planned home births with the assistance of midwives. 93.6% of these families had a normal physiological birth and only 5% were Cesarean sections. In 2013, the rate of Cesarean sections in hospitals in the United States was 32.7%, which is double the rate that World Health Organization recommends.

Scope of Practice

Worldwide Midwives (112 countries), based on official information from the International Confederation of Midwives (ICM) 2017.

The midwife is recognised as a responsible and accountable professional who works in partnership with women to give the necessary support, care and advice during pregnancy, labour and the postpartum period, to conduct births on the midwife's own responsibility and to provide care for the newborn and the infant. This care includes preventative measures, the promotion of normal birth, the detection of complications in mother and child, the accessing of medical care or other appropriate assistance and the carrying out of emergency measures.

The midwife has an important task in health counselling and education, not only for the woman, but also within the family and the community. This work should involve antenatal education and preparation for parenthood and may extend to women's health, sexual or reproductive health and child care.

A midwife may practise in any setting including the home, community, hospitals, clinics or health units.

How to get into Midwifery

If you would like to be a midwife you need to get good grades at high school, especially in maths, english and science. You need to get at least 5 grade C's or above in your GCSE's. You will then have to attend college and do either 3 A-Levels or the equivalent. Work experience in a hospital or caring environment is important too.

Steps

1. Aim to get at least 5 GCSE's at grade A-C, in English, Maths and science.

2. Go to college after this and study A-levels, a science subject or health subject would be better than say studying French which isn't relevant to midwifery. You will need either 3 A levels and 5 GCSE's at grade A-C including maths, science and english, or an access to HE course if you are a mature student with no recent qualifications. Access to health course is the same as having just over 3 A levels.

3. Try to get some work experience in a caring environment like a nursing home, or on a maternity ward. Universities like their students to have a little work experience.

4. When applying to uni make sure you personal statement really shines. This is what will make you stand out from the rest of the applicants. Tell them why you want to be a midwife, what you have to offer, and any work experience you might have. Try to make your personal statement worth reading. But don't ramble on about your favourite TV show or your favourite food as they will not want to know.

5. If you get accepted at your uni. It will be a 3 year degree course as the diploma has been phased out. It is going to be a lot of hard work, but if it what you want then go for it.

How to become a Midwife

Midwives are trained healthcare providers who assist expectant mothers through the process of pregnancy, labor and delivery, in addition to providing postnatal care to both the mother and child. Midwives often assist women who wish to explore natural childbirth, offering emotional and spiritual guidance as well as providing primary physical care. This topic provides information on the role that midwives play, the educational requirements for becoming a midwife, and midwifery career options.

Method 1
Prepare for the Life of a Midwife

1. Understand the multilayered role of a midwife. Midwives have played the role of assisting women through the process of childbirth for centuries. Midwives traditionally operate under the philosophy that pregnancy and the act of giving birth can be a spiritual experience in a woman's life, and it's healthier to have as few instances of medical intervention as possible. Many say they have a calling to do the work they do. Midwives have the following responsibilities:

- Monitor the health of the mother and fetus throughout the pregnancy.

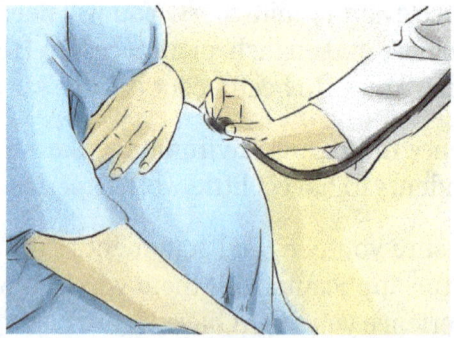

- Provide guidance to the mother on prenatal nutrition and self care as well as emotional well-being.

- Educate the mother on available options for labor and delivery, and empower her to make decisions that are right for her.

- Guide the mother and child through labor and delivery.

- Work with an obstetrician should complications arise.

2. Be ready to assume a high level of responsibility. Midwives are incredibly knowledgeable, highly skilled practitioners who take on the highest responsibility: they act as first responders in the unpredictable process of pregnancy, labor and delivery.

- Since every pregnancy is different and subject to a range of complications, midwives must be able to act confidently in emergency situations. Responsibility for both the mother and child's life lies in the midwives hands.

- Also important is the midwife's responsibility for the emotional and spiritual health of the mother, who looks to the midwife as a leader and guide through the confusing, painful, difficult process of childbirth.

- Women who choose to give birth under the care of an obstetrician may work with a midwife who is responsible for acting as the women's advocate in the hospital setting.

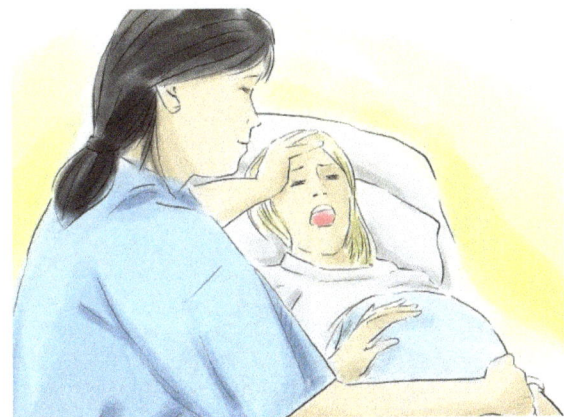

- Midwives are responsible for standing up for their own profession; in some states, it is illegal to practice midwifery.

3. Be willing to make personal sacrifices. Midwives work with women from the beginning of their pregnancy through the labor, delivery, and for months and sometimes years beyond. Due to the intimate, extraordinarily important nature of their work, midwives must be willing to put their clients' needs ahead of their own.

- Midwives must be on call at all times, since they never know exactly when a woman will go into labor.

- Labor can last anywhere from a few hours to a few days, and midwives must be present the entire time.

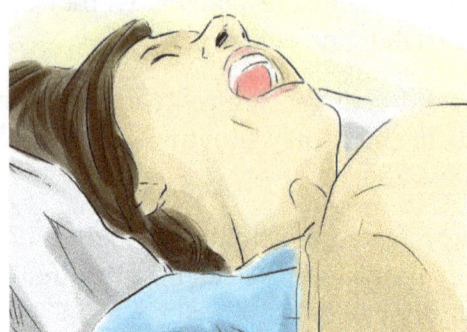

- Midwives are often emotionally present for expectant mothers, giving out their cell phone number and email address and making themselves available for questions or as a shoulder to lean on at stressful moments.

- Some midwives have to be flexible enough to move to a different city or state, since it's difficult to practice midwifery in some locations.

Method 2

Get the Experience you need to become a Midwife

1. Get an undergraduate degree. In order to become a midwife you will need a graduate degree, so

you must start by getting a bachelor's degree. Look into midwifery graduate programs to find out exactly what prerequisites you'll need. You should have a solid foundation in the following areas:

- The sciences. Take courses in chemistry, biology, anatomy, physiology and health.

- The social sciences. Take courses in psychology, sociology, and anthropology.

- Humanities courses such as women's studies and literature. If possible, study the history of the midwifery profession. Asking midwives about their views and experiences will help you gain more perspective on your planned field.

2. Get experience working with midwives. If possible, get an internship at a birthing center, or offer to volunteer. Contact midwives in your area and ask for informational interviews. Ask midwives what steps they took to achieve success in their profession.

- Keep up with the trends in midwifery. This will help you figure out what types of programs to consider.

Method 3

Complete a Midwifery Program and find a Job

1. Apply to midwifery graduate programs. Each midwifery program has a different "personality." Some require a degree in nursing before the midwifery study begins, and others are more focused on the philosophical, political or spiritual aspects of the profession. Find a program that's right for you and start the application process.

- The majority of midwives working in the United States today are Certified Nurse Midwives (CNMs). This certification is recognized in all fifty states.

- It is possible to become a midwife without also being a nurse and become a Certified Midwife (CM). This certification is only recognized by a few states. Choose the professional path that is right for you.

- Your personality is as important as your grades when it comes to getting into midwifery programs. Read books written by midwives and do research on the politics of the profession to inform your personal statement and essay. Demonstrate your passion for becoming a midwife. Explain why you think midwives play an important role in society today.

2. Complete the midwifery program. This will include a set amount of courses, a clinical internship and, depending on the program, a degree in nursing.

3. Pass the national certifying exam. In most countries you are required by law to take and pass an examination in order to get a license to practice midwifery.

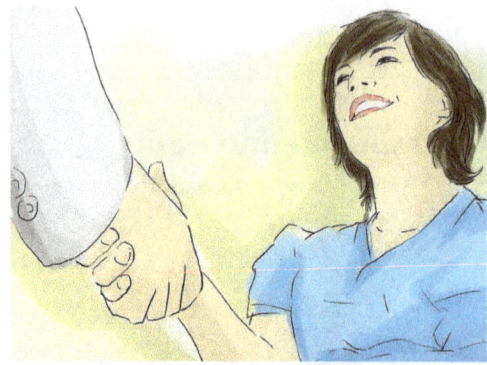

4. Find a job. You can look at hospitals, clinics, and birthing centers. Consider setting up a private practice.

- In addition to practicing as a midwife, you can use your knowledge to work as an educator at the undergraduate or graduate level.

- Health policy is another popular choice for CNMs and CMs.

- Some midwives work at nonprofits or other organizations that provide advocacy for women making their own health decisions.

Prenatal Medical Assistance in Midwifery

Midwives provide prenatal care to pregnant women. Vaginal bleeding, fatigue and back pain are some issues that may arise during pregnancy. Diet and exercise are also provided by midwives. The topics elaborated in this chapter will help in gaining a better perspective about professional midwifery.

Pregnancy

Pregnancy, also known as gestation, is the time during which one or more offspring develops inside a woman. A multiple pregnancy involves more than one offspring, such as with twins. Pregnancy can occur by sexual intercourse or assisted reproductive technology. Childbirth typically occurs around 40 weeks from the last menstrual period (LMP). This is just over nine months, where each month averages 29½ days. When measured from conception it is about 38 weeks. An embryo is the developing offspring during the first eight weeks following conception, after which, the term *fetus* is used until birth. Symptoms of early pregnancy may include missed periods, tender breasts, nausea and vomiting, hunger, and frequent urination. Pregnancy may be confirmed with a pregnancy test.

Pregnancy is typically divided into three trimesters. The first trimester is from week one through 12 and includes conception. Conception is when the sperm fertilizes the egg. The fertilized egg then travels down the fallopian tube and attaches to the inside of the uterus, where it begins to form the embryo and placenta. The first trimester carries the highest risk of miscarriage (natural death of embryo or fetus). The second trimester is from week 13 through 28. Around the middle of the second trimester, movement of the fetus may be felt. At 28 weeks, more than 90% of babies can survive outside of the uterus if provided with high-quality medical care. The third trimester is from 29 weeks through 40 weeks.

Prenatal care improves pregnancy outcomes. Prenatal care may include taking extra folic acid, avoiding drugs and alcohol, regular exercise, blood tests, and regular physical examinations. Complications of pregnancy may include disorders of high blood pressure, gestational diabetes, iron-deficiency anemia, and severe nausea and vomiting among others. Term pregnancy is 37 to 41 weeks, with early term being 37 and 38 weeks, full term 39 and 40 weeks, and late term 41 weeks. After 41 weeks, it is known as post term. Babies born before 37 weeks are preterm and are at higher risk of health problems such as cerebral palsy. Delivery before 39 weeks by labor induction or caesarean section is not recommended unless required for other medical reasons.

About 213 million pregnancies occurred in 2012, of which, 190 million were in the developing world and 23 million were in the developed world. The number of pregnancies in women ages 15 to 44 is 133 per 1,000 women. About 10% to 15% of recognized pregnancies end in miscarriage. In 2013, complications of pregnancy resulted in 293,000 deaths, down from 377,000 deaths in 1990. Common causes include maternal bleeding, complications of abortion, high blood pressure of pregnancy, maternal sepsis, and obstructed labor. Globally, 40% of pregnancies are unplanned.

Half of unplanned pregnancies are aborted. Among unintended pregnancies in the United States, 60% of the women used birth control to some extent during the month pregnancy occurred.

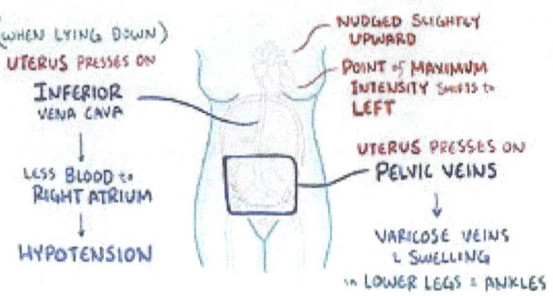

Terminology

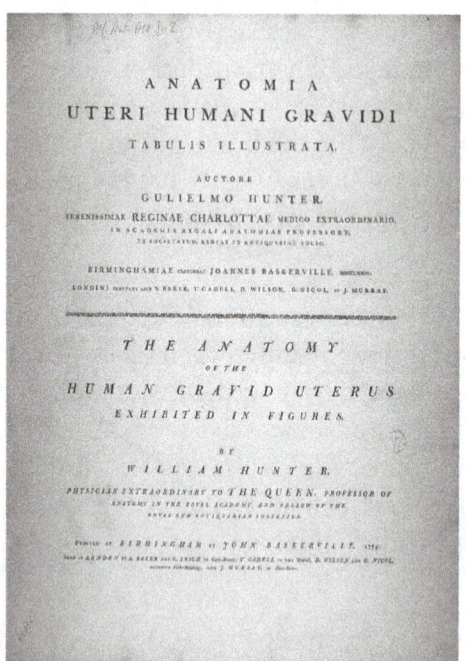

William Hunter, Anatomia uteri humani gravidi tabulis illustrata, 1774

Associated terms for pregnancy are *gravid* and *parous*. *Gravidus* and *gravid* come from the Latin for "heavy" and a pregnant female is sometimes referred to as a *gravida*. Gravidity is a term used to describe the number of times that a female has been pregnant. Similarly, the term *parity* is used for the number of times that a female carries a pregnancy to a viable stage. Twins and other multiple births are counted as one pregnancy and birth. A woman who has never been pregnant is referred to as a *nulligravida*. A woman who is (or has been only) pregnant for the first time is referred to as a *primigravida*, and a woman in subsequent pregnancies as a *multigravida* or as *multiparous*. Therefore, during a second pregnancy a woman would be described as *gravida 2, para 1* and upon live delivery as *gravida 2, para 2*. In-progress pregnancies, abortions, miscarriages and/or stillbirths account for parity values being less than the gravida number. In the case of a multiple birth the gravida number and parity value are increased by one only. Women who have never carried a pregnancy achieving more than 20 weeks of gestation age are referred to as *nulliparous*.

The terms *preterm* and *postterm* have largely replaced earlier terms of *premature* and *postmature*. *Preterm* and *postterm* are defined above, whereas *premature* and *postmature* have historical meaning and relate more to the infant's size and state of development rather than to the stage of pregnancy.

Signs and Symptoms

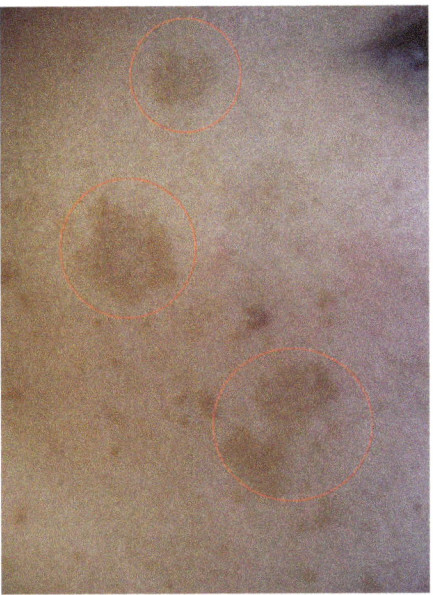

Melasma pigment changes to the face due to pregnancy

The symptoms and discomforts of pregnancy are those presentations and conditions that result from pregnancy but do not significantly interfere with activities of daily living or pose a threat to the health of the mother or baby. This is in contrast to pregnancy complications. Sometimes a symptom that is considered a discomfort can be considered a complication when it is more severe. For example, nausea (morning sickness) can be a discomfort, but if, in combination with significant vomiting it causes a water-electrolyte imbalance, it is a complication known as hyperemesis gravidarum.

Common symptoms and discomforts of pregnancy include:

- Tiredness.

- Constipation

- Pelvic girdle pain

- Back pain

- Braxton Hicks contractions. Occasional, irregular, and often painless contractions that occur several times per day.

- Edema (swelling). Common complaint in advancing pregnancy. Caused by compression of the inferior vena cava and pelvic veins by the uterus leads to increased hydrostatic pressure in lower extremities.

- Increased urinary frequency. A common complaint, caused by increased intravascular volume, elevated glomerular filtration rate, and compression of the bladder by the expanding uterus.

- Urinary tract infection

- Varicose veins. Common complaint caused by relaxation of the venous smooth muscle and increased intravascular pressure.

- Haemorrhoids (piles). Swollen veins at or inside the anal area. Caused by impaired venous return, straining associated with constipation, or increased intra-abdominal pressure in later pregnancy.

- Regurgitation, heartburn, and nausea.

- Stretch marks

- Breast tenderness is common during the first trimester, and is more common in women who are pregnant at a young age.

In addition, pregnancy may result in pregnancy complication such as deep vein thrombosis or worsening of an intercurrent disease in pregnancy.

Chronology

The chronology of pregnancy is, unless otherwise specified, generally given as gestational age, where the starting point is the woman's last normal menstrual period (LMP), or the corresponding age of the gestation as estimated by a more accurate method if available. Sometimes, timing may also be done by fertilization age.

Start of Gestational Age

According to American Congress of Obstetricians and Gynecologists, the main methods to calculate gestational age are:

- Directly calculating the days since the beginning of the last menstrual period.

- Early obstetric ultrasound, comparing the size of an embryo or fetus to that of a reference group of pregnancies of known gestational age (such as calculated from last menstrual periods), and using the mean gestational age of other embryos or fetuses of the same size. If the gestational age as calculated from an early ultrasound is contradictory to the one calculated directly from the last menstrual period, it is still the one from the early ultrasound that is used for the rest of the pregnancy.

- In case of in vitro fertilization, calculating days since oocyte retrieval or co-incubation and adding 14 days.

Estimation of Due Date

Due date estimation basically follows two steps:

- Determination of which time point is to be used as origin for gestational age, as described in section above.

- Adding the estimated gestational age at childbirth to the above time point. Childbirth on average occurs at a gestational age of 280 days (40 weeks), which is therefore often used as a standard estimation for individual pregnancies. However, alternative durations as well as more individualized methods have also been suggested.

Naegele's rule is a standard way of calculating the due date for a pregnancy when assuming a gestational age of 280 days at childbirth. The rule estimates the expected date of delivery (EDD) by adding a year, subtracting three months, and adding seven days to the origin of gestational age. Alternatively there are mobile apps, which essentially always give consistent estimations compared to each other and correct for leap year, while pregnancy wheels made of paper can differ from each other by 7 days and generally do not correct for leap year.

If gestational age has been determined by ultrasound, it is typically accurate within seven days. This means that fewer than 5 percent of births occur on the day of being 40 weeks of gestational age; 50 percent of births are within a week of this duration, and about 80 percent are within 2 weeks.

Physiology

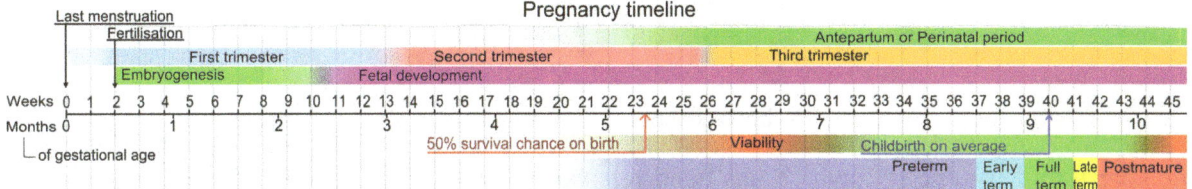

Timeline of pregnancy by gestational age

Initiation

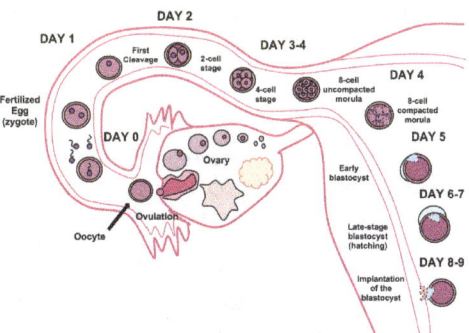

Fertilization and implantation in humans

Through an interplay of hormones that includes follicle stimulating hormone that stimulates folliculogenesis and oogenesis creates a mature egg cell, the female gamete. Fertilization is the event where the egg cell fuses with the male gamete, spermatozoon. After the point of fertilization, the fused product of the female and male gamete is referred to as a zygote or fertilized egg. The fusion of male and female gametes usually occurs following the act of sexual intercourse. Fertilization can also occur by assisted reproductive technology such as artificial insemination and in vitro fertilisation.

Fertilization (conception) is sometimes used as the initiation of pregnancy, with the derived age being termed fertilization age. Fertilization usually occurs about two weeks before the *next* expected menstrual period.

A third point in time is also considered by some people to be the true beginning of a pregnancy: This is time of implantation, when the future fetus attaches to the lining of the uterus. This is about a week to ten days after fertilization. In this model, during the time between conception and implantation, the future fetus exists, but the woman is not considered pregnant.

Development of Embryo and Fetus

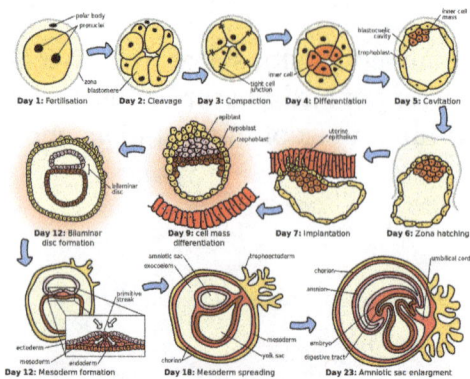

The initial stages of human embryogenesis

The sperm and the egg cell, which has been released from one of the female's two ovaries, unite in one of the two fallopian tubes. The fertilized egg, known as a zygote, then moves toward the uterus, a journey that can take up to a week to complete. Cell division begins approximately 24 to 36 hours after the male and female cells unite. Cell division continues at a rapid rate and the cells then develop into what is known as a blastocyst. The blastocyst arrives at the uterus and attaches to the uterine wall, a process known as implantation.

The development of the mass of cells that will become the infant is called embryogenesis during the first approximately ten weeks of gestation. During this time, cells begin to differentiate into the various body systems. The basic outlines of the organ, body, and nervous systems are established. By the end of the embryonic stage, the beginnings of features such as fingers, eyes, mouth, and ears become visible. Also during this time, there is development of structures important to the support of the embryo, including the placenta and umbilical cord. The placenta connects the developing embryo to the uterine wall to allow nutrient uptake, waste elimination, and gas exchange via the mother's blood supply. The umbilical cord is the connecting cord from the embryo or fetus to the placenta.

After about ten weeks of gestational age, the embryo becomes known as a fetus. At the beginning of the fetal stage, the risk of miscarriage decreases sharply. At this stage, a fetus is about 30 mm (1.2 inches) in length, the heartbeat is seen via ultrasound, and the fetus makes involuntary motions. During continued fetal development, the early body systems, and structures that were established in the embryonic stage continue to develop. Sex organs begin to appear during the third month of gestation. The fetus continues to grow in both weight and length, although the majority of the physical growth occurs in the last weeks of pregnancy.

Electrical brain activity is first detected between the fifth and sixth week of gestation. It is considered primitive neural activity rather than the beginning of conscious thought. Synapses begin forming at 17 weeks, and begin to multiply quickly at week 28 until 3 to 4 months after birth.

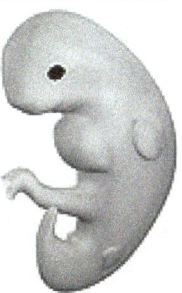

Embryo at 4 weeks after fertilization. (Image from gestational age of 6 weeks). Retrieved 2007-08-28.

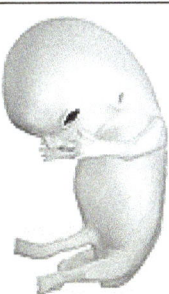

Fetus at 8 weeks after fertilization. (Image from gestational age of 10 weeks). Retrieved 2007-08-28.

Fetus at 18 weeks after fertilization. (Image from gestational age of 20 weeks). Retrieved 2007-08-28.

Fetus at 38 weeks after fertilization. (Image from gestational age of 40 weeks). Retrieved 2007-08-28.

Relative size in 1st month (simplified illustration)

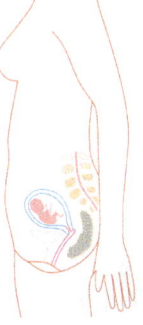

Relative size in 3rd month (simplified illustration)

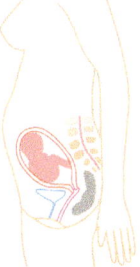

Relative size in 5th month (simplified illustration)

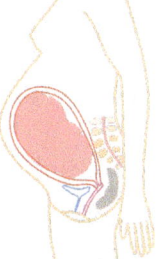

Relative size in 9th month (simplified illustration)

Maternal Changes

During pregnancy, the woman undergoes many physiological changes, which are entirely normal, including cardiovascular, hematologic, metabolic, renal, and respiratory changes. Increases in blood sugar, breathing, and cardiac output are all required. Levels of progesterone and oestrogens rise continually throughout pregnancy, suppressing the hypothalamic axis and therefore also the menstrual cycle.

The fetus is genetically different from the woman and can be viewed as an unusually successful allograft. The main reason for this success is increased immune tolerance during pregnancy. Immune tolerance is the concept that the body is able to not mount an immune system response against certain triggers.

Pregnancy is typically broken into three periods, or trimesters, each of about three months. Each trimester is defined as 14 weeks, for a total duration of 42 weeks, although the average duration of pregnancy is 40 weeks. While there are no hard and fast rules, these distinctions are useful in describing the changes that take place over time.

First Trimester

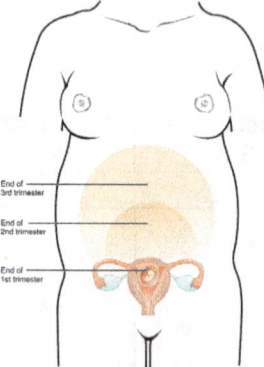

The uterus as it changes in size over the duration of the trimesters

Minute ventilation increases by 40% in the first trimester. The womb will grow to the size of a lemon by eight weeks. Many symptoms and discomforts of pregnancy like nausea and tender breasts appear in the first trimester.

Second Trimester

Weeks 13 to 28 of the pregnancy are called the second trimester. Most women feel more energized in this period, and begin to put on weight as the symptoms of morning sickness subside and eventually fade away. The uterus, the muscular organ that holds the developing fetus, can expand up to 20 times its normal size during pregnancy.

Although the fetus begins to move during the first trimester, it is not until the second trimester that movement, often referred to as "quickening", can be felt. This typically happens in the fourth month, more specifically in the 20th to 21st week, or by the 19th week if the woman has been pregnant before. It is common for some women not to feel the fetus move until much later. During the second trimester, most women begin to wear maternity clothes.

Third Trimester

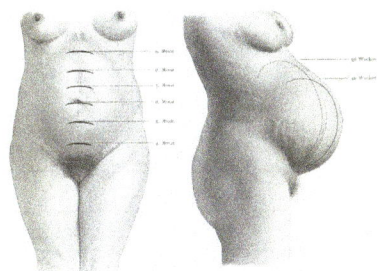

The uterus expands making up a larger and larger portion of the woman's abdomen. At left anterior view with months labeled, at right lateral view labeling the last 4 weeks. During the final stages of gestation before childbirth the fetus and uterus will drop to a lower position.

Final weight gain takes place, which is the most weight gain throughout the pregnancy. The woman's abdomen will transform in shape as it drops due to the fetus turning in a downward position ready for birth. During the second trimester, the woman's abdomen would have been upright, whereas in the third trimester it will drop down low. The fetus moves regularly, and is felt by the woman. Fetal movement can become strong and be disruptive to the woman. The woman's navel will sometimes become convex, "popping" out, due to the expanding abdomen.

Head engagement, where the fetal head descends into cephalic presentation, relieves pressure on the upper abdomen with renewed ease in breathing. It also severely reduces bladder capacity, and increases pressure on the pelvic floor and the rectum.

It is also during the third trimester that maternal activity and sleep positions may affect fetal development due to restricted blood flow. For instance, the enlarged uterus may impede blood flow by compressing the vena cava when lying flat, which is relieved by lying on the left side.

Childbirth

Childbirth, referred to as labor and delivery in the medical field, is the process whereby an infant is born.

A woman is considered to be in labour when she begins experiencing regular uterine contractions, accompanied by changes of her cervix – primarily effacement and dilation. While childbirth is widely experienced as painful, some women do report painless labours, while others find that concentrating on the birth helps to quicken labour and lessen the sensations. Most births are successful vaginal births, but sometimes complications arise and a woman may undergo a cesarean section.

During the time immediately after birth, both the mother and the baby are hormonally cued to bond, the mother through the release of oxytocin, a hormone also released during breastfeeding. Studies show that skin-to-skin contact between a mother and her newborn immediately after birth is beneficial for both the mother and baby. A review done by the World Health Organization found that skin-to-skin contact between mothers and babies after birth reduces crying, improves mother–infant interaction, and helps mothers to breastfeed successfully. They recommend that neonates be allowed to bond with the mother during their first two hours after birth, the period that they tend to be more alert than in the following hours of early life.

Childbirth Maturity stages

Stages of pregnancy term		
stage	starts	ends
Preterm	-	at 37 weeks
Early term	37 weeks	39 weeks
Full term	39 weeks	41 weeks
Late term	41 weeks	42 weeks
Postterm	42 weeks	-

In the ideal childbirth labor begins on its own when a woman is "at term". Pregnancy is considered at term when gestation has lasted between 37 and 42 weeks.

Events before completion of 37 weeks are considered preterm. Preterm birth is associated with a range of complications and should be avoided if possible.

Sometimes if a woman's water breaks or she has contractions before 39 weeks, birth is unavoidable. However, spontaneous birth after 37 weeks is considered term and is not associated with the same risks of a pre-term birth. Planned birth before 39 weeks by Caesarean section or labor induction, although "at term", results in an increased risk of complications. This is from factors including underdeveloped lungs of newborns, infection due to underdeveloped immune system, feeding problems due to underdeveloped brain, and jaundice from underdeveloped liver.

Babies born between 39 and 41 weeks gestation have better outcomes than babies born either before or after this range. This special time period is called "full term". Whenever possible, waiting for labor to begin on its own in this time period is best for the health of the mother and baby. The decision to perform an induction must be made after weighing the risks and benefits, but is safer after 39 weeks.

Events after 42 weeks are considered postterm. When a pregnancy exceeds 42 weeks, the risk of complications for both the woman and the fetus increases significantly. Therefore, in an otherwise uncomplicated pregnancy, obstetricians usually prefer to induce labour at some stage between 41 and 42 weeks.

Postnatal Period

The postnatal period, also referred to as the *puerperium*, begins immediately after delivery and extends for about six weeks. During this period, the mother's body begins the return to pre-pregnancy conditions that includes changes in hormone levels and uterus size.

Diagnosis

The beginning of pregnancy may be detected either based on symptoms by the woman herself, or by using pregnancy tests. However, an important condition with serious health implications that is quite common is the denial of pregnancy by the pregnant woman. About one in 475 denials will last until around the 20th week of pregnancy. The proportion of cases of denial, persisting until delivery is about 1 in 2500. Conversely, some non-pregnant women have a very strong belief that they are pregnant along with some of the physical changes. This condition is known as a false pregnancy.

Physical Signs

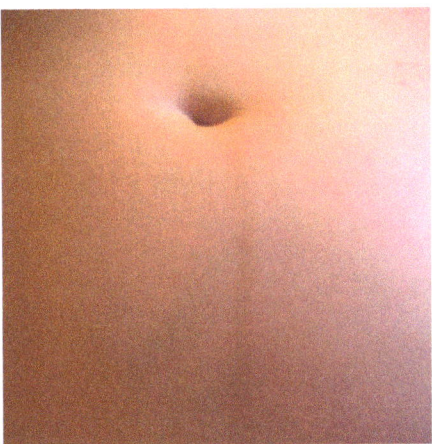

Linea nigra in a woman at 22 weeks pregnant

Most pregnant women experience a number of symptoms, which can signify pregnancy. A number of early medical signs are associated with pregnancy. These signs include:

- the presence of human chorionic gonadotropin (hCG) in the blood and urine

- missed menstrual period

- implantation bleeding that occurs at implantation of the embryo in the uterus during the third or fourth week after last menstrual period

- increased basal body temperature sustained for over 2 weeks after ovulation

- Chadwick's sign (darkening of the cervix, vagina, and vulva)

- Goodell's sign (softening of the vaginal portion of the cervix)

- Hegar's sign (softening of the uterus isthmus)

- Pigmentation of the linea alba – linea nigra, (darkening of the skin in a midline of the abdomen, caused by hyperpigmentation resulting from hormonal changes, usually appearing around the middle of pregnancy).

- Darkening of the nipples and areolas due to an increase in hormones.

Biomarkers

Pregnancy detection can be accomplished using one or more various pregnancy tests, which detect hormones generated by the newly formed placenta, serving as biomarkers of pregnancy. Blood and urine tests can detect pregnancy 12 days after implantation. Blood pregnancy tests are more sensitive than urine tests (giving fewer false negatives). Home pregnancy tests are urine tests, and normally detect a pregnancy 12 to 15 days after fertilization. A quantitative blood test can determine approximately the date the embryo was conceived because HCG doubles every 36 to 48 hours. A single test of progesterone levels can also help determine how likely a fetus will survive in those with a threatened miscarriage (bleeding in early pregnancy).

Ultrasound

Obstetric ultrasonography can detect fetal abnormalities, detect multiple pregnancies, and improve gestational dating at 24 weeks. The resultant estimated gestational age and due date of the fetus are slightly more accurate than methods based on last menstrual period. Ultrasound is used to measure the nuchal fold in order to screen for Downs syndrome.

Management

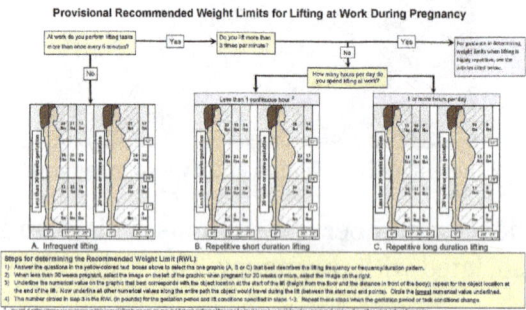

Flowchart showing the recommended weight limits for lifting at work during pregnancy as a function of lifting frequency, weeks of gestation, and the position of the lifted object relative to the lifter's body.

Prenatal Care

Pre-conception counseling is care that is provided to a woman and/ or couple to discuss conception, pregnancy, current health issues and recommendations for the period before pregnancy.

Prenatal medical care is the medical and nursing care recommended for women during pregnancy, time intervals and exact goals of each visit differ by country. Women who are high risk have better outcomes if they are seen regularly and frequently by a medical professional than women who are low risk. A woman can be labeled as high risk for different reasons including previous complications in pregnancy, complications in the current pregnancy, current medical diseases, or social issues.

The aim of good prenatal care is prevention, early identification, and treatment of any medical complications. A basic prenatal visit consists of measurement of blood pressure, fundal height, weight and fetal heart rate, checking for symptoms of labor, and guidance for what to expect next.

Nutrition

Nutrition during pregnancy is important to ensure healthy growth of the fetus. Nutrition during pregnancy is different from the non-pregnant state. There are increased energy requirements and specific micronutrient requirements. Women benefit from education to encourage a balanced energy and protein intake during pregnancy. Some women may need professional medical advice if their diet is affected by medical conditions, food allergies, or specific religious/ ethical beliefs.

Adequate periconceptional (time before and right after conception) folic acid (also called folate or Vitamin B$_9$) intake has been shown to decrease the risk of fetal neural tube defects, such as spina bifida. The neural tube develops during the first 28 days of pregnancy, a urine pregnancy test is not usually positive until 14 days post-conception, explaining the necessity to guarantee adequate folate intake before conception. Folate is abundant in green leafy vegetables, legumes, and citrus. In the United States and Canada, most wheat products (flour, noodles) are fortified with folic acid.

DHA omega-3 is a major structural fatty acid in the brain and retina, and is naturally found in breast milk. It is important for the woman to consume adequate amounts of DHA during pregnancy and while nursing to support her well-being and the health of her infant. Developing infants cannot produce DHA efficiently, and must receive this vital nutrient from the woman through the placenta during pregnancy and in breast milk after birth.

Several micronutrients are important for the health of the developing fetus, especially in areas of the world where insufficient nutrition is common. Multiple micronutrient supplementation containing iron and folic acid improves birth outcomes in developing countries, but has no effect on perinatal mortality. In developed areas, such as Western Europe and the United States, certain nutrients such as Vitamin D and calcium, required for bone development, may require supplementation. Vitamin E supplementation has not been shown to improve birth outcomes. Zinc supplementation has been associated with a decrease in preterm birth, but it is unclear whether it is causative. Daily iron supplementation reduces the risk of maternal anemia. Studies of routine daily iron supplementation for all pregnant women in developed countries found improvement in blood iron levels, without a clear clinical benefit.

Women are counseled to avoid certain foods, because of the possibility of contamination with bacteria or parasites that can cause illness. Careful washing of fruits and raw vegetables may remove these pathogens, as may thoroughly cooking leftovers, meat, or processed meat. Unpasteurized dairy and deli meats may contain *Listeria,* which can cause neonatal meningitis, stillbirth and miscarriage. Pregnant women are also more prone to *Salmonella* infections, can be in eggs and poultry, which should be thoroughly cooked. Cat feces and undercooked meats may contain the parasite Toxoplasma gondii and can cause toxoplasmosis. Practicing good hygiene in the kitchen can reduce these risks.

Women are also counseled to eat seafood in moderation and to eliminate seafood known to be high in mercury because of the risk of birth defects. Pregnant women are counseled to consume caffeine in moderation, because large amounts of caffeine are associated with miscarriage. However, the relationship between caffeine, birthweight, and preterm birth is unclear.

Weight Gain

The amount of healthy weight gain during a pregnancy varies. Weight gain is related to the weight of the baby, the placenta, extra circulatory fluid, larger tissues, and fat and protein stores. Most needed weight gain occurs later in pregnancy.

The Institute of Medicine recommends an overall pregnancy weight gain for those of normal weight (body mass index of 18.5–24.9), of 11.3–15.9 kg (25–35 pounds) having a singleton pregnancy. Women who are underweight (BMI of less than 18.5), should gain between 12.7–18 kg (28–40 lbs), while those who are overweight (BMI of 25–29.9) are advised to gain between 6.8–11.3 kg (15–25 lbs) and those who are obese (BMI>30) should gain between 5–9 kg (11–20 lbs). These values reference the expectations for a term pregnancy. The Friedmann-Balayla Model provides a more accurate calculation of weight gain by gestational age.

During pregnancy, insufficient or excessive weight gain can compromise the health of the mother and fetus. The most effective intervention for weight gain in underweight women is not clear. Being or becoming overweight in pregnancy increases the risk of complications for mother and fetus, including cesarean section, gestational hypertension, pre-eclampsia, macrosomia and shoulder dystocia. Excessive weight gain can make losing weight after the pregnancy difficult.

Around 50% of women of childbearing age in developed countries like the United Kingdom are overweight or obese before pregnancy. Diet modification is the most effective way to reduce weight gain and associated risks in pregnancy. A diet that has foods with a low glycemic index may help prevent the onset of gestational diabetes.

Medication

Drugs used during pregnancy can have temporary or permanent effects on the fetus. Anything (including drugs) that can cause permanent deformities in the fetus are labeled as teratogens. In the U.S., drugs were classified into categories A, B, C, D and X based on the Food and Drug Administration (FDA) rating system to provide therapeutic guidance based on potential benefits and fetal risks. Drugs, including some multivitamins, that have demonstrated no fetal risks after controlled studies in humans are classified as Category A. On the other hand, drugs like thalidomide with proven fetal risks that outweigh all benefits are classified as Category X.

Recreational Drugs

The use of recreational drugs in pregnancy can cause various pregnancy complications.

- Ethanol during pregnancy can cause fetal alcohol syndrome and fetal alcohol spectrum disorder. Studies have shown that light to moderate drinking during pregnancy might not pose a risk to the fetus, although no amount of alcohol during pregnancy can be guaranteed to be absolutely safe.

- Tobacco smoking during pregnancy can cause a wide range of behavioral, neurological, and physical difficulties. Smoking during pregnancy causes twice the risk of premature rupture of membranes, placental abruption and placenta previa. Smoking is associated with 30% higher odds of preterm birth.

- Prenatal cocaine exposure is associated with premature birth, birth defects and attention deficit disorder.

- Prenatal methamphetamine exposure can cause premature birth and congenital abnormalities. Short-term neonatal outcomes show small deficits in infant neurobehavioral function and growth restriction. Long-term effects in terms of impaired brain development may also be caused by methamphetamine use.

- Cannabis in pregnancy has been shown to be teratogenic in large doses in animals, but has not shown any teratogenic effects in humans.

Exposure to Toxins

Intrauterine exposure to environmental toxins in pregnancy has the potential to cause adverse effects on the development of the embryo/fetus and to cause pregnancy complications. Air pollution has been associated with low birth weight infants. Conditions of particular severity in pregnancy include mercury poisoning and lead poisoning. To minimize exposure to environmental toxins, the *American College of Nurse-Midwives* recommends: checking whether the home has lead paint, washing all fresh fruits and vegetables thoroughly and buying organic produce, and avoiding cleaning products labeled "toxic" or any product with a warning on the label.

Pregnant women can also be exposed to toxins in the workplace, including airborne particles. The effects of wearing N95 filtering facepiece respirators are similar for pregnant women as non-pregnant women, and wearing a respirator for one hour does not affect the fetal heart rate.

Sexual Activity

Most women can continue to engage in sexual activity throughout pregnancy. Most research suggests that during pregnancy both sexual desire and frequency of sexual relations decrease. In context of this overall decrease in desire, some studies indicate a second-trimester increase, preceding a decrease during the third trimester.

Sex during pregnancy is a low-risk behavior except when the healthcare provider advises that sexual intercourse be avoided for particular medical reasons. For a healthy pregnant woman, there is no *safe* or *right* way to have sex during pregnancy. Pregnancy alters the vaginal flora with a reduction in microscopic species/genus diversity.

Exercise

Regular aerobic exercise during pregnancy appears to improve (or maintain) physical fitness. Physical exercise during pregnancy does appear to decrease the risk of C-section. Bed rest, outside of research studies, is not recommended as there is no evidence of benefit and potential harm.

The Clinical Practice Obstetrics Committee of Canada recommends that "All women without contraindications should be encouraged to participate in aerobic and strength-conditioning exercises as part of a healthy lifestyle during their pregnancy". Although an upper level of safe exercise intensity has not been established, women who were regular exercisers before pregnancy and who have uncomplicated pregnancies should be able to engage in high intensity exercise programs. In general, participation in a wide range of recreational activities appears to be safe, with the avoidance of those with a high risk of falling such as horseback riding or skiing or those that carry a risk of abdominal trauma, such as soccer or hockey.

The American College of Obstetricians and Gynecologists reports that in the past, the main concerns of exercise in pregnancy were focused on the fetus and any potential maternal benefit was thought to be offset by potential risks to the fetus. However, they write that more recent information suggests that in the uncomplicated pregnancy, fetal injuries are highly unlikely. They do, however, list several circumstances when a woman should contact her health care provider before continuing with an exercise program: vaginal bleeding, dyspnea before exertion, dizziness, headache, chest pain, muscle weakness, preterm labor, decreased fetal movement, amniotic fluid leakage, and calf pain or swelling (to rule out thrombophlebitis).

Sleep

It has been suggested that shift work and exposure to bright light at night should be avoided at least during the last trimester of pregnancy to decrease the risk of psychological and behavioral problems in the newborn.

Complications

Each year, ill health as a result of pregnancy is experienced (sometimes permanently) by more than 20 million women around the world. In 2013 complications of pregnancy resulted in 293,000 deaths down from 377,000 deaths in 1990. Common causes include maternal bleeding (44,000), complications of abortion (44,000), high blood pressure of pregnancy (29,000), maternal sepsis (24,000), and obstructed labor (19,000).

The following are some examples of pregnancy complications:

- Pregnancy induced hypertension
- Anemia
- Postpartum depression
- Postpartum psychosis
- Thromboembolic disorders. These are the leading cause of death in pregnant women in the US.
- PUPPP (Pruritic Urticarial Papules and Plaques of Pregnancy), a skin disease that develops around the 32nd week. Signs are red plaques, papules, and itchiness around the belly button that then spreads all over the body except for the inside of hands and face.
- Ectopic pregnancy, implantation of the embryo outside the uterus.
- Hyperemesis gravidarum, excessive nausea and vomiting that is more severe than normal morning sickness.
- Pulmonary embolism, blood clots that form in the legs that can migrate to the lungs.

There is also an increased susceptibility and severity of certain infections in pregnancy.

Intercurrent Diseases

A pregnant woman may have intercurrent diseases, defined as disease not directly caused by the pregnancy, but that may become worse or be a potential risk to the pregnancy.

- Diabetes mellitus and pregnancy deals with the interactions of diabetes mellitus (not restricted to gestational diabetes) and pregnancy. Risks for the child include miscarriage, growth restriction, growth acceleration, fetal obesity (macrosomia), polyhydramnios (too much amniotic fluid), and birth defects.

- Thyroid disease in pregnancy can, if uncorrected, cause adverse effects on fetal and maternal well-being. The deleterious effects of thyroid dysfunction can also extend beyond pregnancy and delivery to affect neurointellectual development in the early life of the child. Demand for thyroid hormones is increased during pregnancy which may cause a previously unnoticed thyroid disorder to worsen.

- Untreated celiac disease can cause spontaneous abortion (miscarriage), intrauterine growth restriction, small for gestational age, low birthweight and preterm birth. Often reproductive disorders are the only manifestation of undiagnosed celiac disease and most cases are not recognized. Complications or failures of pregnancy cannot be explained simply by malabsorption, but by the autoimmune response elicited by the exposure to gluten, which causes damage to the placenta. The gluten-free diet avoids or reduces the risk of developing reproductive disorders in pregnant women with celiac disease. Also, pregnancy can be a trigger for the development of celiac disease in genetically susceptible women who are consuming gluten.

- Systemic lupus erythematosus in pregnancy confers an increased rate of fetal death *in utero,* spontaneous abortion, and of neonatal lupus.

- Hypercoagulability in pregnancy is the propensity of pregnant women to develop thrombosis (blood clots). Pregnancy itself is a factor of hypercoagulability (pregnancy-induced hypercoagulability), as a physiologically adaptive mechanism to prevent *post partum* bleeding. However, in combination with an underlying hypercoagulable states, the risk of thrombosis or embolism may become substantial.

Medical Imaging

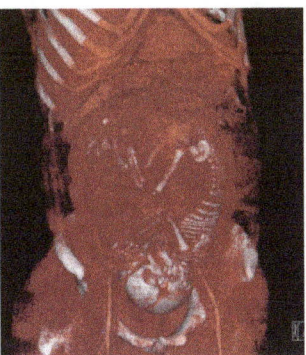

CT scanning (volume rendered in this case) confers a radiation dose to the developing fetus.

Medical imaging may be indicated in pregnancy because of pregnancy complications, intercurrent diseases or routine prenatal care. Magnetic resonance imaging (MRI) without MRI contrast agents as well as obstetric ultrasonography are not associated with any risk for the mother or the fetus, and are the imaging techniques of choice for pregnant women. Projectional radiography, X-ray computed tomography and nuclear medicine imaging result in some degree of ionizing radiation exposure, but in most cases the absorbed doses are not associated with harm to the baby. At higher dosages, effects can include miscarriage, birth defects and intellectual disability.

Epidemiology

About 213 million pregnancies occurred in 2012 of which 190 million were in the developing world and 23 million were in the developed world. This is about 133 pregnancies per 1,000 women between the ages of 15 and 44. About 10% to 15% of recognized pregnancies end in miscarriage. Globally 40% of pregnancies are unplanned. Half of unplanned pregnancies are aborted.

Of pregnancies in 2012 120 million occurred in Asia, 54 million in Africa, 19 million in Europe, 18 million in Latin America and the Caribbean, 7 million in North America, and 1 million in Oceania. Pregnancy rates are 140 per 1000 women of childbearing age in the developing world and 94 per 1000 in the developed world.

The rate of pregnancy, as well as the ages at which it occurs, differ by country and region. It is influenced by a number of factors, such as cultural, social and religious norms; access to contraception; and rates of education. The total fertility rate (TFR) in 2013 was estimated to be highest in Niger (7.03 children/woman) and lowest in Singapore (0.79 children/woman).

In Europe, the average childbearing age has been rising continuously for some time. In Western, Northern, and Southern Europe, first-time mothers are on average 26 to 29 years old, up from 23 to 25 years at the start of the 1970s. In a number of European countries (Spain), the mean age of women at first childbirth has crossed the 30-year threshold.

This process is not restricted to Europe. Asia, Japan and the United States are all seeing average age at first birth on the rise, and increasingly the process is spreading to countries in the developing world like China, Turkey and Iran. In the US, the average age of first childbirth was 25.4 in 2010.

In the United States and United Kingdom, 40% of pregnancies are unplanned, and between a quarter and half of those unplanned pregnancies were unwanted pregnancies.

Globally, an estimated 270,000 women die from pregnancy-related complications each year.

Infertility

Modern reproductive medicine offers many forms of assisted reproductive technology for couples who stay childless against their will, such as fertility medication, artificial insemination, *in vitro* fertilization and surrogacy.

Abortion

An abortion is the termination of an embryo or fetus, either naturally or via medical methods. When done electively, it is more often done within the first trimester than the second, and rarely in the third. Not using contraception, contraceptive failure, poor family planning or rape can lead to undesired pregnancies. Legality of socially indicated abortions varies widely both internationally and through time. In most countries of Western Europe, abortions during the first trimester were a criminal offense a few decades ago but have since been legalized, sometimes subject to mandatory consultations. In Germany, for example, as of 2009 less than 3% of abortions had a medical indication.

Legal Protection

Many countries have various legal regulations in place to protect pregnant women and their children. Maternity Protection Convention ensures that pregnant women are exempt from activities such as night shifts or carrying heavy stocks. Maternity leave typically provides paid leave from work during roughly the last trimester of pregnancy and for some time after birth. Notable extreme cases include Norway (8 months with full pay) and the United States (no paid leave at all except in some states). Moreover, many countries have laws against pregnancy discrimination.

In 2014, the American state of Kentucky passed a law which allows prosecutors to charge a woman with criminal assault if she uses illegal drugs during her pregnancy and her fetus or newborn is considered harmed as a result.

In the United States, laws make some actions that result in miscarriage or stillbirth crimes. One such law is the federal Unborn Victims of Violence Act.

How to Cope with Pregnancy Discomforts

Carrying a growing baby in the womb can bring about an onslaught of uncomfortable physical pains and irritations. Knowing how to alleviate many of these pains can make this part of the pregnancy process less of a burden, and help make your pregnancy as successful as possible.

Part 1

Minimizing the Morning Sickness

1. Learn to control and eliminate morning sickness. Morning sickness can be a difficult aspect of pregnancy, as the associated nausea and vomiting is both unpredictable and unpleasant. However, learning about ways to control it can help pregnant women better manage morning sickness for a more comfortable pregnancy.

- Try eating smaller, more frequent snacks.

- Avoid anywhere there are extremes of odors, such as the butcher's, the perfume counter, the fish market, a smoky room, moldy areas, etc.

- Keep healthy nibbles with you at all times. A small bag of crackers is easy to carry in your purse, and many women find them to be helpful in minimizing nausea.

- Some women find it best to eat a piece of toast or similar bland item *before* getting out of bed in the morning. Keeping a box of saltines or other bland crackers by your bedside can be an easy way for you to have a soothing bite before getting up.

- Avoid processed foods and stick to healthy sources of food (protein, complex carbohydrates, lots of green and leafy veggies).

- Go to bed earlier; avoid stress.

- Ginger, lemon and lavender can help, in tea, aromatherapy or edible forms.

Part 2

Alleviating Lower Body Disorders

1. Try alleviating constipation associated with pregnancy. As a result of the physiological changes associated with the growing baby, many woman suffer from constipation during pregnancy. This constipation can be better controlled by consuming specific food and drink and performing exercises that can help.

- Another issue you may find yourself having to deal with is constantly wanting to urinate. This can cause earlier-than-desired sleep interruptions! If you experience this discomfort, you'll find it's usually in effect during the first 13 weeks or so of pregnancy and then again in the third trimester. Don't dehydrate yourself though; instead, drink a lot during the day but less in the evenings to try to alleviate many toilet trips during the night. Then again, it is a form of training for what's to come.

  - If you experience burning or stinging sensations when urinating, speak to your doctor; you may have a urinary tract infection.

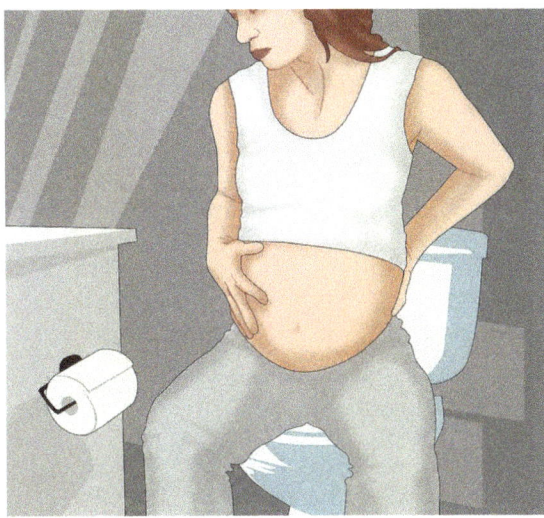

2. Prevent hemorrhoids during pregnancy. Learn to maintain a schedule of going to the bathroom to help eliminate hemorrhoids associated with pregnancy.

Part 3

Increasing your Energy Levels

1. Reduce fatigue during pregnancy. Tiredness is a commonplace issue for many pregnant women. By learning to control your sleep schedule, you can better manage your tiredness during the day.

- Learn to love naps. Nap when you're home, over the weekend, during a lunch break. Again, this is more training for what's to come! Also, get others to help more with housework, any lifting/shifting/moving heavy items, grocery shopping, etc. At work, ask for reduced travel or changed tasks if you feel too tired as a result. Avoid going out at nights, as this can increase your tiredness; meet up with friends and family on weekends or for lunch instead.

- If you're already a mom, nap when the children do. Ask a neighbor or friend to mind the kids for a bit while you catch up on some lost sleep.

Part 4

Coping with Aches and Pains

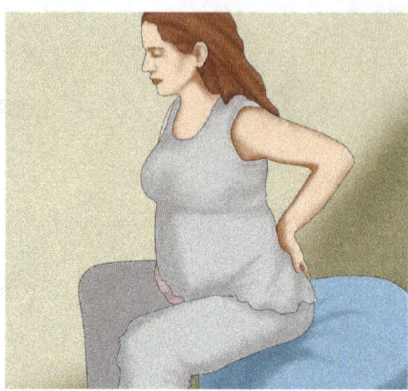

1. Manage your back pain during pregnancy. Pregnant women frequently suffer from back pain because of the physical stress of carrying a baby, but there are steps that help better control the discomfort.

- Avoid standing or sitting for long periods of time. If this requires changes in your routine, then ensure that the changes occur.

- Wear flat shoes that have excellent support. Visit a shoe clinic if you don't know what good support in a shoe is all about.

- If you must lift things, always bend from your knees.

- Don't twist or jerk around, especially not suddenly.

- Get someone else to put other children into backseat car restraints.

- Use warm (not hot) baths to relieve backache.

- Use warm heat packs or warm hot water bottles to relieve backache.

- Talk to your doctor if nothing is helping you.

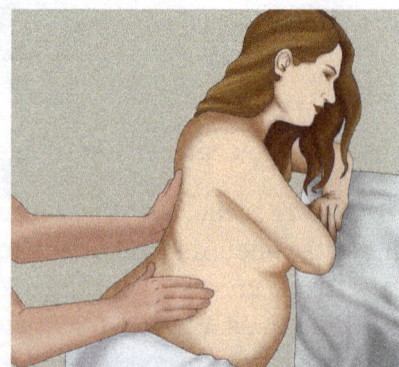

2. Receive a massage from your friend or partner. Massage techniques geared toward pregnant women can ease pain, and are easy to teach to a friend.

3. Learn to manage your round ligament pain. Physical therapy, yoga and rhythmic body movements can all help pregnant women overcome pain associated with the round ligament during pregnancy.

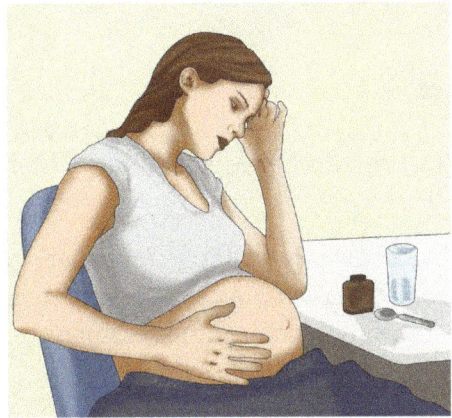

4. Take safe precautions when you're sick. If you get a fever while you're pregnant, learn how to reduce your fever safely to prevent putting yourself and your baby at risk.

- Ask your doctor for safe medications. Some medications that you'd consider safe when not pregnant can be harmful to the growing fetus, so always check before taking anything.

5. Eliminate heartburn. Take an empty glass and pour an adequate amount of baking soda (around a teaspoon) into it. Pour room temperature water into the glass, filling it. This will leave the water a whitish color. Drink in small amounts, and drink whenever you have heart burn, and/or before a meal/snack.

How to Stop Vaginal Bleeding During Pregnancy

Many women experience vaginal bleeding at some point in their pregnancy, especially in the first trimester when the pregnancy is just beginning. In many cases (especially early on, and if the bleeding is minimal) this can be completely normal. However, continued bleeding can be worrisome and warrants evaluation by a physician, particularly if the bleeding is accompanied by pain, cramps, fever, dizziness or fainting. It is important to know strategies to handle and control bleeding if it occurs, and also to know when to see your doctor for additional help and treatment.

Method 1

Assessing and Controlling the Bleeding

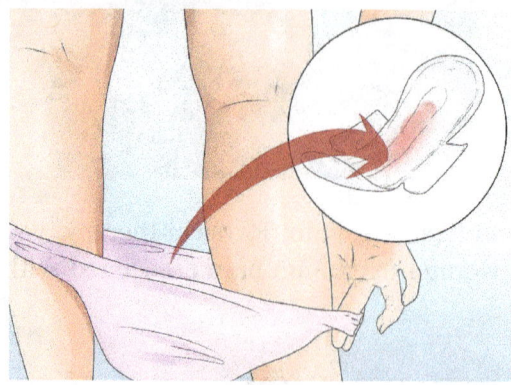

1. Keep track of the bleeding. It is very important to have an idea about the amount of blood loss during an episode of bleeding. This will help your doctor to make a possible diagnosis as well as establish a management plan. Start monitoring the amount of blood you are losing as soon as you notice the bleeding.

- You can do this by keeping a sanitary pad in your underwear until it is soaked. Count how many pads are soaked from 8 am one day to 8 am the next day. Keep a written record of this number, then bring it to your doctor for assessment.

- Also keep track of other characteristics of the bleeding, such as whether it is painful or painless, and intermittent or constant bleeding. This information describing your bleeding will be helpful to your doctor in figuring out what is at cause in the matter.

- Take note of the color of your blood (pink versus red versus brown), as well as the presence or absence of blood clots or other "tissue masses" that may come out alongside the blood. If you do have any tissue masses come out of your vagina alongside the blood, you may want to collect these in a container to show to your doctor, as this could be of assistance to her in diagnosing the cause of your problem.

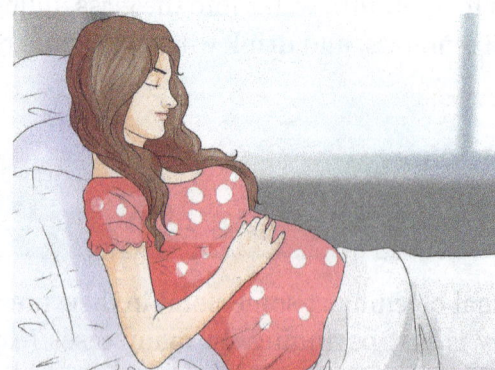

2. Get plenty of bed rest. For minor bleeding in early pregnancy, rest is the ideal treatment.

Physicians usually advocate complete bed rest for the first few days following the episode of bleeding.

- If the bleeding does not stop or diminish with rest, it is important to see your doctor for a more detailed assessment.

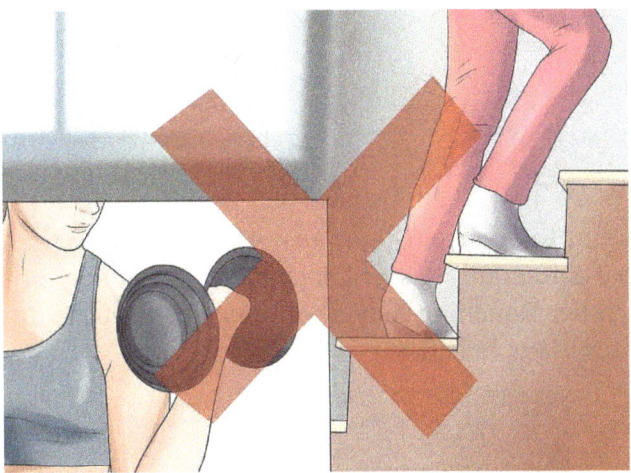

3. Avoid heavy work. Your physician will definitely advise you to avoid strenuous or heavy work such as weightlifting, climbing stairs frequently, running, cycling, etc. These activities cause jerking of the uterus and can rupture the delicate, newly-formed blood vessels in the placenta. Avoidance of these kind of activities is absolutely necessary, even if you only notice a tiny amount of bleeding.

- You should limit your physical activities and avoid heavy work for at least two weeks after the bleeding stops.

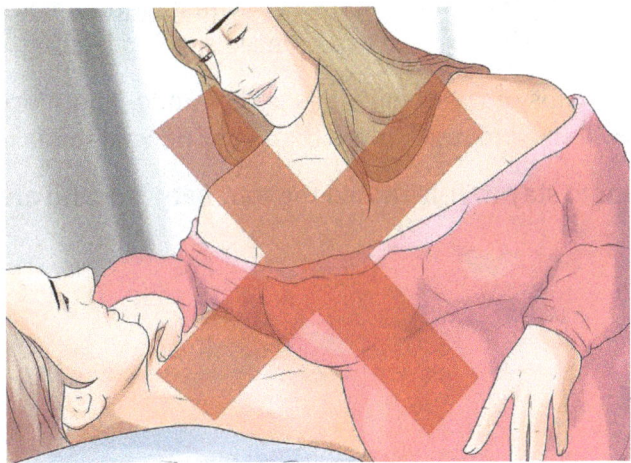

4. Put intercourse on hold for the time being. Sometimes intercourse can induce or aggravate bleeding from the vagina.

- If you experience bleeding during pregnancy, you should avoid intercourse until your doctor tells you it's safe. Normally, you will have to wait at least two to four weeks after bleeding has stopped.

5. Do not use tampons or try to douche. Do not insert anything into the vagina following vaginal bleeding. Absolutely avoid using tampons or douching, as these may injure the cervix or vaginal wall causing further bleeding. Douching may also introduce bacteria and other microorganisms into the vagina, leading to serious infection.

6. Stay hydrated. It's very important that you drink adequate amounts of fluid during a bleeding episode. This is particularly true if you have experienced severe bleeding.

- Drink at least eight cups of water daily to stay hydrated, and more. Bleeding correlates to fluid loss, so you will need to drink more than your normal to make up for the lost fluid.

- It is also important to stay well-hydrated for your baby's health and wellbeing.

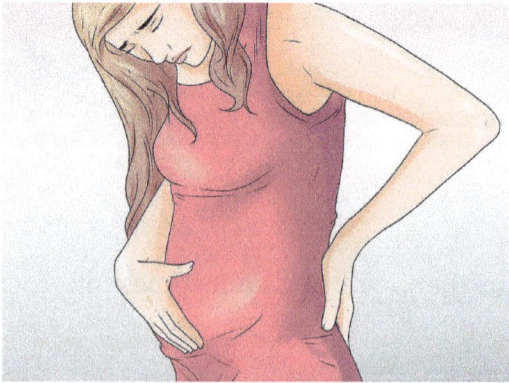

7. Be aware of causes of vaginal bleeding in pregnancy. This can help to differentiate what may be going on in your particular case.

- Bleeding is actually quite common in the first trimester (in the first 12 weeks of pregnancy) and occurs for about 20 – 30% of women. Many of these cases of bleeding are benign, meaning they are not worrisome for the mother or the baby and may be due to the fetus implanting in the wall of the uterus or other physiologic changes of pregnancy.

- There are, however, more worrisome possibilities associated with higher volumes of blood loss and/or pain in the first trimester as well. These include the possibility of "ectopic pregnancy" (the baby has implanted in the fallopian tubes rather than the uterus), "molar pregnancy" (a rare condition in which abnormal tissue grows inside your uterus rather than a fetus), or a miscarriage.

- In 50% of cases of vaginal bleeding within the first 20 weeks of pregnancy, it indicates that a miscarriage is occurring.

- Bleeding later in pregnancy (in the second or third trimester) is more likely to be worrisome. Causes include problems with the placenta, problems with the uterus (especially if you have had a previous C-section), premature labor (defined as the onset of labor before 37 weeks), or also of course labor itself (if you are near the time of your due date).

- Additional causes of bleeding that may be unrelated to the pregnancy specifically include "trauma" (or injury to the vaginal wall) from sexual intercourse, cervical polyps (masses around the cervix that may bleed and that can be present in women irrespective of whether or not they are pregnant), cervical dysplasia (abnormal cells that can lead to cancer), and/or cervical cancer (one of the most prevalent forms of cancer for women who are not regularly screened with Pap tests).

8. Calculate your due date and consider whether or not your bleeding could mean that your labor has started. Pregnancy normally lasts for 40 weeks or 280 days. You can use this information to calculate your due date — just add nine calendar months and seven days from the first day of last menstrual period. For example, if your last period began 1st January, 2014, your due date is 8th October, 2014.

- Bleeding near your due date may indicate that your labor has begun. The typical range is from 10 days before to 10 days after the due date. You should immediately report to your doctor if your suspect that you might be in labor.

9. Know when to seek help from a medical professional. Any bleeding during pregnancy should be discussed with your physician in a timely manner. If the bleeding is accompanied by any of the following symptoms, it is recommended to be seen by a doctor as soon as possible in the emergency room for quick assessment and treatment:

- Severe pain or cramps

- Dizziness or fainting (signs of large blood loss)

- Tissue that comes out of your vagina alongside the blood (could be a sign of miscarriage)

- A fever and/or chills (could be a sign of infection)

- Severe bleeding that does not slow down or stop.

Method 2

Knowing when to Seek Medical Help

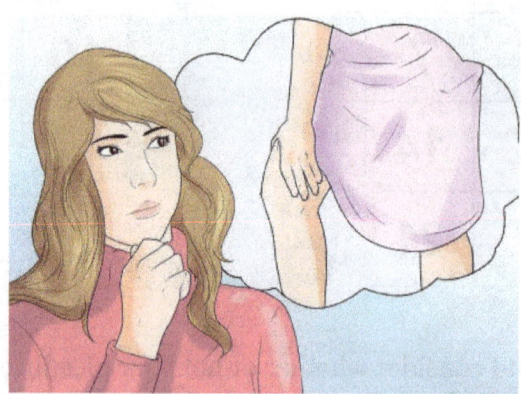

1. Know that you can ignore very light bleeding. If you are bleeding very little (only a few drops), the blood is brown in color, it lasts less than one or two days, and is not associated with pain or cramps, then you can usually ignore it. Most likely it is implantation bleeding or the result of stretched blood vessels.

- Regardless of how light the bleeding is, you should avoid heavy work for a few days and meticulously monitor the amount of bleeding.

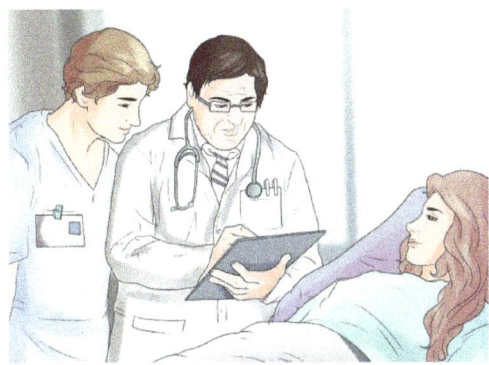

2. Seek medical help if you experiencing heavy bleeding. Any type of profuse bleeding during pregnancy should be regarded as an emergency. Profuse bleeding roughly means any amount of bleeding more than usual menstrual bleeding.

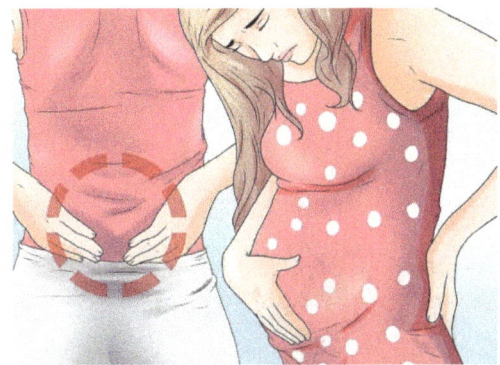

3. Pay attention to any pain or cramps you feel. Pain that comes and goes indicates contractions of the uterus, which means that the uterus is trying to expel the fetus. In early pregnancy, pain and cramping may be a sign of miscarriage and in third trimester it may indicate that you are going into labor. Therefore, if you experience any pain or cramping, you should contact your doctor immediately.

- True labor pain is regular and occurs at intervals. It gradually increases in intensity and duration and it associated with "show" (expulsion of mucus mixed with blood).

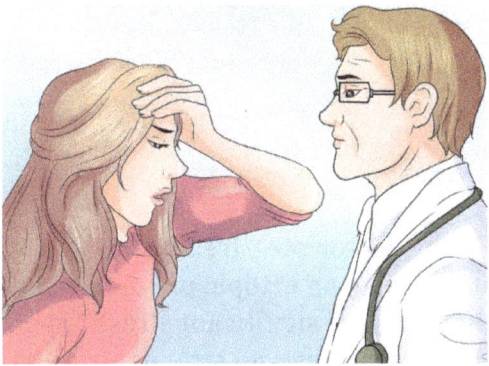

4. Seek help if you are dizzy or feeling faint. Dizziness or feeling faint are symptoms of massive blood loss.

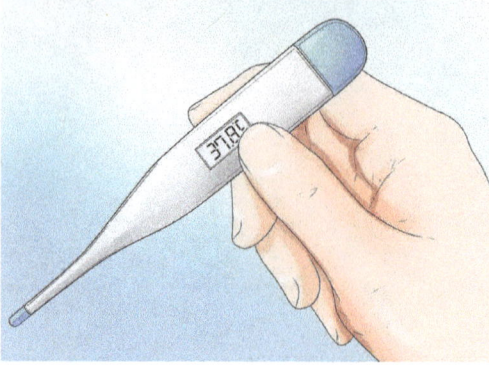

5. Check your temperature. Bleeding accompanied by fever usually indicates an infection, such as infection in your uterus following natural miscarriage or abortion. As a result, any signs of fever should be brought to the attention of your doctor immediately.

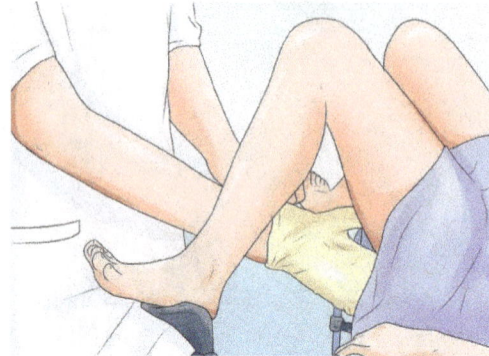

6. Seek immediate help if you are passing tissue through your vagina. Passing a fleshy mass through your vagina is a serious indication of miscarriage. If this happens, you should contact your doctor immediately so he can evacuate the uterus if needed and thus control the bleeding.

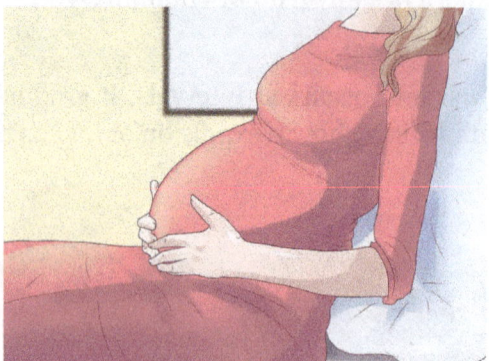

7. Follow the instructions of your doctor post-treatment. Regardless of what caused vaginal bleeding (whether it was a miscarriage, an ectopic pregnancy outside the uterus, an infection, or the onset of labor), it will have caused significant stress to your body. In the great majority of cases your doctor will strongly advise rest, no strenuous exercise, often abstaining from sex for a little while, and drinking lots of water. Be sure to heed your doctor's advice for recovery in order to maximize the speed at which you recover, as well as to prevent any other complications.

How to Alleviate Back Pain During Pregnancy

Back pain and pressure during pregnancy is a very common, and often very uncomfortable, problem. Weight gain, hormonal changes in preparation for childbirth, changes in your posture and how you walk, and stress can all cause back pain ranging from mild to severe. There are many options for relieving this discomfort.

Method 1

Exercising to Relieve Back Pain

1. Exercise regularly. Continuing physical activity during uncomplicated pregnancies has been shown to be beneficial and not risky. However, if your back pain develops late in pregnancy, you should be cautious about easing slowly into new routines.

- Look for pregnancy-safe ways to strengthen your core, abdominal, and back muscles. Avoid traditional crunches and oblique exercises, which can put pressure on important veins and separate abdominal muscles from each other. Instead, try standing crunches or tucking your tailbone while standing. You may also try getting on your hands and knees and touching alternate elbows with your knees, switching between sides.

- Walking, swimming, and stationary cycling are particularly safe options for exercise during pregnancy. Ask a doctor or physical therapist for other suggestions.

- Stand with your back to a wall. Bend your knees and work to straighten your spine.

- Engaging in high impact exercises prior to pregnancy, such as running and jogging, have been shown to reduce the risk of pelvic girdle pain in pregnancy.

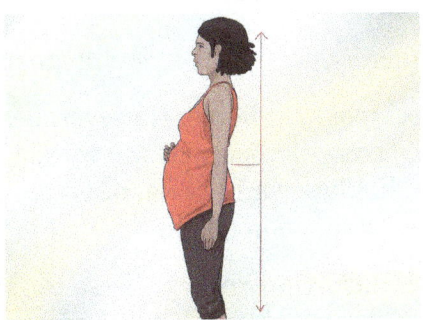

2. Maintain good posture. As your center of gravity shifts forward during pregnancy, you might

start to strain muscles in order to avoid falling over. Practicing good posture can shift your center of gravity back and reduce strain.

- When standing, envision an imaginary cord pulling your body up into perfect alignment from above your head. Use a comfortably wide stance, don't lock your knees, and rest one foot occasionally on a step stool if you have to stand for a long time.

- When sitting, sit up straight and don't slouch your shoulders. Instead, keep your shoulders back and relaxed.

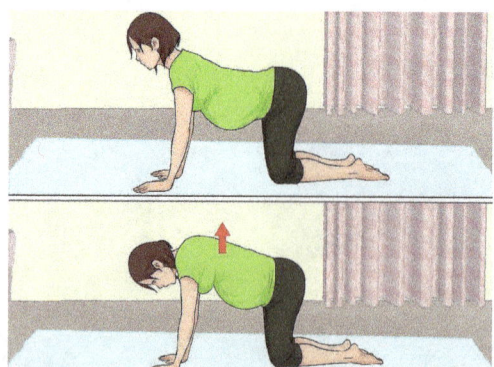

3. Stretch your lower back. Get on your hands and knees and alternate rounding and then flattening your back. Hold each position for several seconds, but be gentle, gradually working up to ten repetitions. This is sometimes called "cat and cow" stretching.

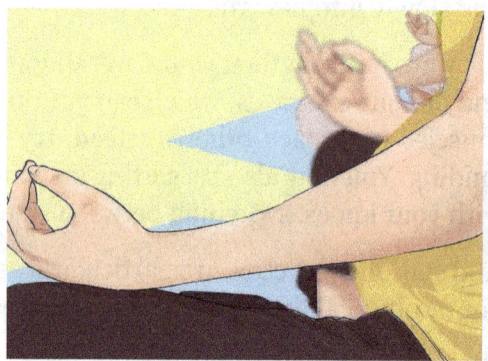

4. Enroll in a prenatal yoga class. In addition to relieving back pain, prenatal yoga can improve sleep, reduce stress, and alleviate other symptoms such as nausea and headaches. It may also strengthen the muscles you will use in childbirth.

- Always let your yoga instructor know that you are pregnant.

- You can also do gentle yoga poses at home. However, be sure to avoid poses that involve lying on your stomach, lying on your back after 16 weeks, inversions (going upside-down), strong twists, back bends, holding your breath, or taking short, forceful breaths. If something feels difficult or like a strain, don't do it.

- There are many safe poses during pregnancy. These include hip-opening squats (malasana), chair pose (utkatasana), warrior poses I and II (virbhadrasana), tree pose (vrksasana), and legs up the wall pose (viparita karani).

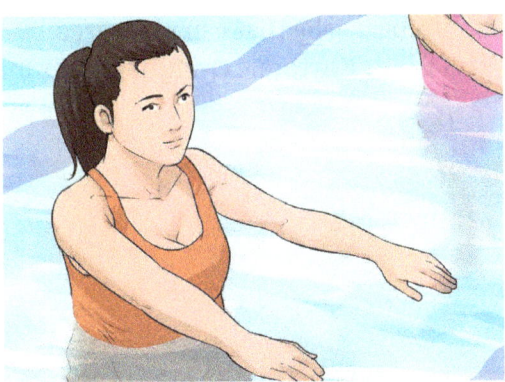

5. Swim or do prenatal water exercises. In addition to being a great workout, water exercise relieves pressure from your back and joints. Since the water supports your weight, even walking or floating in the pool will help relieve the pressure.

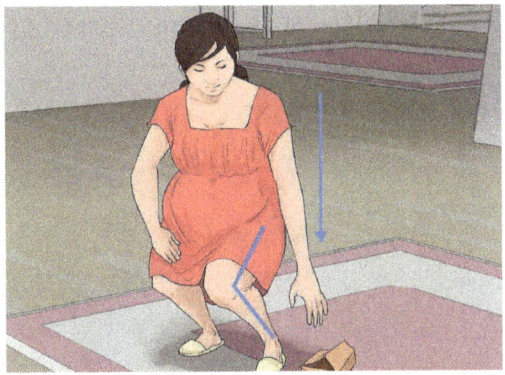

6. Squat and lift with your legs when picking something up. Do not bend at your waist or lift with your back muscles. Ask for help if you need it.

- When carrying bags, try to distribute the weight evenly. Carry a similar amount of weight in each hand.

Method 2

Treating Back Pain

1. Distinguish between normal back pain and early labor. Always call your doctor if you suspect that

a symptom may be a sign of labor. A backache that can't be eased by changing positions or seeking comfort other ways can be a sign of labor. Rhythmic cramping pains may also be a sign of early labor.

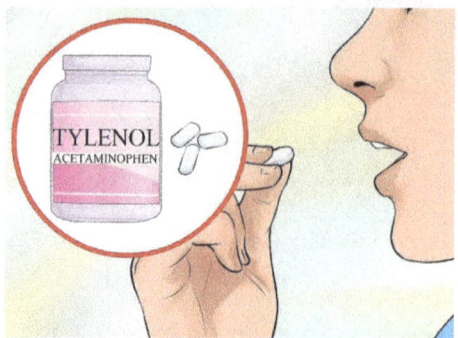

2. Use pain medication. You should consult with your doctor about what medications are safe to use. In general, acetaminophen (Tylenol) is usually safe during pregnancy, while aspirin and non-steroidal anti-inflammatory drugs (NSAIDs) such as ibuprofen or naproxen are not.

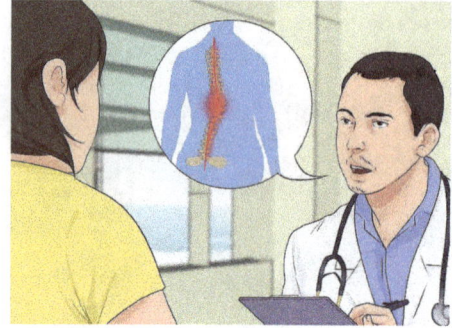

3. Consult an osteopath or chiropractor. An osteopath or chiropractor can assess your back pain and offer therapeutic options or refer you to the right health professional. If you are going to consult one, make sure you go to someone who specializes in pregnancy and has had years of experience in this. You can reach out to the local chiropractic or osteopath society for a referral.

- In a recent study, it was found that 6.1 % of pregnant women consult an osteopath.

- A chiropractor and osteopath may perform osteopathic manipulation therapies, and have been shown to be helpful in women with low back pain while pregnant.

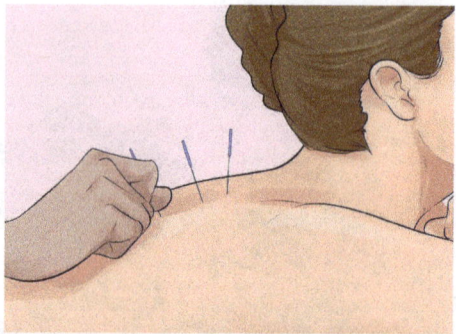

4. Try acupuncture. Find a certified acupuncturist with experience in treating pregnant women. Acupuncture has been shown to relieve lower back pain in pregnant women.

- Ask for recommendations from friends or other medical practitioners when searching for an acupuncturist. Ask a potential acupuncturist about what kind of training and continuing education she receives, what her recommended course of treatment for you is, and whether she can work with your insurance (if applicable). Work with someone who makes you feel comfortable and whose office is convenient.

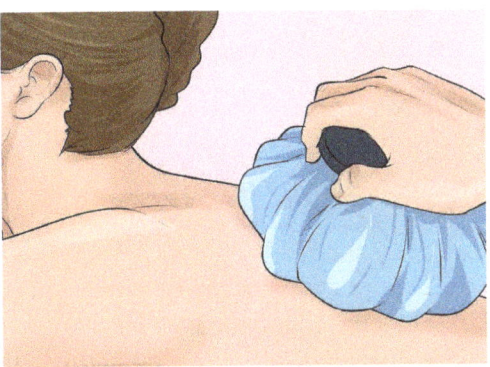

5. Apply a heating pad or ice packs. You may get relief by alternating between ice packs and heat.

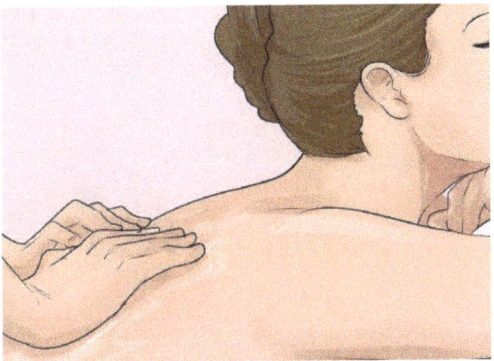

6. Get a massage. Ask a loved one to gently rub your back. You may also get a prenatal massage from a trained massage therapist.

7. Seek counseling to deal with stress. Ask your physician, midwife, friends, or faith leader about finding a good counselor. You might need to speak with a few therapists before you find a good match. Ask a potential therapist about their experience treating your issue and about their areas of expertise. You might also find relief from talking about your stress or worries with a trusted friend or relative.

Method 3

Supporting your Back

1. Wear flat shoes with good arch support. Sensible footwear can help you walk evenly without putting excess pressure or strain on your back. Research has shown that during week 20 and 32 of pregnancy, there is a shift in where the full pressure of the body is distributed over the foot. That's why it's important to see a foot specialist to see if an arch support may be useful for you.

- Avoid high heels as well as shoes that offer little to no support for your arches or ankles, such as flip-flops or "Crocs." The back of the shoe should be rigid and vertical. Lacing shoes may also provide more support.

2. Use a lumbar support pillow when sitting. You might appreciate having a pillow in the office and another in the car. Elevating your feet on a footstool may also help relieve back pressure while sitting.

3. Sleep on your side using extra pillows. Bend one or both knees. The pillows should be placed strategically to help relieve aches and pains. Use a firm pillow for your head and place another pillow between your legs. Place a small pillow under your abdomen to relieve pelvic and back pressure while you sleep. Some pregnant women find full-length body pillows to provide relief.

- Be careful when you're getting in and out of bed to avoid straining your spine.

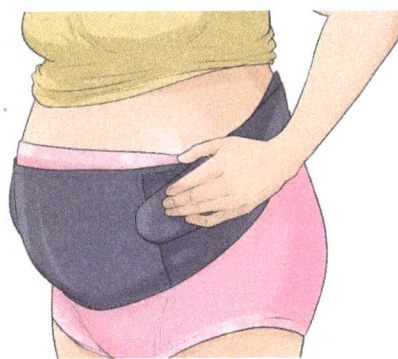

4. Wear a maternity support belt. Available in a variety of shapes and sizes, these thick elastic bands are worn under the belly cradle and around the hips to support your abdominal muscles. Models are also available with bust and shoulder straps to provide relief for all-over back pain.

- Support hose might also offer relief.

How to Reduce Fatigue During Pregnancy

Many pregnant women experience bouts of fatigue from time to time. You may feel sluggish and tired and your energy levels will be lower than normal. At times, the fatigue can be so overwhelming that you may be unable to be productive at work or keep up with your normal activities. Often, fatigue is most noticeable during the first three months and the last three months of pregnancy. Normal hormonal changes cause some of these symptoms, and the extra strain on your body to accommodate a new life is also part of the cause. In addition, you may have a disrupted sleep pattern or psychological changes that make you feel mentally as well as physically drained. It is very important that you receive regular prenatal care and stick to a healthy diet; however, there are other things you can do to reduce fatigue.

Method 1

Eating to Reduce Fatigue

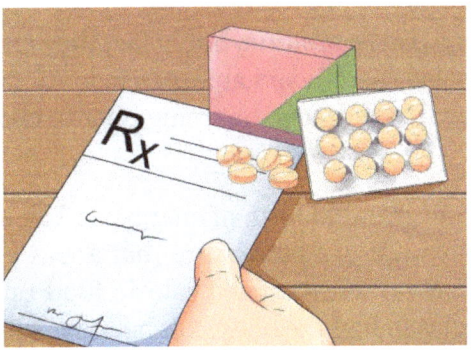

1. Take your prenatal vitamins. Pregnant women have many increased nutritional needs, and if

you don't get the proper nutrition, you are more likely to feel fatigued. Prenatal vitamins are specially formulated to help supply the additional nutritional needs for pregnancy. Remember to take them every day.

- Be sure to use a prenatal that contains vitamin B12, which helps fight fatigue.

- Also be sure that your vitamin contains at least 27 grams of elemental iron. Pregnancy-induced anemia can cause extreme fatigue for some women, and if your doctor tests your blood and determines that you have this condition, you may need to increase your iron up to 60 grams a day.

- If you have trouble remembering to take your prenatal vitamins, set them on your dining room table or wherever you eat dinner every day. You can also try setting a timed reminder on your phone to sound an alarm every day when you need to take your vitamin.

2. Eat for energy. Pregnant or not, the body gets its energy from food. A healthy diet can make the difference between chronic fatigue and energy. You need three major macronutrients for energy: protein, carbohydrates, and fat.

- Protein provides much of the energy your body needs to do the hard work of growing a human. When pregnant, you need about 70 grams of protein every day-- considerably more than the 45 grams recommended for non-pregnant women. Consider healthy food sources such as beans, dairy, tofu, chicken, and fish.

- Carbohydrates often get a bad reputation, but in fact they are one of the body's main sources of energy and vital to your health and ability to fight off fatigue. About half of your daily calories should be from carbohydrates, but remember to choose healthy sources like unrefined grains.

- Fats provide the most concentrated form of energy, and also help you to absorb some vital vitamins. While pregnant, you need to ensure that about a quarter of your daily calories come from fat. Avoid low-fat and reduced-calorie food options, which don't provide as many energy-filled calories to fuel the body. Eat healthy, whole foods with naturally occurring fats like avocado, nut butters, vegetable or coconut oil. Avoid margarine and saturated fats.

3. Eat several small meals. Instead of eating three large meals a day, increase the number of meals you eat, but reduce the amount of food at each meal. This gives the body more boosts of energy throughout the day to fight pregnancy-induced fatigue.

- Despite that popular cliché "eating for two," you shouldn't double your food intake while pregnant; instead, increase your caloric intake by about 300 calories per day. Make sure your added calories contain protein and carbohydrates for energy, but ensure that they are nutritious calories and not junk food. For example, three hundred nutritious, fatigue fighting calories can be found in an apple, sliced and spread with your favorite nut butter; or in a cup of Greek yogurt with a handful of almonds and berries.

4. Increase your water intake. It can be hard enough to drink enough water for non-pregnant women; during pregnancy, you need to increase your intake of water substantially to combat dehydration and fatigue. In fact, one of the first symptoms of dehydration is fatigue.

- Aim for a dozen eight-ounce glasses of water a day, if you live in a temperate area. In hot, humid areas, you will need even more.

- If you have trouble stomaching all that water, add some variety to make things more interesting. Try adding fresh fruit to your water or drinking non-caffeinated tea. You can also eat juicy fruits and vegetables like watermelon, lettuce, or tomatoes.

- Try to not drink water two to three hours before bedtime to reduce the urge to get up to urinate.

5. Don't rely on caffeine for energy. Even if you drank lots of caffeinated beverages prior to pregnancy, it's important that you only consume a moderate amount of caffeine while pregnant. Studies have shown that it is safe to drink a small amount of coffee, black tea, or hot cocoa while pregnant, but keep it to a minimum.

- Limit your caffeine to no more than 200 mg per day. That's the amount found in one twelve ounce cup of black coffee or four cups of black tea.

- Never drink energy drinks, energy shots, or pure caffeine while pregnant. These have questionable health risks even when you're not pregnant, and are linked with miscarriage and birth defects.

Method 2

Changing your Habits

1. Get more rest. One of the first symptoms of pregnancy is exhaustion, caused by a rapid increase in the hormone progesterone. Progesterone is vital for a healthy pregnancy, but causes sleepiness for almost every pregnant woman. You may find that your typical seven hours of sleep at night is no longer sufficient. Make rest a priority, especially during your first trimester.

- Go to bed earlier at night, or set your alarm a bit later in the morning. Better yet, do both: pregnant women sometimes need up to three more hours of sleep than they did prior to pregnancy.

- Take power naps during the day. When you are on break at work, get a quick ten minute doze to help recharge your batteries.

2. Give yourself a break. your activity levels, such as household chores, to a lower level than before you were pregnant. Ask a spouse, relative, friend, or even a hired helper for assistance.

- While pregnant, your body goes through so many metabolic changes and does so much work each day that it is almost as if you are running a daily marathon! Keep this in mind when you feel like you're being lazy.

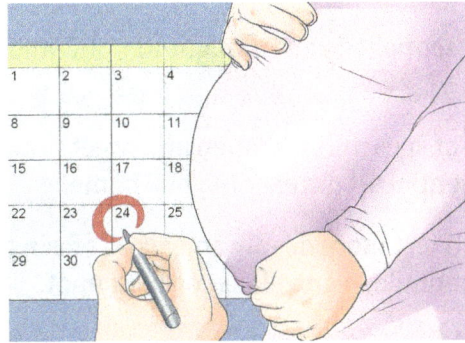

3. Reduce your commitments. If it is at all possible, cancel plans for social activities and reduce your schedule at work. In most cases, the fatigue lifts a bit after the first trimester, and you will be able to resume many of your activities at that time.

- Ask for vacation time or a reduced workweek for a few weeks if you find that your fatigue interferes with your ability to work.

4. Exercise daily. One cause of pregnancy fatigue is restlessness at night and the inability to fall into a deep sleep. But exercising every day can help you to sleep more deeply and have more restorative rest. Try to get at least 30 minutes of exercise every day.

- Even if all you do is go for a walk, swim, or do some yoga, daily exercise will also help increase your circulation and keep your muscles toned. This may also help you with the birthing process.

Method 3

Trying Home Remedies to Fight Fatigue

1. Try aromatherapy. Certain essential oils are thought to uplift and energize. These may also help regulate your sleep patterns.

- Try mixing a drop each of spearmint, grapefruit, sweet orange, and lime essential oils and diffusing them in an essential oil diffuser in your home.

- At bedtime, help yourself rest more deeply and avoid tossing and turning by using oils such as lavender, neroli, chamomile, ylang ylang, or bergamot.

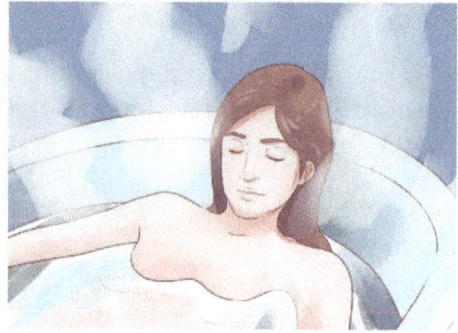

2. Relax with a massage or soaking in a warm bath. You can help fight fatigue by increasing the quality of your rest. While there are certain precautions you should take, massages, warm baths, and other relaxation techniques are great ways to experience a deeper rest.

- Look for a massage therapist who has experience with prenatal massage. You may need to lie on a special massage mat or lie on your left side instead of lying on your tummy or flat on your back.

- Remember to keep your bath warm and not hot. Temperatures too high can raise the body temperature of both mom and fetus, potentially leading to pregnancy complications or even miscarriage. Try taking a warm bath with a few drops of your favorite relaxing essential oil.

- Do not use a hot tub! It is fine to take warm baths while you are pregnant, but it is not safe to use a hot tub while you are pregnant.

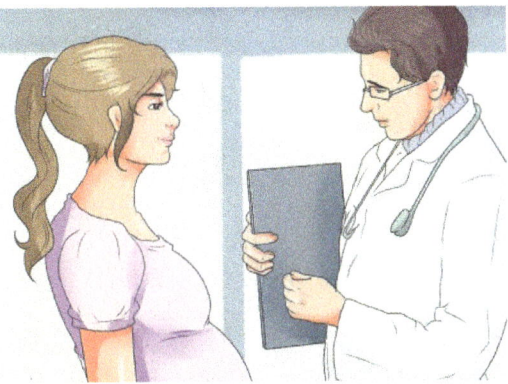

3. Consider acupuncture. Special acupuncture techniques are trusted in many parts of the world as excellent ways to reduce fatigue by stimulating certain parts of the body and brain. This is thought to release endorphins in the body, which are chemicals that cause a rise in energy.

- Look for a licensed acupuncturist with experience working with pregnant patients.

4. Try Bach Flower Remedies. These are homeopathic solutions developed in the 1930s, which involve distilling certain types of flowers in brandy and water. While there is no scientific evidence to suggest that they work, many people report feeling less tired.

- Try olive or hornbeam, which are specifically meant to combat fatigue. You can purchase these online or from some health food stores.

How to take Care of your Skin During Pregnancy

Pregnancy causes many changes in a woman's body and hormonal makeup. A pregnant woman's body produces more hormones — particularly estrogen and progesterone — which causes a number of noticeable changes. To maintain healthy and beautiful skin during pregnancy, you may need to reconsider your skincare routine. You need to learn what products are safe for you — and your baby — to use on your skin during your pregnancy.

Method 1

Expecting Changes During your Pregnancy

1. Prepare for some skin changes. You're carrying a developing baby who is growing inside your body and making room for itself. Your little bundle of joy may be creating noticeable marks in the form of stretch marks. Even post-baby, hormones can also be a factor in causing these skin abrasions. One way of combating stretch marks is using cocoa butter, which is a safe lotion to help fade skin blemishes.

- It is recommended to only gain the amount of weight that your doctor recommends. Excess weight gain can increase stretch mark formation.

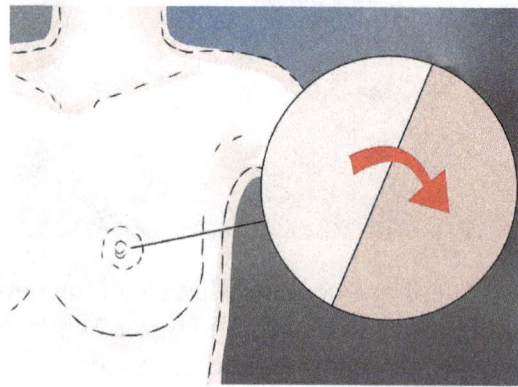

2. Notice your skin's pigmentation. You may notice darker skin splotches due to hyperpigmentation. When you're pregnant and your hormones are going haywire, increased melanin in your skin may cause noticeable difference. It may cause patches of your skin to darken, especially around the areolas.

- You may also notice the pregnancy line, or linea nigra. This is a vertical line that appears going down the center of your stomach. It is normally too light to see, but it may darken and become visible during pregnancy.

- There is nothing to worry about with skin pigmentation, but if you notice linea nigra, it may indicate you need more folic acid (a B vitamin). Talk to your doctor about this.

3. Avoid popping pimples. You may relive your teenage years with an increase in acne. Since your body goes through a lot of hormonal changes during a pregnancy, you may develop acne or other skin abrasions. Mostly, your skin will clear up after your pregnancy. But, serious rashes like Chloasma (or sometimes called "Mask of Pregnancy") can occur and needs to be treated by a doctor.

Method 2

Avoiding Harmful Products and Chemicals

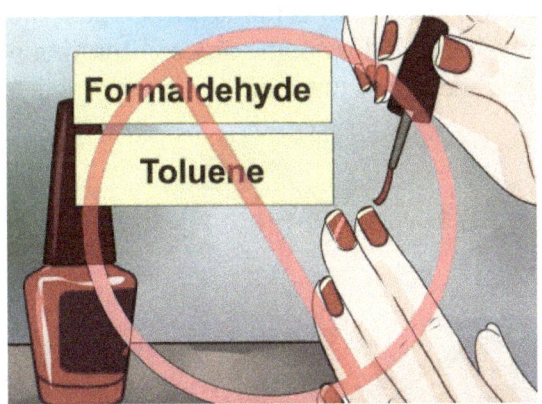

1. Think about your nail routine. Nail polishes and nail polish remover can have harsh chemicals like formaldehyde and toluene. Both of these chemical are preservatives and can do serious harm if absorbed. You do not have to completely forego pretty nails, just be sure to pick nail polishes that do not have nasty chemicals like Formaldehyde in them

2. Talk to your doctor about wrinkle cream and acne medication. Accutane (isotretinoin), Retin-A (tretinoin), and tetracyclines can all be dangerous to your developing fetus, may cause serious birth defects, and should be avoided. Wrinkle cream may also contain Retinol, which can also be dangerous.

- If you have concerns about wrinkles or acne while pregnant, it is important you discuss this with your doctor and find a treatment that is safe for both you and your baby.

- Botox should not be used to treat wrinkles while pregnant, either.

3. Wait to whiten your teeth. Teeth-whitening products that contain peroxide may not be safe to use while pregnant. There is not enough research to support that it is safe to bleach or have your teeth whitened, so it's best to wait until after you have given birth and are finished breastfeeding. In fact, it is illegal in some countries for dentists to perform whitening procedures on pregnant women.

- Some whitening toothpastes, too, contain peroxide. The levels are so low they should not affect your pregnancy, but talk to your doctor first. Look for stain-reducing, rather than whitening, toothpaste.

4. Avoid tanning and spray tans. There is not clear evidence that tanning will harm your baby, but using a tanning bed is the leading cause of skin cancer and should always be avoided. Tanning may also potentially break down folic acid, which is important in building your baby's nervous system. Avoid spray tans, as you can inhale chemicals that could harm your baby.

- In addition, overheating by tanning or laying out in the sun can increase your risk for birth defects.

- Wear sunscreens containing zinc oxide or titanium dioxide.

- Talk to your doctor before using self-tanner. There is not enough evidence to show that self-tanning lotion is safe for use while you are pregnant, but it is thought the chemical that browns your skin (dihydroxyacetone) is not absorbed past the first layer of skin. Still, you should check with your doctor before using any self-tanning products, or just make peace with being a little pale while you're pregnant.

Method 3

Picking Products That Will Work for you

1. Consult with experts. Talk with your doctor, or your dermatologist. If you have any questions or concerns, don't hesitate to talk to your doctor about what products you can use. If you develop a problem with your skin like a rash or persistent acne, the doctor can prescribe you safe options such as a topical cream.

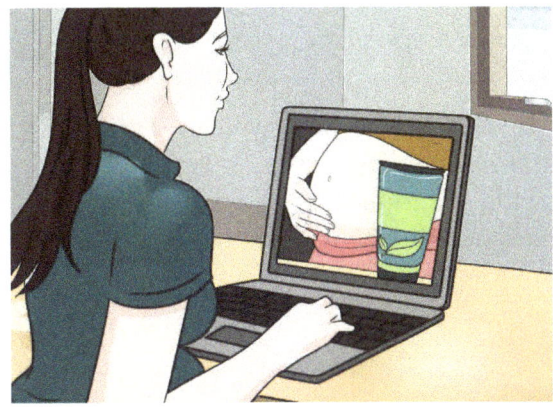

2. Be wise and do your research. Once you know what you need and what can harm you, you need to look for products that will work for your skin, body, and baby. There are plenty of resources on the internet for expecting mothers, including popular pregnancy forums hosted by well-known parenting magazines.

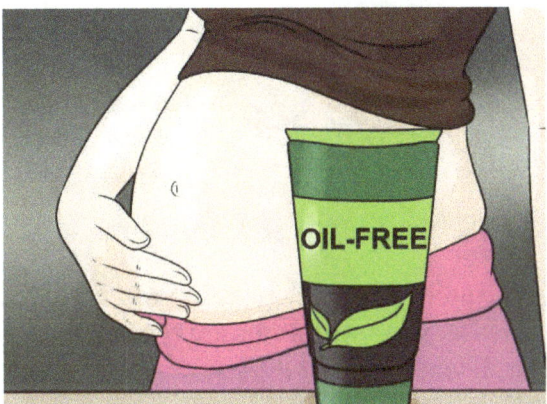

3. Go green! Use natural, oil-free products on your skin. These products avoid harsh chemicals and are often more environmentally friendly. Some even are specifically blended for pregnant women.

4. Keep an eye on advertisements. There a number of products that specialize in sulphate-free or oil-free beauty alternatives. Check out magazines like Parenting, American Baby, or Baby Talk for specialized advertisements.

How to Screen for Depression During Pregnancy

It's estimated that between 14-23% of pregnant women struggle with symptoms of depression. During pregnancy, many hormonal changes occur, which can directly affect symptoms of depression and anxiety. Coupled with situational stressors, depression can occur during pregnancy. While some women experience moodiness during pregnancy, it's important to address any potential depression so that you can properly treat it.

Part 1

Identifying Symptoms of Depression

1. Examine physical symptoms. Indications of depression can include several physical symptoms. It's important to determine whether your symptoms are typical of pregnancy or if they seem more extreme or enduring for longer. If you've suffered from some of the following symptoms more days than not for two or more weeks in a way that affects your normal functioning, it may be related to depression:

- Decreased energy/feeling constantly exhausted
- Feeling restless; fidgeting often
- Feeling overly lethargic or making slow movements

2. Look at possible emotional symptoms of depression. Pregnancy often affects emotions, and it's

important to differentiate between emotional changes that are part of a normal pregnancy and those that may be due to depression. Check to see if you have had emotional symptoms of depression for two or more weeks that have affected your functioning at home, school, or work. Emotional symptoms that may indicate that you have depression include:

- Feeling worthless

- Difficulty concentrating, problems with memory

- Persistent sadness, crying

- Low mood, feeling numb

- Feeling irritable, angry or aggressive

- Decreased interest in activities you used to enjoy

- Feeling unmotivated or detached from your typical routine

- Having thoughts of harming yourself or the baby

3. Recognize behavioral symptoms. You or other people may see changes in the way you act that differ from your normal behavior. While it's typical to experience some hormonal changes during pregnancy that can affect your behavior, it's important to determine whether your behavior changes are within the range of 'normal' or if they may be related to depression. If you notice behavior changes that impair your functioning and that last 2 or more weeks, it's time to consider depression. Behavioral symptoms can include:

- Changes in sleep habits (sleeping too much or too little, such as staying up all night or wanting to sleep all day even if you slept well at night)

- Changes in eating habits (beyond what may be considered "normal" in pregnancy, such as binge eating or not wanting to eat at all)

- Socially withdrawing from friends and family, isolating yourself

- Engaging in reckless behavior (like things that may harm the fetus, like drinking)

4. Ask yourself if there's a family or personal history of depression. Look at your family members and ask yourself if there's a family history of depression. Then, ask yourself whether you've previously experienced depression at any point in your life. If so, you are at a higher risk for developing depression.

- Does anyone in your immediate family (parents, siblings) suffer from depression or take medication to treat depression? What about your extended family (grandparents, aunts/uncles, cousins)?

- Have you ever taken medication, seen a therapist, or struggled with symptoms of depression in the past?

Part 2

Screening Medical or Physical Contributions

1. Acknowledge physical discomforts. Dealing with the changes and pain from pregnancy can become wearing day after day. From morning sickness to back pain to minimal sleeping positions, the physical stress from pregnancy can deplete normal ability to cope and leave you drained and exhausted.

- Are you finding it more difficult to respond to stress due to the pain you experience regularly? Do you feel like you have a shorter fuse or that your discomfort is making you excessively sad or irritable? How is your pregnancy affecting your emotional state?

- Help your body relax by taking warm baths, using a heating pad for muscle aches, and using good posture.

2. Recognize problems in your pregnancy. If you're struggling with a high-risk pregnancy or have increased medical complications with your pregnancy, you may be at higher risk for depression. Dealing with stress and the fear of any problems with your baby can be too much to handle.You may also feel frustrated or unhelpful if you're not allowed to work or do things you could previously do with ease.

- Are you feeling worthless or unneeded in your family due to a complicated pregnancy? Are you bedridden and frustrated at your lack of independence? Are these issues affecting your emotional or mental health? These situations can contribute to depression.

- Make sure you stay in contact with your medical practitioner and communicate any questions you may have about your pregnancy.

3. Ask yourself if fertility treatments have affected your well-being. If you've endured several months of fertility treatments, it's likely that your body and emotions are under stress. Especially if you tried tirelessly to get pregnant and now are, you may be worried to lose the baby you tried so hard to conceive. The fertility process is a difficult one and emotionally taxing. Once you're pregnant, it can stay difficult. All of these factors can make you more prone to depression.

- Have you found it more difficult to manage your emotions since fertility treatments? How have the treatments and resulting stress from the treatments affecting your mental and emotional health?

- Think about the stressors your body, mind, and emotions have experienced during and after treatments. Find ways to express these feelings healthfully, such as through talking to a friend or a therapist.

Part 3

Expressing Emotional Factors

1. Acknowledge past pregnancy loss. A previous loss such as a miscarriage can impact your feelings about the current pregnancy. You may find yourself excessively worried about the baby and if it will survive. Acknowledge the loss and allow yourself to work through the grief and disappointment.

- Do you find yourself constantly worried about the baby's health? Have you fully healed from the past loss? Does this affect your own well-being and emotional health?

- If you've experienced a pregnancy loss, don't hesitate to reach out for help. Your friends and family want to support you. Talk about the baby and use the name. It's okay to acknowledge what would have or could have been.

- For more information, check out How to Cope With Grief.

2. Ask a friend. If you think you may be depressed, ask a friend to reflect back to you any changes to your emotional health that he or she has noticed. Ask someone you know will be honest with you, such as a sibling or best friend. Share how you've been feeling and if he or she has noticed changes in your behavior, emotions, or moods.

3. Seek therapy. If you have suspicions that you may be depressed during your pregnancy, seek a

mental health professional. You can talk about your symptoms and how you feel. A therapist can give you a diagnosis and help emotionally support you through the pregnancy. She or he can help you find coping strategies to help lift the depression, help shift negative thoughts, give you tools to help adjust behaviors, and arm you with how to prevent future depression.

Part 4

Examining Home Life Difficulties

1. Examine relationship problems. If you're struggling with your romantic relationship with your partner, it can trigger depression. Some people try to stick it out and assume that having the baby will dissolve all the problems; it won't. The baby will only add strain to the relationship.

- Do you find yourself taking your stress out on your partner? Are issues between you and your partner more tumultuous than before you were pregnant? Think about how your relationship may have changed since becoming pregnant.

- Holding on to relationship stress can affect the growing fetus and increase the likelihood of the baby developing behavior problems in childhood. Let go of anger and resentment and work through relationship problems as quickly as possible.

- If your relationship is struggling, get counseling. Don't delay on getting the help you need. For more information, check out How to Tell if You Need to See a Therapist.

2. Deal with financial concerns. It's normal to be concerned about affording a new baby. However, financial difficulties may cause a significant amount of stress and contribute to depression. Before the baby comes, create a budget to help you feel more in control and reduce finance related stress.

- Try to make small changes to save money. For example, you can purchase generic items, watch for sales, clip coupons, buy frequently used items in bulk, or limit entertainment purchases, such as eating out or going to the movies.

- Consider DIY options to save money, such as making your own baby food or making reusable cloth diapers.

- Ask friends and family if they would be willing to help you with childcare after your baby is born. Friends and family members may also be willing to donate items to you such as baby clothes, a car seat, a baby monitor, or a stroller.

3. Acknowledge a past history of abuse. A history of abuse as a child may contribute to your risk of suffering from major depression as an adult. Abuse may take the form of sexual abuse, physical abuse, emotional abuse, and neglect. No matter what type of abuse you suffered as a child, it is important to seek help as an adult.

- If you were abused as a child, seek help from a therapist to work towards recovery.

- If you've experienced past abuse, check out How to Love Yourself After a Long Battle in an Abusive Relationship.

- If you're experiencing current abuse, please report it and seek help. See How to Leave an Abusive Relationship.

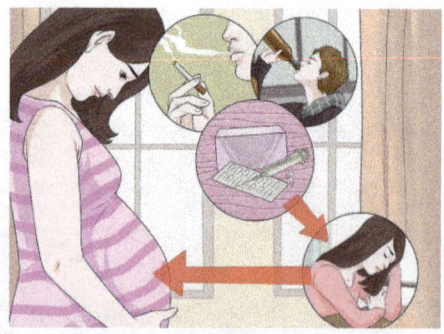

4. Look at major risk factors. If you are young, single, or have an unplanned pregnancy, you have a higher risk for depression. Other risk factors include a maternal age, lifestyle choices (like taking drugs, drinking alcohol, or smoking), medical history (like previous pregnancy complications), and carrying multiples. Think about how these factors may affect your well-being during pregnancy. You may need additional support during your pregnancy to avoid developing depression.

How to use Prenatal Massage Techniques

The University of Miami School of Medicine conducted a study that demonstrated prenatal massage techniques can help pregnant women sleep better. Massages during pregnancy can also improve anxiety, decrease pain in legs and hips and manage stress hormones. Keeping the mother and baby safe should be the first priority of any prenatal massage. Use prenatal massage techniques by working with the proper equipment, utilizing light pressure and paying attention to the changes that a pregnant woman's body is undergoing.

Steps

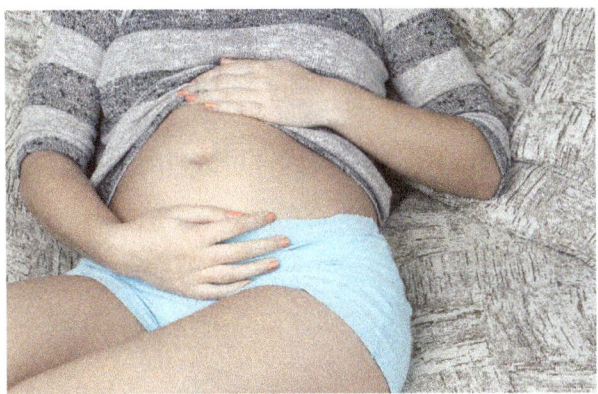

1. Wait until your second trimester to have a prenatal massage. The highest risk of miscarriage is during weeks 1 to 12 of a pregnancy, so most massage therapists avoid massaging women in their first trimester.

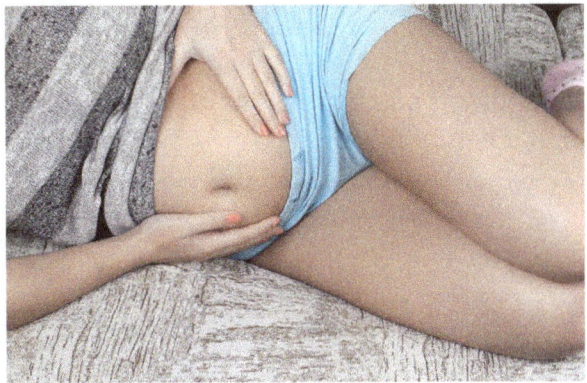

2. Lay on your side for a prenatal massage. There are specialty tables available with a uterus-sized cutout to allow a woman to lay on her stomach, but those tables can still apply dangerous pressure to the abdomen and pull on uterine ligaments.

- Use pillows to prop yourself on your side. Specialty pillows for prenatal massages are called bolsters.

- Have a massage sitting in a chair if it is more comfortable for you to sit. You do not need to be laying down to enjoy prenatal massage techniques.

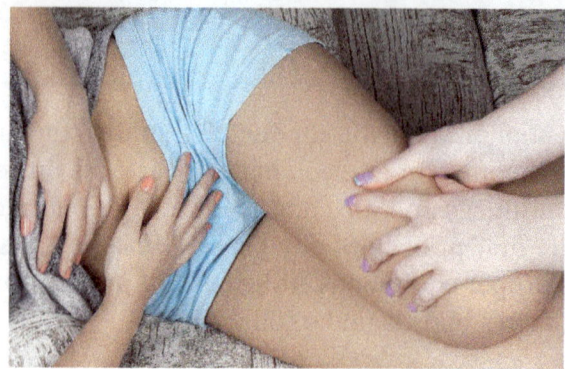

3. Work with a massage therapist who is experienced in prenatal massage. There are practitioners who are certified in this type of massage. Special training is offered on techniques that are safe and beneficial to pregnant women.

- Ask your massage therapist about certification or training in prenatal techniques. Each state has different standards and there is no national certification or program.

4. Avoid the pressure points in ankles and wrists. Prenatal massage should never include pressure on the areas that stimulate the uterus and the pelvis. Massaging the ankles and wrists is a technique often used to induce labor naturally.

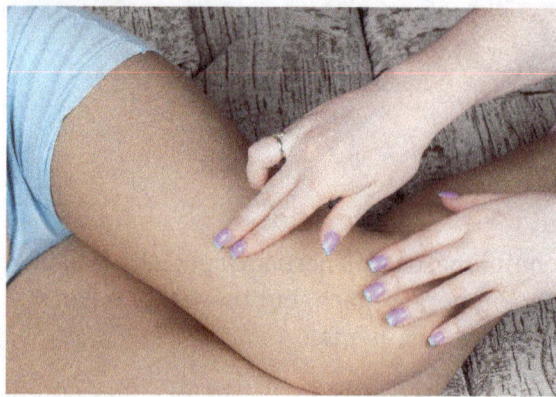

5. Adjust to lighter strokes during your massage. Prenatal techniques will involve less pressure than a Swedish massage or a deep tissue massage or any type of massage you might get when you are not pregnant.

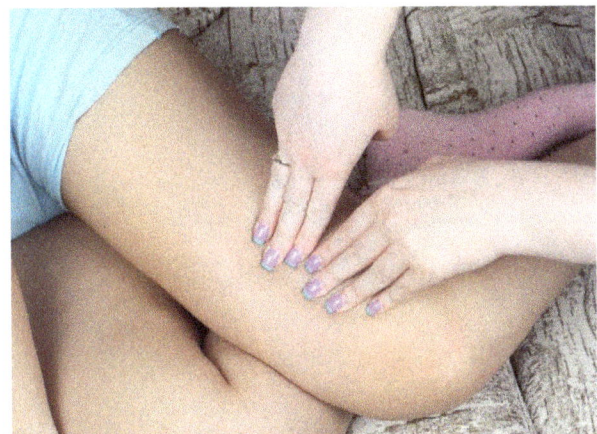

6. Watch the amount of pressure applied to your legs. The amount of blood a pregnant body produces is much higher, and the level of anticoagulants in the blood is also increased while the body prepares for labor and delivery.

- Avoid the calves and inner thighs. When you are pregnant, your risk of blood clots increases and strong massaging of your lower legs and inner thighs could dislodge a clot.

- Make sure all leg strokes move towards the heart. This prenatal technique will keep your circulation healthy and your risks low.

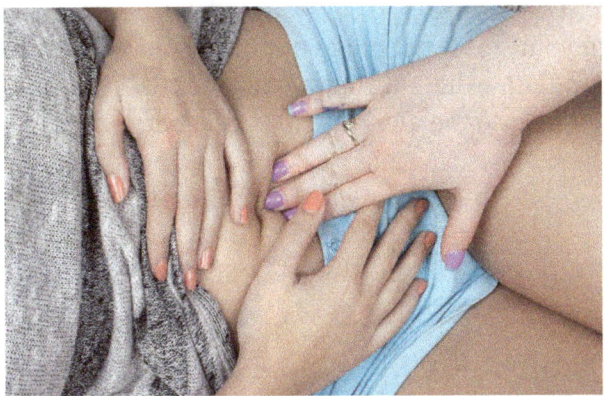

7. Keep the abdomen off limits. Most massage therapists will not touch the belly at all. If you do want your massage to include your stomach, the technique should be nothing more than light fingertips on the skin with no pressure.

How to Manage Anxiety During Pregnancy

An expectant mother may have a host of worries: her baby's health and well-being, her changing body, or even how to support her growing family. Although anxiety during pregnancy is common (researchers say as much as 33% experience anxiety or depression), it's nice to have practical strategies at hand to help you manage it. You can minimize the stress and anxiety you feel while pregnant by incorporating relaxation into your daily life and eliminating sources of anxiety.

Part 1

Doing Relaxation Exercises

1. Do deep breathing exercises. Taking slow, controlled breaths stimulates your body's natural relaxation response. Breathing deeply helps slow the heart rate, relieve muscle tension, and promote sleep. Plus, of all relaxation techniques, deep breathing is the most accessible to pregnant mothers—you can do this almost anywhere.

- For beginners, try deep breathing at home where you can sit or lie in quiet without interruptions. Sit comfortably on a couch or floor cushion. Or, lie down on your left side with a pillow beneath your right side (and a pillow between your legs, if desired).

- Breathe in through your nose, noticing your abdomen expanding gently. Hold the breath for a few counts and then exhale through your mouth. You should see your abdomen deflating a little as you release the air. Repeat as needed.

2. Try progressive muscle relaxation. This exercise helps you develop self-awareness to the tension in your body. You can do this in different settings to help you control your anxiety. To start, choose a place that is quiet and distraction-free.

- Sit or lie down comfortably. Start at your head (or your toes) and gradually move up through your body contracting and relaxing different muscle groups.

- For example, if you start at your head, you will wrinkle your forehead and eyebrows for a few seconds. Notice the tension. Then, release these muscles and notice how the tension melts away. Move on the next muscle group until you complete the entire body.

3. Do visualization exercises. Visualization, or guided imagery, is a relaxation technique that can help you achieve calm by envisioning a peaceful, stress-free environment. You can listen to a recorded audio/video of these exercises or you can simply use your imagination.

- As an example, imagine that you are walking along a windy, sunny beach. Activate all your senses to hear the roaring waves as they meet the shore. Listen to birds circling overhead. Smell the salty water. Feel the sand in between your toes and the water as it washes it clean with each wave.

- Perform this visualization exercise for as long as you'd like to relax after a stressful day.

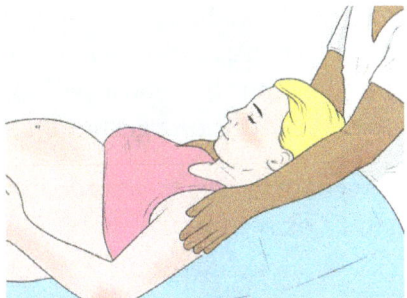

4. Get a massage. Massage is a wonderful treat for soothing your tired muscles during pregnancy. Luckily, massage therapy also offers a host of benefits like reducing joint and muscle pain, decreasing anxiety, reducing depressive symptoms, and improving labor outcomes.

- You can spring for a professional massage at a spa with a certified massage therapist, or you can ask your partner to massage your achy muscles.

5. Engage in regular self-care. In addition to using relaxation techniques to relieve stress, you may also find relaxation while engaging in soothing activities. Self-care is a terrific way to manage your anxiety on a daily basis by taking time out to do things that bring you pleasure.

- Self-care activities that help you ease tension and anxiety will depend on your individual preferences. Activities may include taking a relaxing soak in the tub, reading a new book, listening to music, chatting with your best friend, or watching the sunset.

Part 2

Nurturing your Health and Wellness

1. Engage in light exercise. Certain types of yoga, gentle stretching, walking, and swimming are all generally approved for pregnant women. In addition to combating stress, getting your body and your baby moving has many advantages, such as promoting better sleep, improving mood and energy, and minimizing pregnancy complications like constipation, bloating and backaches. Staying active while pregnant also lowers your risk of getting gestational diabetes.

- Although exercise is usually recommended by your doctor, be sure to discuss it with him or her beforehand to verify that it's okay in your situation.

2. Get enough sleep. Pregnancy can result in sleep disturbances for women who've never had trouble getting shut-eye. Side effects of pregnancy like nausea, stress, and changing hormone levels all play a role in you not getting enough rest. Although getting adequate sleep can be challenging, there are tips you can follow to improve your sleep quality and quantity. These include:

- Doing relaxation exercise to manage stress.

- Exercising at least 30 minutes per day (as long as your doctor says it's okay).

- Sleeping on your left side to improve blood flow and comfort.

- Cutting back on fluids a few hours before bed.

- Eating several small meals throughout the day and avoiding spicy, fried, or acidic foods that cause heartburn.

- Not forcing yourself to sleep; if you can't go to sleep, get up and do something like reading, journaling, or taking a bath.

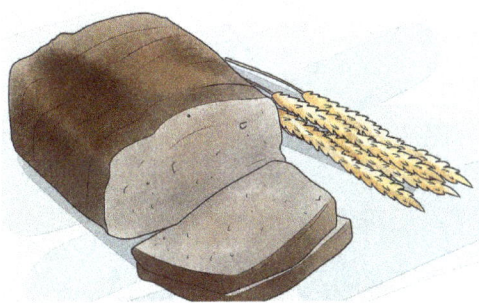

3. Watch your diet. Consuming whole foods with adequate nutrients not only supports your physical health but will also help you manage anxiety. Choose balanced and nutritious foods, including fruit and vegetables, lean sources of protein, seafood (which has been shown to ease anxiety), whole grains, and healthy fats found in nuts, avocadoes, and olive oil.

- Pregnant women should avoid raw eggs, soft mould-ripened cheeses, deli meats, uncooked or partially cooked meat, and fish with high mercury content. In addition refrain from drinking alcohol and caffeine to prevent complications.

4. Reduce your caffeine intake. It is important to cut back on your caffeine intake during pregnancy because caffeine may cross the placenta and increase your baby's heartrate. However, cutting back on caffeine may also help to reduce your anxiety.

- Avoid having more than 200 milligrams of caffeine per day. This is about the equivalent of two 8 ounce cups of brewed coffee.

5. See a therapist. If you have trouble managing anxiety and stress on your own, schedule an appointment with a mental health provider. A therapist with experience treating anxiety in pregnancy can work with you to relieve worries and concerns and promote relaxation.

- Cognitive-behavioral therapy has been shown to be particularly effective in the treatment of anxiety disorders. Consider this option before pharmacological treatments, as there is little research to show how anxiety medications affect your baby.

- You may also want to discuss non-pharmacological options with your therapist, such as biofeedback, pet therapy, and outdoor therapy.

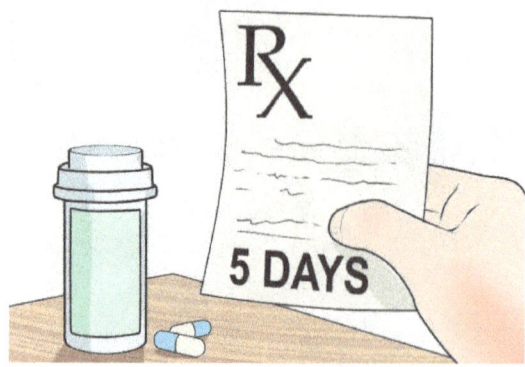

6. Take medication under your doctor's supervision. If your anxiety is severe, your doctor may recommend that you take prescription medication to manage your symptoms. You may have some concerns about how anxiety medications will affect your baby. There may be some risks depending on what medication you take.

- Therefore, if you are unable to reduce anxiety on your own, or if you are suffering from anxiety and depression at the same time, medication may be a practical option. Your doctor may suggest medication to minimize the likelihood of these conditions worsening or evolving into more severe conditions like postpartum depression or psychosis.

- Talk with your doctor to determine if medication is a good choice for your situation.

7. Join a support group. Leaning on your network of family and friends is incredibly important to reducing your stress and anxiety during pregnancy. However, it can also help to express your feelings and concerns in a support group with others who are experiencing anxiety, too.

- Talk to your doctor or mental health provider to help you locate a local support group for pregnant women. These other women can help alleviate fears, answer common questions and ease concerns you have as your pregnancy progresses.

Part 3

Reducing Stressors

1. Educate yourself about pregnancy. If this is your first pregnancy, much of your anxiety may come from feeling unprepared. Reading up on pregnancy as well as talking with your doctor and health care providers can help you feel better equipped to handle the next several months. Feeling informed can address many of your worries and concerns and reduce the stress that you are experiencing.

- While becoming informed about pregnancy may be empowering to some women, in others, it may heighten anxiety. If certain information you read about pregnancy creates anxiety within you, limit your exposure to this kind of literature. Plus, if you read something in a book or online that causes concern, speak with your doctor so that they can address your concerns and alleviate your worries.

2. Practice positive thinking. It can be easy to fall into a negative thinking trap when you are pregnant. You may find yourself thinking about a lot of worse-case scenarios that only heighten your anxiety. Attack negative thought patterns and "what ifs" with positive thinking.

- When you find yourself thinking negatively or worrying, talk to your partner, a close friend or a family member who can help you put your fears into perspective. Simply say "I'm really worried that my baby will be premature..." This person can provide a realistic sounding board for you.

- You can also challenge such thoughts on your own by stopping yourself and replacing such worries with more positive statements. For example, you say "I'm really worried that my baby will be premature..." To combat these worries, remind yourself that the majority of pregnancy complications won't actually happen, but, if they do, you will take the necessary actions to ensure your baby's health.

3. Learn how to say "no." If you're a woman who's guilty of playing superhero, being pregnant is an experience that forces you to cut back. It's impossible and probably risky for you to maintain the same levels of activity and obligations as you did before your pregnancy.

- Force yourself to take it easy and start bowing out of excessive responsibilities. Say "no" to unreasonable demands on your time. Look through your daily routine and search for ways you can cut back on duties or include more rest and relaxation. You may be feeling stressed because you are trying to wear all the hats you did before you had a growing baby inside of you.

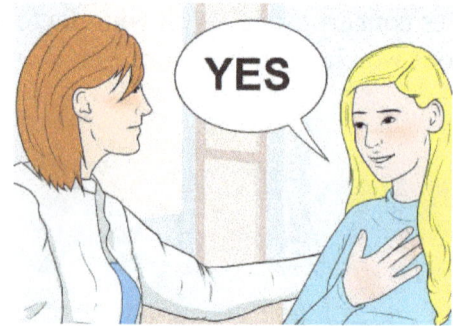

4. Say "yes" to offers to help. Another way to manage stress during pregnancy is to accept your friends' and relatives' offers to assist you. Don't try to do it all yourself. At some point near the end of your pregnancy, you will have to loosen the reins and start letting others help out more anyway. If you're already feeling stressed, start early and delegate chores and tasks to those around you. Odds are, they will be happy to lighten your load.

Techniques for Labour Assistance

Midwives provide care to reduce pain during childbirth. The woman's body goes through physiological changes that midwives monitor and assess. The aspects elucidated in this chapter are of vital importance and provide a better understanding of labor assistant in midwifery.

How to Induce Labor at Home

Your pregnancy due date is typically calculated at 40 weeks of pregnancy. If you are beyond 40 weeks, you may be uncomfortable, impatient and excited to get the birthing process started. Before you turn to medical interventions to induce labor, try a number of natural ways at home to start labor.

Method 1

Eating Certain Foods

1. Eat pineapple. Pineapple is one fruit that may trigger labor. It contains bromelain, which may help soften and "ripen" the cervix. This is a key stage in bringing on labor.

- Eat pineapple plain, drink pineapple juice, or make a fruit smoothie with pineapple.

2. Eat spicy foods. Some people swear by spicy foods as a catalyst for labor. Mexican food or foods

with hot chilis might help bring on labor. Be careful that these foods don't give you indigestion in this late stage of pregnancy.

- Some research shows that eating spicy foods might actually stave off labor, thanks to the capsaicin in some spicy foods. Capsaicin overtake naturally-occurring endorphins that help relieve pain.

3. Eat licorice. Black licorice is said to stimulate labor. Get natural licorice that contains less sugar. You can also get licorice in pill form. Licorice can stimulate cramps in the bowel by having a laxative effect. Bowel cramps may help induce uterine cramps.

4. Eat garlic. When you eat enough garlic, you may stimulate your bowels. This can cause you to empty your bowels, which gives room for the baby to move lower in your body. Once the baby moves down, it engages more with your uterus and cervix, readying your body for labor.

- Prepare foods with lots of garlic, as long as it doesn't give you indigestion.

5. Eat plenty of fiber. Foods that are rich in fiber will help you avoid being constipated. If you are

constipated, you will have a full bowel or rectum, which takes up space that the baby may need to move lower down in your body. Eat plenty of fruits and vegetables during the last few weeks of your pregnancy. Eating prunes and other dried fruits can help as well.

6. Drink red raspberry leaf tea. This tea can strengthen and tone the uterus, and can help the muscles start to contract. Brew a cup by pouring 6 ounces of boiling water over one tea bag. Let it steep for 3 minutes. Let it cool and drink.

- Make red raspberry leaf iced tea in the summer for a refreshing drink.

7. Drink cumin tea. Cumin can be used for digestive problems and also to start menstruation and to relieve bloating. Brew a cup of tea using cumin seeds to bring on labor.

- Add some sugar or honey to counteract the bitterness of the tea.

Method 2

Positioning your Body

1. Rest on all fours. Resting on all fours will help the baby into a good position. When the baby's

head puts downward pressure on your cervix, the cervix starts to efface, or shortens and thins out. Resting on all fours for 10 minutes at a time, several times a day, can help move the baby's head into the optimal position.

2. Don't recline backward on the couch. You are probably exhausted at this late stage of pregnancy and ready to just relax. But reclining or sitting back on the couch can be counterproductive to making sure the baby is in the right position for labor. Instead, lay on the couch on your left side, slightly rolled forward. Prop yourself up with cushions to make it comfortable.

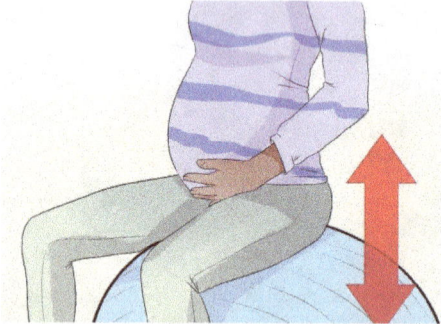

3. Bounce on a birth ball. A birth ball is a large bouncy ball (they are also used in exercising) that can help you sit comfortably towards the end of pregnancy. You can also use this ball to help you cope with labor. Sitting or bouncing on the ball, while spreading your legs wide, can help the baby move downward.

Method 3

Getting Physical Activity

1. Go for a walk. Walking can help stir the baby into moving downward in your body. Once the

baby's head puts pressure on the cervix, labor isn't far behind. Try walking for 15-20 minutes. Getting out in the fresh air can also be beneficial.

- Try walking up a steep hill. This will force your body to lean forward at an angle. Leaning at a 40-45 degree angle can help the baby move in the right downward direction.

2. Try galloping. Galloping, or moving one leg forward and hopping the back leg to catch up, can help jar the baby slightly. Be careful when trying this to make sure you don't trip over your feet.

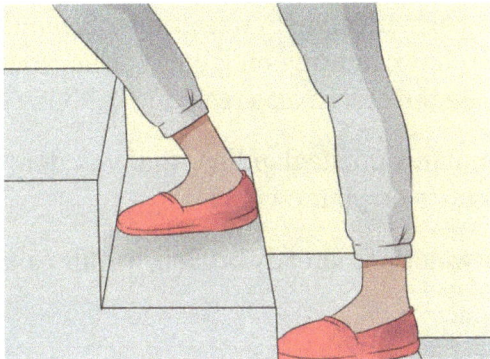

3. Walk up a few flights of stairs. Walking up stairs will force your body to lean at an angle (about 40-45 degrees), which can help the baby move lower down in your body. Be sure to hold onto the handrail to make sure you are ascending the stairs safely.

- Pounding your feet on each step can also help.

4. Clean the house. Doing a semi-strenuous activity can help bring on labor. Cleaning out the

garage, vacuuming, or mopping the floors gets your body moving, which can activate labor. You'll have the added bonus of having a clean house when the baby is born.

Method 4

Preparing your Body for Labor

1. Have sex. Having sex with a partner can help release prostaglandins, which are similar to hormones in your body. Prostaglandins can bring on labor. Sperm from an ejaculation inside the vagina can help to soften and dilate the cervix, also readying the body for labor.

- Having an orgasm stimulates prostaglandins, so if you don't feel comfortable having sex, you can still have an orgasm on your own.

- Do not have sex if your water has already broken, as this can put you at risk for infection.

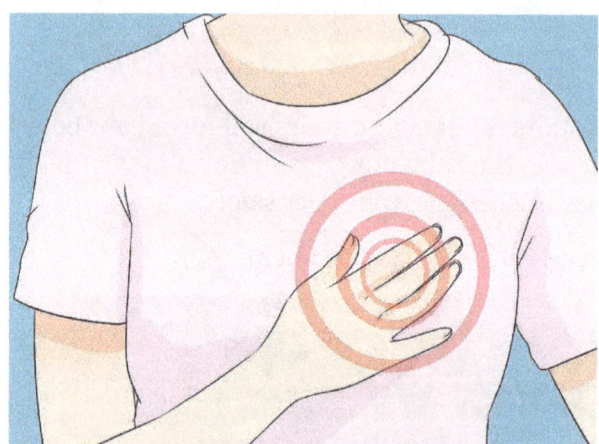

2. Stimulate your nipples. Nipple stimulation is another way to induce uterine contractions. Use your thumb and forefinger to roll the nipple for 2 minutes. Give it a rest for 3 minutes. Continue this process for about 20 minutes. If you don't feel any contractions, increase the rolling part to 3 minutes, with the rests lasting 2 minutes.

- Use olive oil on your fingers to prevent irritation.

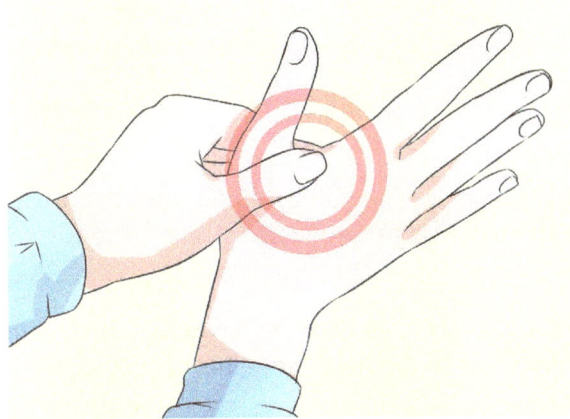

3. Use acupressure. Acupressure is similar to acupuncture, a traditional Chinese bodywork technique that promotes relaxation and healing. According to this healing technique, the body has acupoints through which energy flows. Applying direct, firm pressure to two of these points may help induce labor. To use acupressure:

- Locate the pressure points, which are in the webbing between your thumb and your index finger and on your lower leg about 3 inches (8 cm) above the inside of your ankle bone.

- Pinch the webbing of your hand. Rub for 30-60 seconds by moving in a circular motion.

- Press firmly with the tip of a finger or two fingers on the spot on your leg. Rub in a circular motion.

- With either of these pressure points, stop rubbing when you have a contraction. Start rubbing again when the contraction stops.

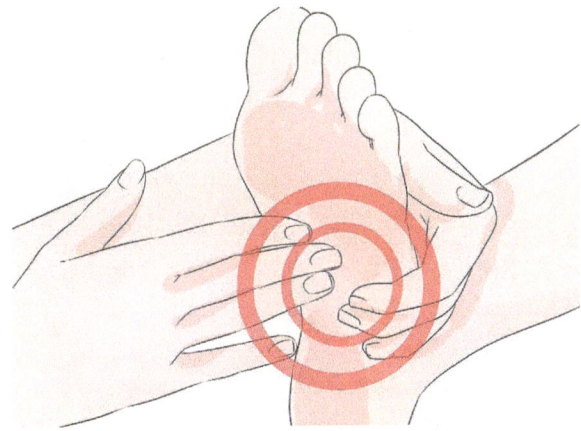

4. Use reflexology. Reflexology is a method of using pressure points in the feet to trigger labor within 24-48 hours. Use the pressure points that correspond to the pituitary, bladder, solar plexus, and ovaries and uterus to activate your body into labor. Put direct, firm pressure on one of these points, or rub in a circular motion with firm pressure.

- Pituitary: Located on the big toe, this pressure point will activate the pituitary gland, which releases hormones like oxytocin.

- Bladder: Located on the bottom of the foot near the instep, this pressure point can help the muscles around your uterus contract, which can in turn start uterine contractions.

- Solar plexus: Located in the center of your foot sole, this point will help you relax and feel more balanced.

- Ovaries and uterus: Located on your inner ankle, just below the malleolus (the bony part of the ankle that sticks out), this pressure point may be tender. This can jumpstart uterine contractions.

- Do not attempt reflexology before you reach 38 weeks, which can put you at risk for preterm labor. Definitely do not try it in the first trimester of pregnancy, as it can put you at risk for a miscarriage.

5. Try castor oil. Inducing labor by ingesting castor oil happens by causing intestinal cramps and stimulating the bowels. By contracting intestinal and bowel muscles, you can cause uterine contractions. These methods will cause diarrhea, which can be extremely uncomfortable.

- Mix 2 ounces of castor oil in a glass of juice. Drink it all at once.

- Alternately, you can try an in-home enema. However, use this method only once, and proceed with extreme caution. It can clear out your bowels and leave you quite dehydrated and uncomfortable.

Method 5

Using Herbal Treatments

1. Take evening primrose oil. Evening primrose oil contains prostaglandins, which is the

hormone-like substance that induces contractions and helps soften the cervix. Take this oil orally in 500mg capsules 3 times a day.

- Alternately, insert a capsule at bedtime into the vagina. The moist environment of the vagina will melt the capsule and disperse the gel throughout the cervix.

2. Take cohosh. Cohosh root is a medicinal plant that can be used to treat symptoms of menstruation, menopause and osteoporosis, and to induce labor. It is available as black or blue cohosh root, typically in water-based or alcohol-based tincture form. Follow the dosing instructions on the package.

- Black cohosh is thought to be more effective than blue cohosh.

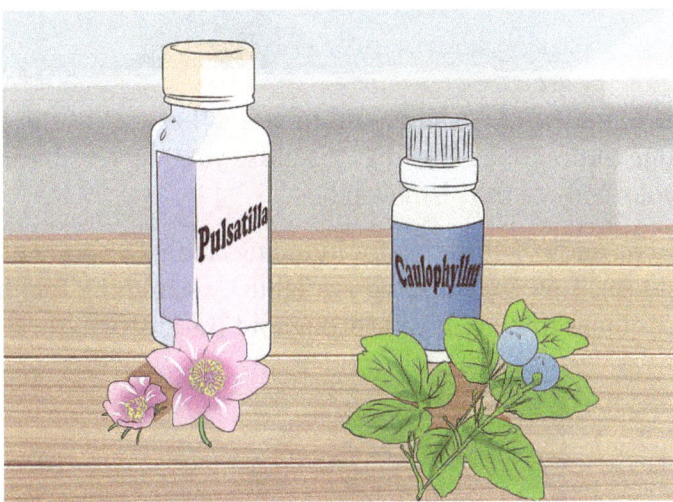

3. Try homeopathic remedies. Homeopathic remedies such as pulsatilla and caulophyllum can be used to stimulate labor. Pulsatilla is often used to treat menstrual symptoms, as well as headaches and insomnia. Caulophyllum can also help tone the uterine muscles, which helps with productive contractions.

- Follow the dosing instructions on the package for both of these remedies.

Method 6

Relaxing your Body

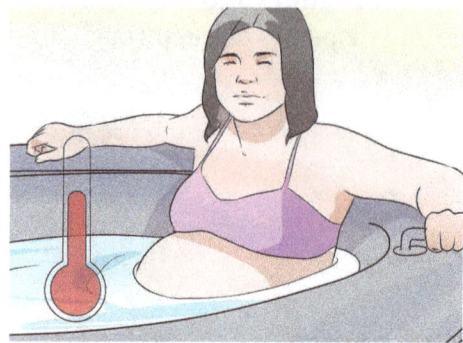

1. Take a warm bath. Sitting in a warm bath can help you relax your body and release tension in your muscles. Put a few drops of lavender essential oil into the water to help calm your mind.

- Make sure the water is not so hot that your skin turns red. You don't want to stress the baby with excessive heat.

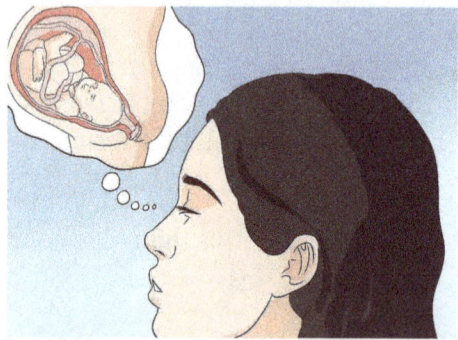

2. Try visualization. Sit in a meditative state and imagine the start of the birth process. Breathe deeply and visualize your contractions starting. Visualize your cervix dilating. Imagine your baby moving further down your body to the birth canal.

- Search online for an audio meditation for inducing labor. These are often available as down-loadable mp3 tracks. They may also be available by searching for "hypnobirthing," which uses similar techniques to sustain you throughout the entire natural birthing process.

3. Have a good cry. Crying can release tension in your body, which can help your body relax enough

to bring on labor. This point in your pregnancy can be a very stressful time, so give yourself the opportunity to cry it out.

- Grab a box of tissues and watch a good tearjerker movie to get the tears started if you need to.

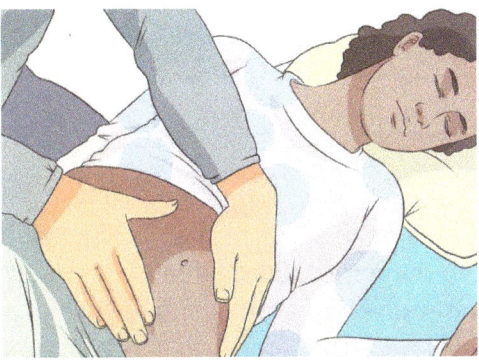

4. Get a massage. Getting a relaxing massage can be a great way to help your body stay calm. Make sure your massage practitioner is knowledgeable about giving prenatal massage. When you are getting your massage, lie down on your left side with a pillow between your knees to support your body.

Method 7

What to Expect from a Professional

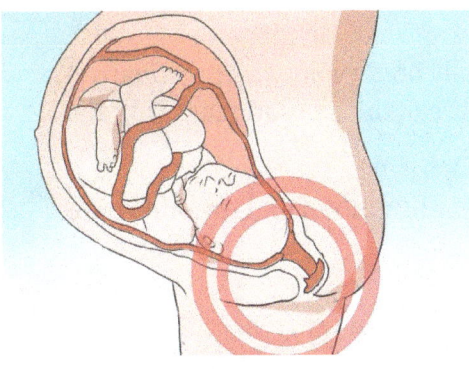

1. Know when a would doctor will induce labor. If you are committed to a home birth, you should still have a doctor or midwife present. Most doctors will not rush to induce labor unless there are extenuating circumstances, including when:

- Your water breaks, but there are no contractions.

- You are two weeks past your due date.

- You have an uterine infection

- You have gestational diabetes, high blood pressure, or not enough amniotic fluid.

- There is a problem with the placenta or baby's positioning/growth.

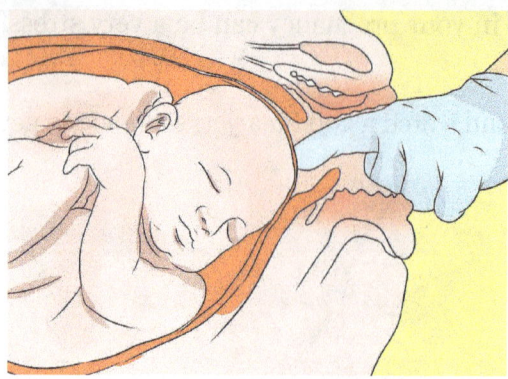

2. Expect the doctor's first action to be to strip the membrane from the amniotic sac. With gloved fingers, the doctor will reach into the cervix and rub the membrane of the amniotic sac until it separates from the uterine wall. Naturally-released hormones then usually kick-start labor.

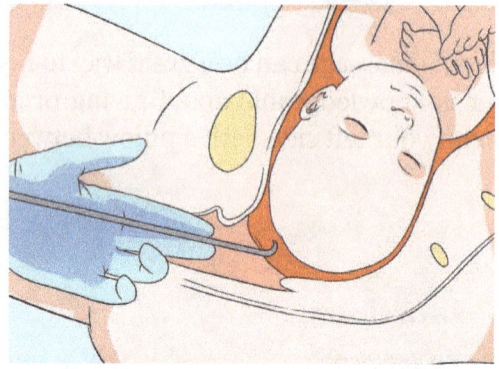

3. Expect the doctor to potentially break your water manually. Known medically as a "amniotomy," the doctor uses a thin hook to break the amniotic sac. This almost always brings on labor within a few hours.

- While it is short, this may be painful and uncomfortable.

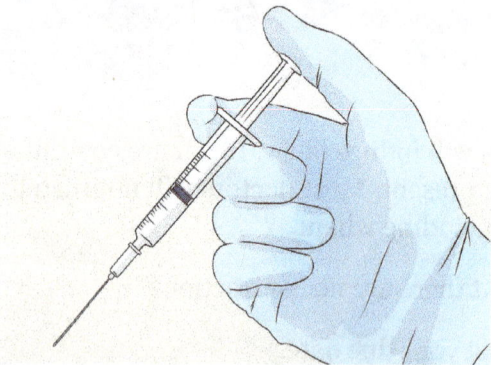

4. Prepare to be prescribed prostaglandin, a natural hormone. It may be applied directly to the vagina or taken orally. This usually happens in a hospital, and it thins out the cervix to prepare it for labor.

- This often leads to strong cramping and some pain.

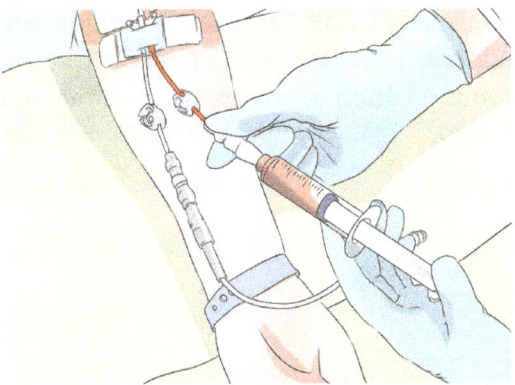

5. Expect to be prescribed oxytocin through an IV at the hospital. This is generally for slowed or stalling labor. In emergencies, like those outlined above, it can also help induce labor.

- Labor induced with oxytocin often leads to more frequent contractions.

6. With your doctor, understand the risks of inducing labor. These strategies do not always work, especially if the body is not quite ready to go into labor. If you've tried to induce labor and it failed, it is imperative to get to a medical facility. The following risks and precautions should be carefully minded:

- Infection (especially if water has broken)

- Tears in the uterine wall

- Late pre-term babies (beginning labor prematurely)

- Irregular contractions.

How to Speed up Early Labor

Entering early labor can be exciting when you're anxious to meet your baby. Early labor refers to the time between the onset of labor and when the cervix is dilated three centimeters. In some cases, unfortunately, you may enter early labor only to have your symptoms stall. Prolonged labor lasts for about 20 hours and it usually results in labor becoming latent in the early stages. It can be incredibly frustrating to suddenly have labor stall. Luckily, there are many things you can do to speed up labor, from shifting your position to creating a soothing atmosphere. In rare cases, medical intervention may be necessary.

Method 1

Moving Around to Help the Baby Shift

1. Get up and walk around. Walking can help the baby shift in the uterus, causing it to the descend towards the pubic bone. This sends a signal to your body that the baby is ready to be born, which may trigger labor to progress.

- Walking up and down stairs can be especially helpful to shift a baby in the right position for birth.

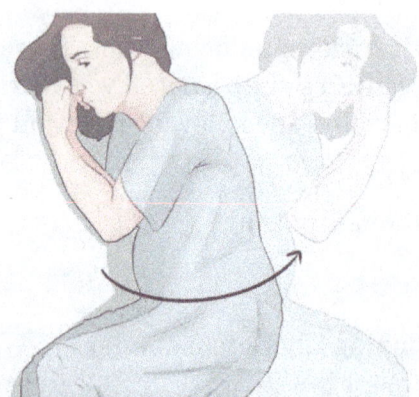

2. Shift around when you're lying down. Even if you're too tired to be walking up and down the stairs, you can move around in bed to help the baby reposition. Shift from your back to your side, for example, and then switch it up again a few minutes later. Staying in the same position will not help the baby move to speed up labor.

- Going from a sitting to standing position can be helpful. Try to get out of bed a few times an hour. If possible, walk around the room a bit before lying back down.

- Try lying on your left side. This increases blood flow to the baby and can improve pain.

3. Get on all fours. Your back will feel better, and you'll help the baby rotate into the face-down position he or she needs to take in order to come out. Get on the floor and gently hold yourself up on your hands and knees. Kneel on a pillow if that's more comfortable.

- However, it's a good idea to talk to your doctor before you try this or any other unusual stretches or movements. You want to make sure such motions are safe for your specific pregnancy.

Method 2

Trying other Methods

1. Relax and wait. Usually, the best thing you can do during prolonged labor is relax and accept you need to wait. If your doctor thinks your pregnancy is progressing normally, there is not a lot for you to do other than try to remain calm. As you usually do not have to go to the hospital during early labor, do things around your home to wind down like reading a soothing book or watching a movie you enjoy.

2. Create a soothing environment. While further studies are needed some evidence suggests stress could stall pregnancy. It certainly couldn't hurt to create a soothing, stress-free environment for yourself and it may help you get through early labor faster.

- Evaluate the room and take note of anything you don't like. Is the television too loud? Are the lights more bright? Do you want more privacy?

- Make any adjustments you need to create a soothing room for yourself. This may result in early labor picking up again.

3. Take a soothing bath. A nice warm bath can be relaxing, and can also help if you're feeling any physical pain from labor. While you're waiting for labor to progress, draw yourself a nice, warm bath and linger in the water until you feel calm.

4. Try to sleep. While sleep does not always speed up labor, it can make the time feel like it's going by faster. It's also a good idea to sleep during the early stages of pregnancy, when you're able to get rest. Eventually, you will progress to later stages where you'll need to push. Sleeping can help you build up strength.

- If you went into early labor during the night, it's particularly important to try to get some sleep.

5. Try nipple stimulation. Nipple stimulation has been known to speed up early labor for some. If you're having trouble getting through early labor, you can roll your nipples between your thumb and pointer finger. You can also rub your fingers with your palm. If you want, you can have a partner or a nurse do this for you.

- However, some women's fingers are very sensitive throughout the course of pregnancy. If your nipples are sore, do not cause yourself discomfort by engaging in nipple stimulation.

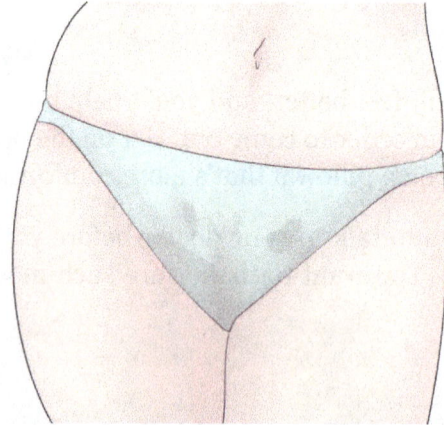

6. Have an orgasm. There is some evidence that having an orgasm can help labor progress. If you want, you can try to engage in sexual activity with your partner to bring about an orgasm. You can also try masturbation.

Method 3

Seeking Medical Solutions

1. Ask your doctor about any drugs you're taking. If you took drugs early in your pregnancy, they may be slowing down labor. In this case, flushing drugs from your system can help you advance through early labor. Talk to your doctor about any drugs you took and ask them for advice about how to get the drugs out of your system quicker.

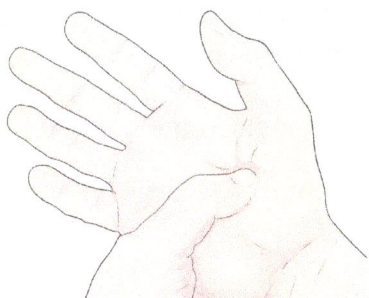

2. Apply acupuncture. If you can, book an acupuncture appointment during early labor. Pressing down on certain pressure points may affect hormones and speed labor.

- If your partner or midwife knows acupuncture, you can simply have them speed up your labor.

3. Have a doctor or midwife break your water. If your labor has been stalled for a long time, a doctor or midwife may suggest manually breaking your water to help labor progress. This is usually done during active labor, however, but may be done earlier in rare cases. Only go this route if your doctor or midwife suggest it, as you should not attempt to manually break your water on your own.

4. Try a hormonal drip. A hormonal drip administers Syntocinon, an artificial form of oxytocin which is a hormone that helps with labor. Your doctor will need to monitor your baby's heartbeat if a hormonal drip is used. It may help speed up a labor that has stalled.

How to Break your Water

Your water breaks when the fluid filled sac in which your baby is in ruptures. This usually occurs at the beginning of labor. You may suddenly feel a lot of fluid come out of your vagina all at once or it may be a trickle that comes and goes. If you are unsure if your water has broken, go to the hospital and get checked by a doctor. Under some circumstances your doctor may decide that it is necessary to break your water as a part of inducing labor. Do not try to break your water or induce labor yourself. The pregnancy should continue naturally unless there is a medical risk to you or your baby.

Part 1

Having a Doctor Break your Water

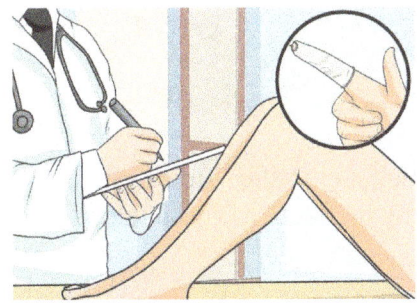

1. Let the doctor break your water if necessary. The doctor may suggest manually breaking your

water as a way of inducing labor. This is called an amniotomy. This will likely only be done if your cervix is dilating and the baby is in your pelvis in the birthing position. The doctor will put a probe inside you that has a hook on the end, sort of like a crochet needle. The hook will be used to puncture the amniotic sac. You will likely feel the water flow out when it breaks.

- This procedure may be uncomfortable but it will not harm you or the baby. The hospital may monitor the baby's heart rate throughout the procedure.

2. Recognize when your water breaks. Women's experiences when their water breaks are highly variable. Some women experience an obvious flood of fluid while other women have difficulty identifying it. If you are unsure, call your doctor or midwife. When your water breaks you may feel:

- Wetness in your vagina and underwear that is different from your normal pregnancy discharge.

- A small amount of fluid that starts and stops. It may be difficult to distinguish this from a trickle of urine.

- A continuous, but small flow.

- A sudden and unmistakable amount of water.

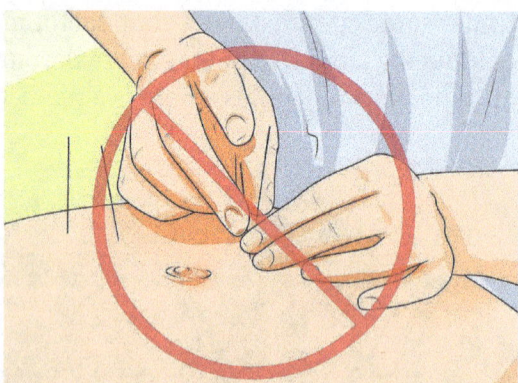

3. Do not try to induce labor yourself. Scientific studies suggest that commonly suggested methods of trying to start labor are generally ineffective. These include:

- Acupuncture

- Homeopathy

- Caster oil

- Enemas

- Hot baths with ginger oil. This has not been shown to shorten labor. Do not take ginger orally because it may increase your risk of bleeding.

- Sex. Having sex won't cause any problems for you or the baby if you have it before your water breaks. Afterwards you should not have sex because it may increase the risk of infection.

Part 2

Considering the Risks and Benefits of Induction

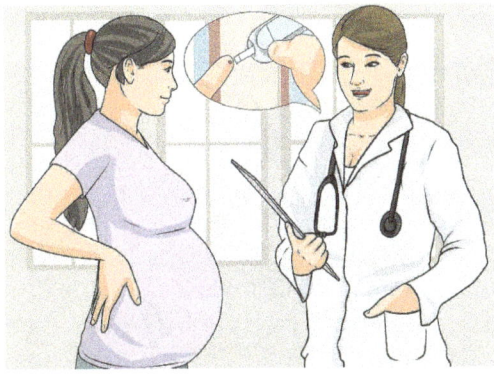

1. Ask your doctor why you should be induced. Generally you will only be induced if there is a reason why it is likely to be better for you and the baby. Reasons for induction include:

- You are in your 42nd week of gestation and labor isn't starting.

- You have an infection in your uterus.

- The baby isn't developing sufficiently.

- There isn't enough amniotic fluid in the sac.

- The placenta is separating from the wall of the uterus and / or starting to break down.

- You have diabetes or high blood pressure.

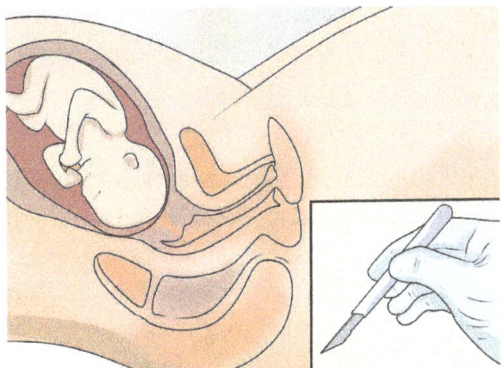

2. Do not have an optional induction. Some women want to schedule the birth ahead of time and

then be induced. The American College of Obstetricians and Gynecologists (ACOG) is not against elective induction but they do try to discourage across the board induction of everyone. Patients must be at least 39 weeks before induction will be considered. Risks include:

- If your cervix is not dilated enough, you will need a C-section.

- Manually rupturing the amniotic sac increases your infection risk.

- Inducing labor makes it more probable that the umbilical cord will slip into the vagina before the baby. If this happens as the baby passes through the baby will press on the umbilical cord and cut off its oxygen supply during the birth. This is very dangerous for the baby.

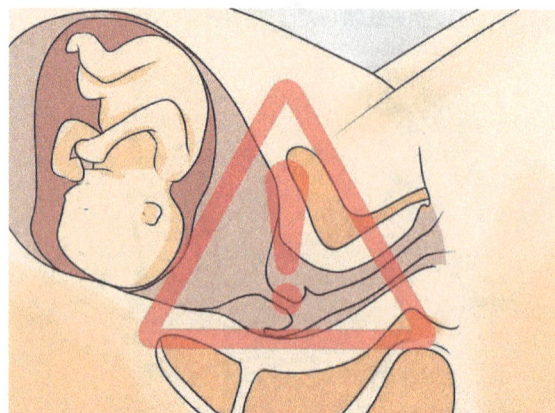

3. Accept that induction may not be an option. There are situations when a C-section, instead of a natural birth is necessary. Under these circumstances, induction is unsafe for you and the baby:

- The position of the placenta or baby makes a natural birth dangerous. This includes if the placenta is blocking your cervix or if the baby is not in the correct position. For example, if the baby is crosswise in the transverse fetal position you cannot be induced.

- There are concerns about whether you can physically give birth. This includes if your birth canal may be too small for the baby to fit through or if your uterus has been weakened by a prior surgery or C-section that makes it likely to rupture.

- Active infections, such as herpes or HIV, may also make a C-section safer.

How to Check a Cervix for Dilation

Cervical dilation happens as a pregnant woman gets closer to her labor and delivery. The cervix dilates in order to unblock your baby's path from your uterus to the birth canal, and finally to your arms. The cervix needs to dilate from one to 10 centimeters (3.9 in), at which point you can deliver your baby. In most cases, licensed professionals such as doctors, nurses, and midwives will check to see how far your cervix is dilated, but you also might want to get a sense for yourself. By feeling your cervix and watching for other signs like mood and noises, you can check your cervix to see how much it's dilated.

Part 1

Preparing to Check your Cervix Manually

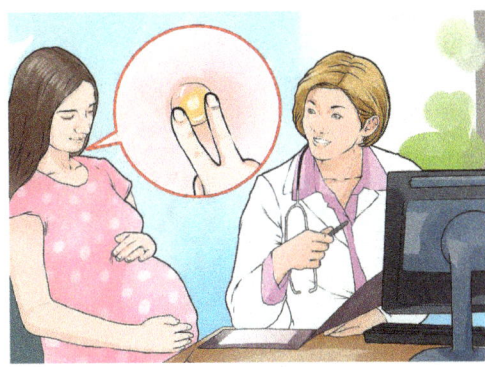

1. Talk to your medical professional. Having a safe pregnancy is important to a healthy birth and baby. Making sure you're getting proper obstetrical care from a doctor, nurse practitioner or midwife can help ensure not only that your pregnancy is progressing normally but also that it's safe for you to check your cervix for dilation.

- Be aware that beginning in your ninth month of pregnancy, your doctor will begin looking for signs that your labor is getting closer. This includes palpitating your abdomen and performing an internal exam to check your cervix. He or she will see if the baby has "dropped," which means that the cervix has begun to dilate and get softer.

- Ask your doctor any questions you may have, including if the baby has dropped. You should also ask if it is safe to check dilation on your own. If your pregnancy is safe, then you can proceed.

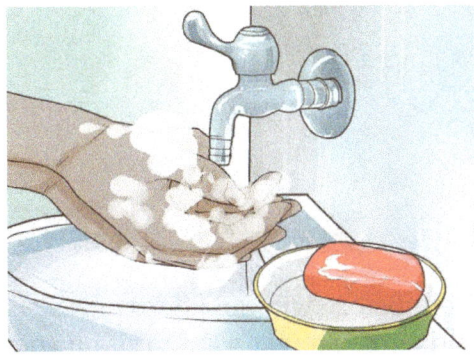

2. Wash your hands. Having dirty hands can spread bacteria and germs that cause infection. Checking your cervix requires inserting a hand or fingers into your vagina. It's extremely important to your health and that of your unborn baby to wash your hands before you check your cervix for dilation.

- Use any type of soap and some warm water to clean your hands. Wet your hands with running water and apply your soap, lathering well. Rub your hands vigorously for at least 20 seconds, making sure to scrub each surface of your hands. Rinse off the soap and then dry your hands thoroughly.

o   Use a hand sanitizer of at least 60% alcohol if you don't have soap. Apply enough of the sanitizer for both hands to the palm of one hand. Just as with soap, rub your hands together and make sure you cover every surface including nails. Keep rubbing until your hands are dry.

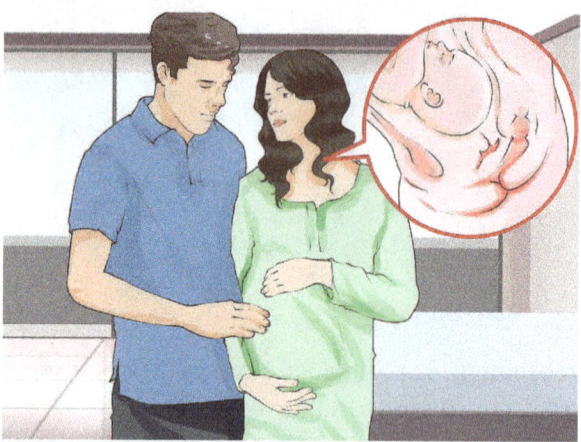

3. Reach out for help. If you're a bit worried or scared about doing the exam on your own, ask your partner or another loved one for help. Allow the person to help as much as you are comfortable with and like. Support can come in the form of holding a mirror or your hand or even offering calming words.

4. Get into a comfortable position. Before you can effectively check your cervix for dilation, you need to be in a comfortable position. You might want to sit on your toilet or lie on your bed with your legs spread, just do what is most comfortable for you.

- Take off your clothes on your lower half before you start. This way, you don't have to awkwardly remove them when you're comfy.

- Sit or squat on the toilet with one foot on the floor and the other on the toilet seat. You can also squat on the floor or lie on your bed if these are more comfortable

- Remember that you have nothing about which to be ashamed. You're doing something completely normal and natural.

Part 2

Checking your Cervix at Home

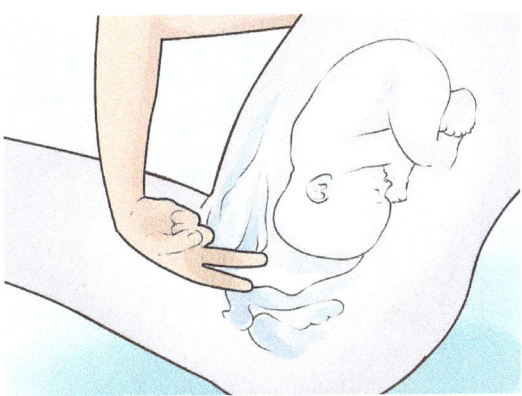

1. Insert two fingers into your vagina. You'll need to start your exam by getting an initial sense of how far you may be dilated. Instead of putting your entire hand into your vagina, which may cause discomfort, use your pointer and middle fingers to start checking your cervix.

- Remember to wash your hands thoroughly with soap and water before inserting your fingers in your vagina.

- Locate the entrance of your vagina with the tips of your fingers. The back of your hand should be facing your spine and your palm should face upwards. Angle your fingers back towards your anus to most effectively feel your cervix. If you feel any pain or extreme discomfort, remove your fingers.

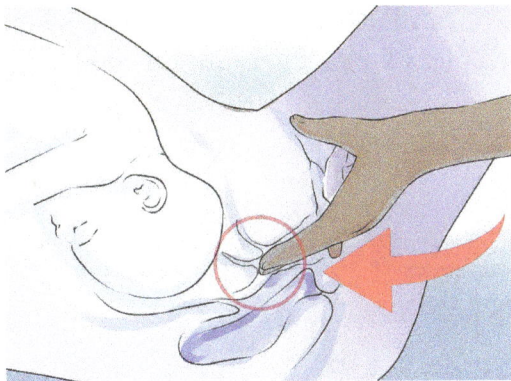

2. Push your fingers to your cervix. A woman's cervix feels like a pair of puckered lips when pregnant. After you've inserted your fingers into and up your vaginal canal, keep pushing them until you reach what feels like the puckered lips.

- Be aware that some women have a high cervix and others have a low cervix. You may need to insert your fingers further up your vaginal canal or may reach it relatively quickly. The cervix is basically the "end" of your vaginal canal no matter its position in your body.

- Use a gentle touch to feel for your cervix. Pressing or poking it with your fingers can lead to bleeding.

- Recognize that one finger may easily slip into the middle of your cervix if it is dilating. What you may feel at the center of the opening is your bag of waters that covers the baby's head. You may find this has the sensation of a latex balloon filled with water.

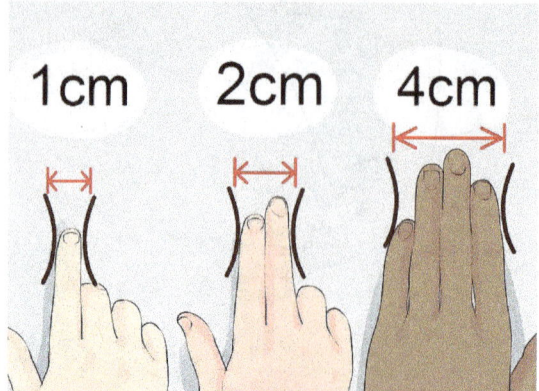

3. Continue using your fingers to feel how far you're dilated. Once a woman is dilated 10 centimeters, she'll generally ready to deliver her baby. If one of your fingers entered the middle of the cervix easily, you can use additional fingers to figure out how far along your dilation is.

- Keep in mind the following: if you can slip one finger into the middle of your cervix, you're about one centimeter dilated. Likewise, if you can insert five finger widths into your cervix, you're about 5 centimeters dilated. As your labor progresses, your cervix will go from feeling tight to like an elastic band. At 5 centimeters, it may feel like and have the thickness of a rubbery circle jar ring used in canning.

- Continue to insert fingers gently into your vagina until you're using your entire hand or it causes discomfort. Remove your hand to see how many finger widths you used. This can give you a general idea of how far your cervix is dilated.

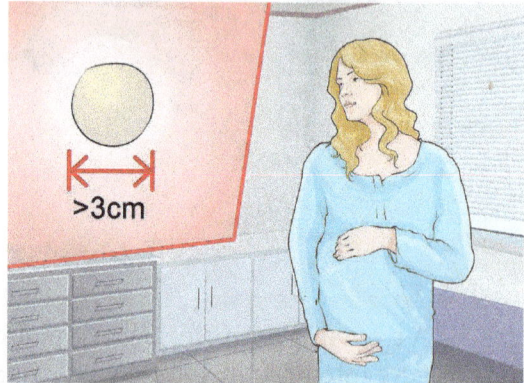

4. Go to your delivery center. If you're cervix is dilated more than 3 centimeters, it generally means you are in the active phase of labor. You should go to the delivery center you've chosen or prepare your home if you're having a home birth.

- Be aware that your contractions can also help indicate that you should go to the delivery center. They will be more regular and stronger. They should be about five minutes apart and last for 45-60 seconds.

Part 3

Looking for Additional Signs of Cervical Dilation

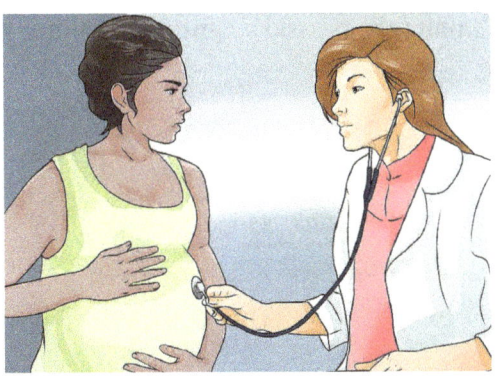

1. Listen for the sounds of dilation. There are many indicators of dilation that don't require inserting your fingers into your vagina. This can be especially helpful if you are in a lot of pain or discomfort. Most women will make some type of sound when they're in labor. Listening to what types of sounds you're making can cue you into how much you're cervix has dilated. The following sounds can accompany the various stages of labor and cervical dilation:

- At 0-4 centimeters dilated, you may not be making much noise and can talk through a contraction with little effort.

- At 4-5 centimeters, it may be difficult to nearly impossible to talk. Your noises may still be quiet.

- Between 5-7 centimeters, you may make louder and staccato noises. It should be nearly or completely impossible to talk through contractions.

- Between 7–10 centimeters (2.8–3.9 in), you may be making very loud noises and shouldn't be able to talk through a contraction.

- If you're a silent laborer, you can also check your dilation. Tell someone to ask you a question at the start of a contraction. The less you are able to say a sentence, the farther along your dilation is.

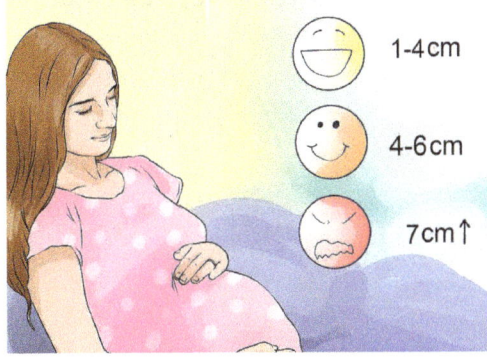

2. Pay attention to your emotions. Childbirth is an inherently emotional experience for the woman in labor. Watching what emotions you're experiencing can cue you into how far your cervix is dilated. You may have the following emotions during labor:

- Happiness and laughter between 1-4 centimeters

- Smiley and laughing at little things between contractions between 4-6 centimeters

- Irritation at jokes and small talk around 7 centimeters until birth.

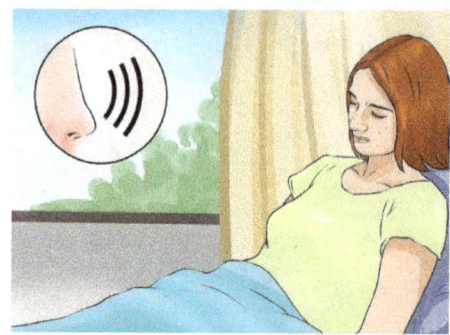

3. Smell for dilation. Many people will notice certain scents when a woman gets to between 6 and 8 centimeters dilated. The smell of labor is deep, heavy, and dusky—not musky. If you notice a distinct change to these scents in the smell of the room in which you're laboring, your cervix may be between 6 and 8 centimeters dilated.

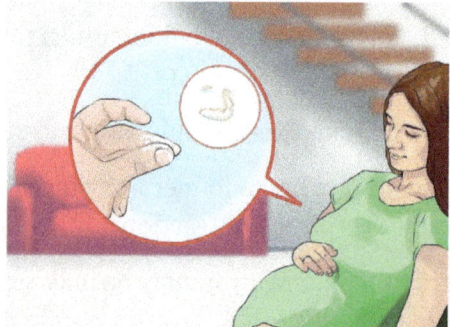

4. Look for blood and mucous. Some women may see a stringy mucus discharge at 39 weeks that is tinged pink or brown with blood. This bloody show may continue through the early stages of labor. At 6-8 centimeters dilated, however, a lot of blood and mucus may be present. Looking for these substances can indicate that you're somewhere between 6-8 centimeters dilated.

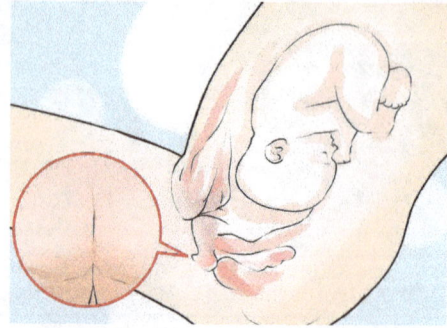

5. Examine the purple line. The purple line is located in your natal cleft, or what some people call the butt crack. This line can be a measure of how far you're dilated, with it reaching the top of your cleft at full dilation. You may need someone to help you examine your purple line.

- Recognize that in the early stages of labor that the purple line will be closer to the anus. As your labor progresses, it will creep up between your buttocks. At full dilation, the purple line will extend to the top of your natal cleft.

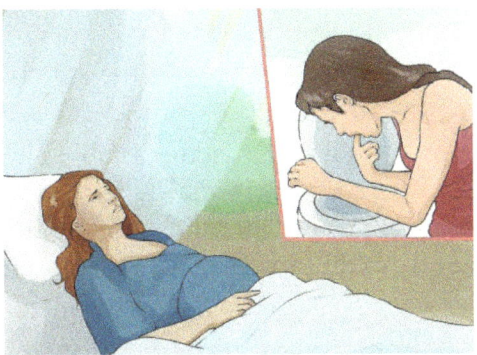

6. Scan how your body feels. Many women experience physical signs of dilation that are visible without a vaginal examination. In general, many will feel like they have the flu as they get close to 10cm and/ or the pushing phase. Scanning your body for these signs and symptoms can help you figure out how much your cervix has dilated. In most, cases, a combination of these signs can indicate how you're your cervix is dilated.

- Feeling like you have to vomit, having a flushed face and feeling warm to the touch can mean you're about 5 centimeters dilated. You may also tremble uncontrollably. Vomiting alone may be the result of emotions, hormones, or fatigue.

- Seeing if your face is flushed with no other signs can be a good indicator that you're 6-7 centimeters dilated.

- Be aware that trembling uncontrollably without any other signs can indicate fatigue or fever.

- See if you're curling your toes or standing on your toes, which is a sign you're between 6 and 8 centimeters dilated.

- Check your buttocks and upper thighs for goose bumps, which is a good sign that you're at 9-10 centimeters.

- Recognize that having involuntary bowel movements is also a sign of full dilation. You may also see or feel the head at your perineum.

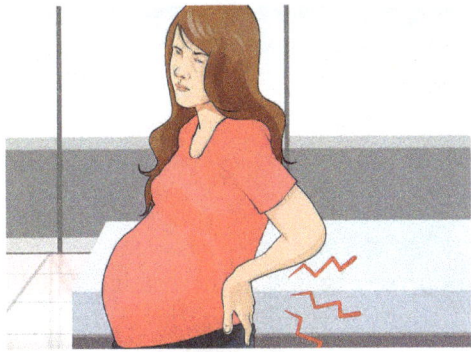

7. Feel for pressure in your back. As your baby descends into the birth canal, you will feel pressure

at different points along your back. The more you dilate, the farther down your back the pressure will be lower. It will generally move from the rim of your pelvis down to your tailbone.

How to Deliver a Baby

Whether you're an expectant parent or an unsuspecting cabbie, the time may come when you are called upon to help deliver a baby with no professional help in sight. Don't worry — people have to do this all the time. Most of what you need to do is help the mother relax and let her body do the work. That being said, there are steps you can take to ensure that everything goes as smoothly as possible until help arrives.

Part 1

Preparing for the Birth

1. Call for help if possible. Contact emergency services. That way, even if you have to deliver the baby yourself, help will arrive soon if you experience complications. The dispatcher should also be able to either talk you through the delivery or connect you to someone who can.

- If the mother has a doctor or midwife, call that person too. The medical professional can often stay on the phone and help guide you through the process.

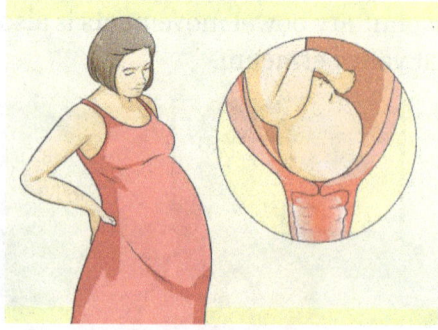

2. Determine how far labor has progressed. The first stage of labor is called the "latent" stage, where the body is getting ready to deliver by dilating the cervix. It can take a *long* time, especially if this is the woman's first child. The second, or "active" stage occurs when the cervix has completely dilated.

- Women may not experience as much pain or discomfort during this stage as later stages.

- If the woman is fully dilated, and you can see the baby's head crowning, she's in stage two. Wash your hands, skip to the next section and get ready to catch the baby.

- Unless you have been trained to do so, don't try to examine the cervix. Just watch to see if the head begins to appear.

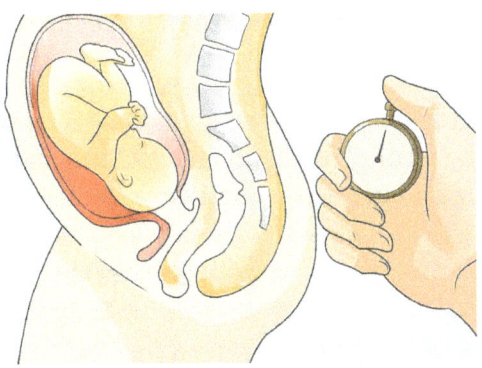

3. Time contractions. Time the contractions from the beginning of one to the beginning of the next, and note how long they last. The further along labor is, the more regular, stronger, and closer together contractions become. Here's what you need to know about contractions:

- Contractions that are 10 minutes apart or less are a sign that the mother has entered labor. Physicians recommend that you contact the hospital when contractions are 5 minutes apart and last 60 seconds, and this activity has been going for an hour. If this is the case, you probably have time to make it to the hospital if you live close to one.

- First-time mothers are likely to give birth when contractions are three to five minutes apart and last 40 to 90 seconds, increasing in strength and frequency for at least an hour.

- If the contractions are two minutes or less apart, buckle down and get ready to deliver the baby, especially if the mother's had other children and they were fast labors. Also, if the mother feels like she's going to have a bowel movement, the baby is probably moving through the birth canal, creating pressure on the rectum, and is on its way out.

- If the baby is preterm then you should contact the mother's physician and emergency services at any signs of labor.

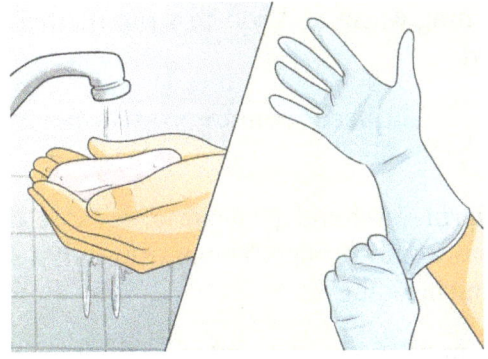

4. Sanitize your arms and hands. Remove any jewelry, such as rings or watches. Wash your hands

thoroughly with antimicrobial soap and warm water. Scrub your arms all the way up to your elbows. If you have the time, wash your hands for five minutes; if you don't have time for that, wash them thoroughly for at least one minute.

- Remember to scrub in between your fingers and under your nails. Use a nail brush or even a toothbrush to clean under your nails.

- Wear sterile gloves if available. Don't wear things like dishwashing gloves, which are likely loaded with bacteria.

- To finish (or if you don't have access to soap and water), use an alcohol-based hand sanitizing product or rubbing alcohol to kill off any bacteria and viruses that may have been on your skin. This helps prevent giving the mother or the baby an infection.

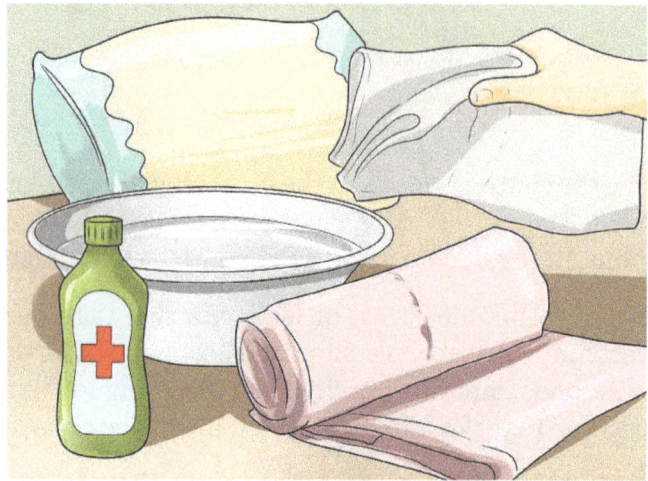

5. Prepare a birthing area. Get set up so that you have everything you'll need within easy reach, and so the mother is as comfortable as possible. There will be a mess afterwards, so you may want to have the birthing area somewhere you don't mind getting messy.

- Collect clean towels and clean sheets. If you have clean waterproof tablecloths or a clean vinyl shower curtain, these are excellent at preventing blood and other fluids from staining furniture or carpeting. In a pinch, you can use newspapers, but they are not as sanitary.

- Get a blanket or something warm and soft to wrap the baby in. The infant must be kept warm once it's delivered.

- Find a few pillows. You might need them to prop up the mother as she's pushing. Cover them with clean sheets or towels.

- Fill a clean bowl with warm water and get a pair of scissors, a few lengths of string, rubbing alcohol, cotton balls, and a bulb syringe. You may find that sanitary napkins or paper towels are helpful to stop the bleeding later.

- Get a bucket in case the mother feels nauseated or the need to vomit. You may also want to get a glass of water for the mother. Labor is hard work.

6. Help the mother stay calm. She may feel panicky, rushed, or embarrassed. Do your best to remain calm and reassuring to help her relax.

- Ask the mother to undress from the waist down. Provide her with a clean sheet or towel to cover up, if she'd like.

- Encourage her to breathe. Avoid hyperventilation by speaking in a low, soothing voice and verbally directing her breathing. Encourage her to inhale through her nose and out through her mouth in an even, rhythmic manner. If you're still having trouble, hold her hand and take deep, slow breaths along with her.

- Reassure her. This is probably not the birthing experience she had in mind, and she might be worried about potential complications. Tell her help is on the way, and you'll do the best you can in the meantime. Remind her that people have given birth outside of hospitals for thousands of years, and it's more than possible to come through it safely.

- Validate her. The mother may feel scared, angry, giddy, or any combination of those feelings. Validate whatever she is feeling. Don't try to correct her or argue with her.

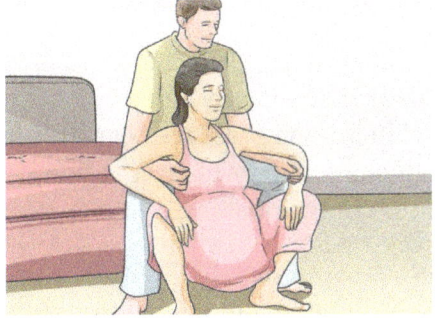

7. Help the mother find a comfortable position. She might want to walk around or crouch down during this stage of labor, especially when a contraction hits. As she starts to transition to the second phase, she might want to settle into a position to give birth or cycle through a few different ones. Switching between positions may help the labor progress more smoothly, but let her decide what's working for her body. Here are four standard positions, and the pros and cons of each:

- Squatting. This puts gravity to the mother's advantage, and can open the birth canal 20%-30% more than other positions. If you suspect the baby is breech (emerging feet-first), suggest this position as it gives the baby room to rotate. You can help the mother in this position by kneeling behind her and supporting her back.

- All-fours: This position is gravity-neutral and can ease back pain, and the mother might instinctively choose it. It can provide pain relief if the mother has hemorrhoids. Position yourself behind her if that's the case.

- Side-lying: This leads to a slower descent through the birth canal, but can lead to a more gentle stretching of the perineum and may reduce tearing. Have the mother lie on her side, with her knees bent, and lift the top leg. She might also need to prop herself up on an elbow.

- Lithotomy position (lying back). This is the most common position used in hospitals, with the woman lying flat on her back and her legs bent at the knee. It allows maximum access for the caregiver, but it puts a lot of pressure on the mother's back and is not considered ideal. It also may make contractions slower and more painful. If she seems to prefer this position, try putting a few pillows under her back to ease the pain.

Part 2

Delivering the Baby

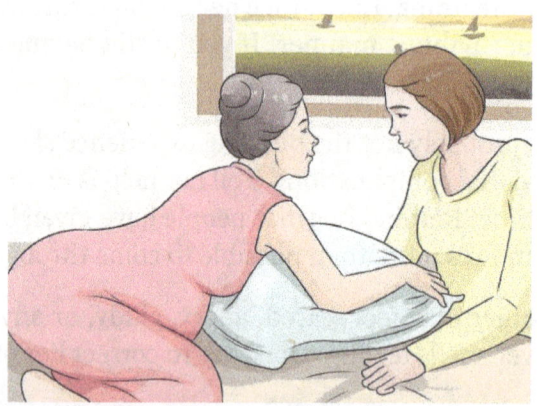

1. Guide the mother in pushing. Don't encourage her to push until she feels an unstoppable pressure to do so — you don't want to waste her energy and make her exhausted too early. When women are ready to push, they may feel increased pressure near their lower back, perineum, or rectum. It may even feel to her as though she is ready to have a bowel movement. When she is ready, though, you can help guide her through the pushing.

- Ask the mother to curl forward and tuck her chin. This curved position will help the baby through the pelvis. When pushing, it can be helpful if the mother holds her knees or legs with her hands and pulls her legs back.

- The area around the vagina will bulge out until you see the top of the baby's head (crowning). As soon as the baby crowns, it's time for the mother to push in earnest.

- Encourage her to focus her abdominal muscles to push *down*, as you might do when you're trying to urinate faster or have a bowel movement. This can help avoid straining or directing the pushing force upward toward the neck and face.

- Three to four pushes, lasting 6-8 seconds each, are considered appropriate per contraction. However, it is important to encourage the mother to do whatever comes naturally to her.

- Keep encouraging deep, slow breathing. Pain can be controlled to different extents through mental relaxation and by concentrating on deep breathing instead of panicking or being distracted by everything that is going on. Different people have different levels of mental control, but deep, slow breathing is always a benefit during childbirth.

- Understand that the woman may urinate or have a bowel movement during labor. This is normal and is not a cause for concern. Don't even bother mentioning it -- you don't want to embarrass the mother.

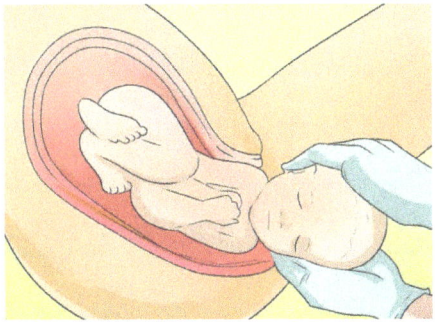

2. Support the baby's head as it emerges. This step isn't complicated, but it's important. Pay extra attention to these tips:

- *Do not pull on the baby's head or the umbilical cord*. This can cause nerve damage.

- If the cord is wrapped around the baby's neck, which is fairly common, *gently* lift it over the baby's head or carefully loosen it so the baby can slip through the loop. *Do not pull on the cord.*

- It's natural -- and in fact desirable -- for the baby to pass through the pelvis face-down. If the baby's face is facing toward the mother's back, don't worry. This is actually the best position for delivery.

- If instead of the head emerging you see the feet or buttocks coming first, you have a breech birth. See instructions for that situation below.

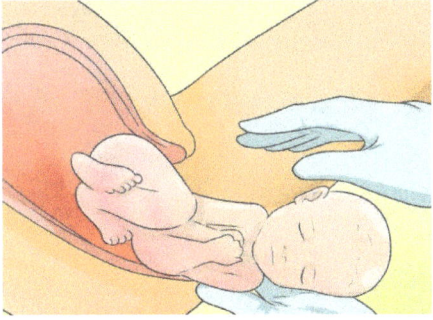

3. Prepare for the baby's body to emerge. When the baby's head rotates to one side (which it will probably do on its own), be prepared for the body to come out with the next push.

- If the baby's head does not rotate to one side, ask the mother to push again. The baby will likely rotate spontaneously.

- If the baby's head doesn't rotate without help, gently turn it to one side. This should help a shoulder emerge with the next push. Don't push it if you feel any resistance.

- Deliver the other shoulder. Gently lift the body toward the mother's stomach to help the other shoulder come through. The rest of the body should follow quickly.

- Keep supporting the head. The body will be slippery. Make sure you're still providing enough support for the baby's neck, which isn't strong enough to support the head on its own.

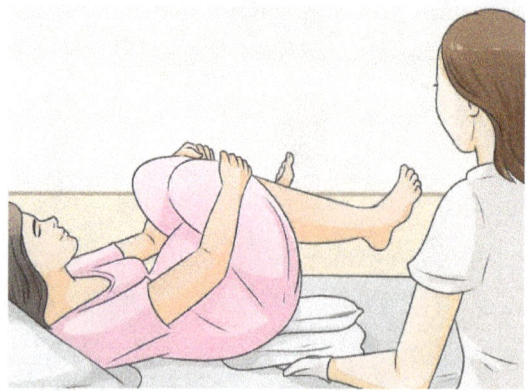

4. Manage complications. Hopefully, all goes well, and you've successfully delivered a healthy baby by now. If the delivery seems stalled, though, here's what you can do:

- If the head comes out, and the rest of the body doesn't come out after she pushes three times, have the mother lie on her back. Instruct her to grab her knees and pull her thighs toward her stomach and chest. This is called the McRoberts position, and it's very effective at helping push the baby out. Have her push hard with each contraction.

- Never push on a mother's abdomen to try to help deliver a stuck baby.

- If the feet come out first, see the section on breech birth below.

- If the baby is still stuck *and* paramedics are still nowhere near the scene then you could try to guide the baby's head gently downward toward the mother's rectum. This should only be attempted as a last resort, and should not be attempted at all if medical attention will be arriving soon.

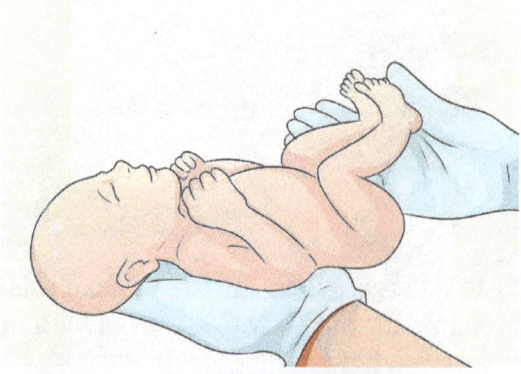

5. Hold the baby, so the fluids in its mouth and nose drain. Hold the delivered baby with two

hands, one supporting its neck and head. Tilt the head down at about a 45-degree angle to allow the fluids to drain. The feet should be slightly above the head (but don't hold the baby by the feet).

- You can also wipe any mucus or amniotic fluid from the nose and mouth area with clean, sterile gauze or cloth.

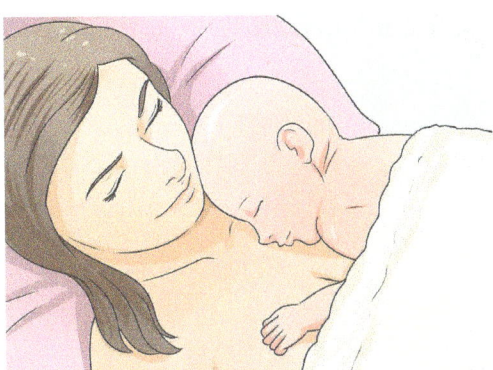

6. Place the baby on the mother's chest. Ensure full-skin contact, and cover them both with clean towels or blankets. The skin-to-skin contact encourages a hormone called oxytocin, which will help the mother deliver the placenta.

- Position the baby so that its head is still slightly lower than the rest of the body, so fluids can keep draining. If the mother is lying down and the baby's head is on her shoulder, and its body is on her breast, this should happen naturally.

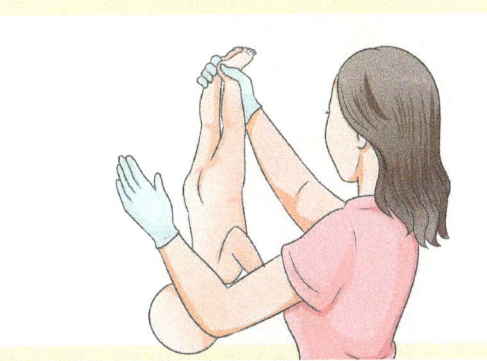

7. Make sure the baby is breathing. It should be crying slightly. If it's not, you can take a few steps to help make sure the airway is clear.

- Rub the body. Physical touch will help the baby breathe. Rub over its back firmly with a blanket while it's still on its mother's chest. If that's not helping, turn the baby so that it's facing the ceiling, tilt the head back to straighten the airway, and keep rubbing the body. It might not cry, but doing this ensures that the baby gets the air it needs.

- Rubbing vigorously with a clean towel can also help stimulate the baby to breathe.

- Manually clear fluids. If the baby gags or turns blue, wipe fluids out of the mouth and nose with a clean blanket or cloth. If that doesn't do the trick, squeeze the air out of a bulb syringe, put the tip in the nose or mouth, and release the bulb to suck the fluid into the bulb. Repeat until all the fluid is cleared, emptying the bulb between uses. If you don't have a bulb, you can use a drinking straw.

- If nothing else has worked, try flicking the soles of the baby's feet with your fingers, or gently popping its bottom. Don't slap the baby.

- If none of this helps, perform infant CPR.

Part 3

Delivering a Breech Birth

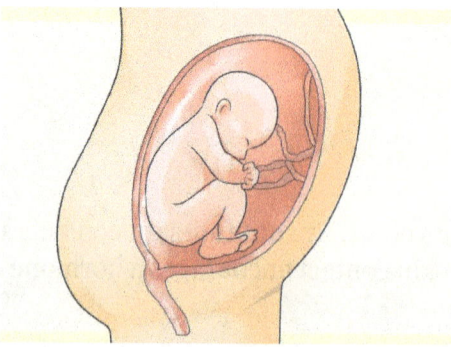

1. Know that a breech birth is unlikely. If it happens, a breech birth is a circumstance where the feet or buttocks enter the pelvis first instead of the head coming out.

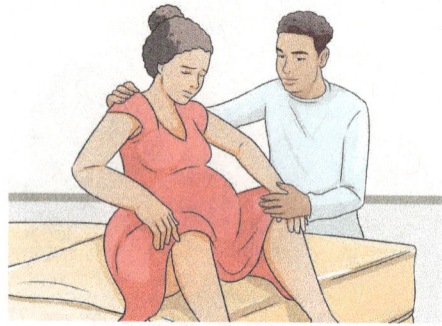

2. Position the mother. Have her sit at the edge of a bed or other surface and pull her legs to her chest. As a precaution, put down pillows or blankets where the baby is likely to fall.

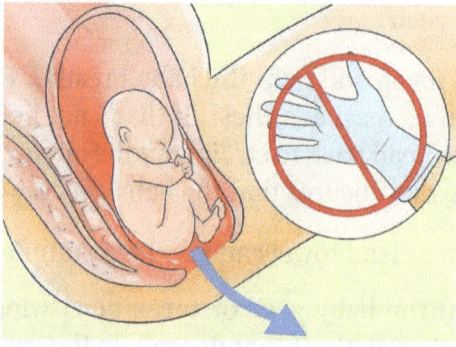

3. *Do not* touch the baby until the head comes out. You'll see its back and bottom hang down, and

you'll want to grab it, but don't. You want to avoid touching the baby until the head is delivered because your touch could stimulate the baby to gasp while the head is still submerged in amniotic fluid.

- Try to make sure the room is warm, as a drop in temperature could also cause the baby to gasp.

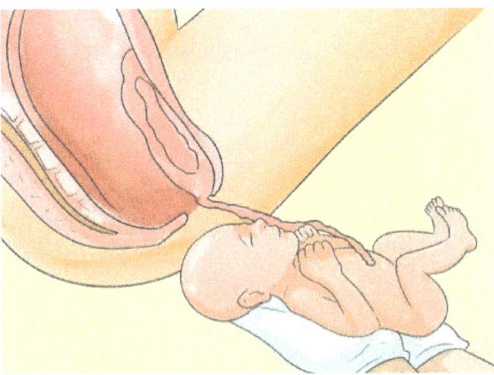

4. Catch the baby. Once the head is delivered, grab the baby under the arms and bring it up to the mother. If the head doesn't come out in the push after the arms come out, have the mother squat and push.

Part 4

Delivering the Placenta

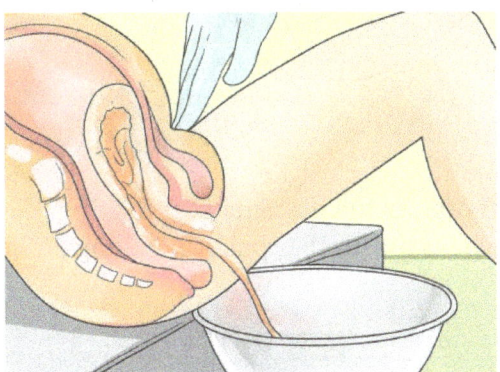

1. Prepare for the placenta. Delivering the placenta is the third stage of labor. It will arrive anywhere between a few minutes to an hour after the baby is delivered. The mother will probably feel an urge to push after a few minutes; this is helpful.

- Put a bowl close to the vagina. Right before it emerges, blood will come out of the vagina, and the cord will get longer.

- Have the mother sit up and push the placenta into the bowl.

- Rub the mother's stomach below her belly button firmly to help slow down the bleeding. It might hurt her, but it's necessary. Keep rubbing until the uterus feels like a large grapefruit in the lower belly.

2. Let the baby breastfeed. If the cord isn't stretched too tightly by doing so, encourage the mother to breastfeed as soon as possible. This will help stimulate a contraction and encourage the delivery of the placenta. It may also help slow bleeding.

- If breastfeeding isn't an option, stimulating the nipples can also help stimulate delivering the placenta.

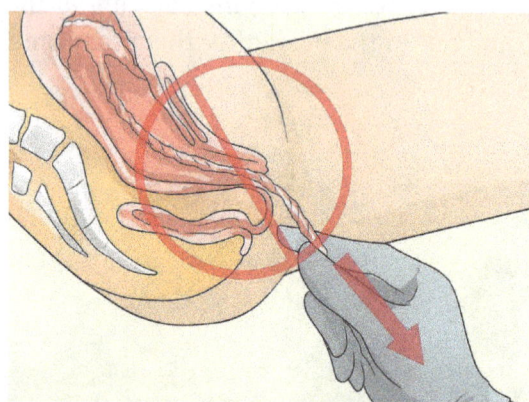

3. Don't pull on the umbilical cord. As the placenta is delivering, don't tug on the cord to hurry it along. Let it come out on its own as the mother pushes. Pulling on it could cause severe damage.

4. Bag the placenta. Once the placenta is out, place it in a trash bag or a container with a lid. When and if the mother goes to a hospital, the doctor might want to inspect the placenta for any abnormalities.

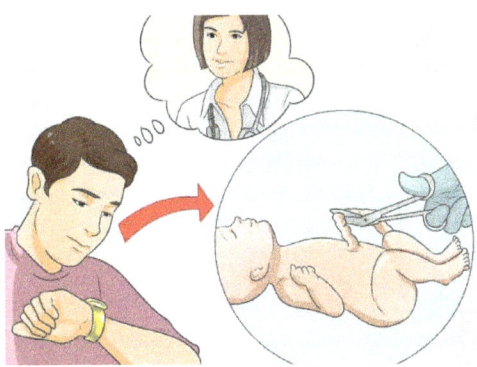

5. Decide whether to cut the cord. You should only cut the umbilical cord if professional medical attention is hours away. Otherwise, leave it alone and just make sure it's not pulled tight.

- If you do need to cut the cord, first feel the cord gently for a pulse. After about ten minutes, the cord will stop pulsing because the placenta has separated. Don't cut it before then.

- Don't worry about pain. There are no nerve endings in an umbilical cord; neither mother nor child will feel pain when its cut. The cord will, however, be slippery and difficult to handle.

- Tie a string or lace around the cord, about three inches from the baby's belly button. Tie it tightly with a double knot.

- Tie another lace about two inches away from the first one, again using a double knot.

- Using a sterile knife or scissors (that have been boiled in water for 20 minutes or wiped down with rubbing alcohol), cut between the two laces. Don't be surprised if it's rubbery and tough to cut; just take your time.

- Cover the baby again when the cord is cut.

Part 5

Caring for the Mother and Baby

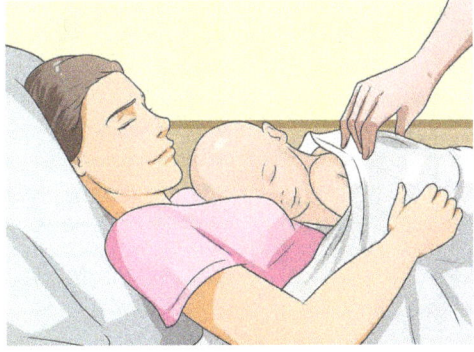

1. Keep the mother and baby warm and comfortable. Cover them both in blankets, and encourage the mother to keep the baby on her chest. Replace any wet or dirty bedding, and move them to a clean, dry area.

- Control pain. Put an ice pack on the mother's vagina for the first 24 hours to ease soreness and pain. Offer her acetaminophen/paracetamol or ibuprofen if she's not allergic.

- Give the mother something light to eat and a drink. Avoid carbonated drinks and fatty or sugary foods, as these could cause nausea. Toast, crackers, or light sandwiches are good options. The mother may want to rehydrate with an electrolyte-containing sports drink.

- Put a diaper on the baby. Make sure it's below the umbilical cord. If the cut cord smells bad (signaling an infection) clean it with alcohol until it doesn't smell anymore. If you have a small hat available, put it on the baby, so it doesn't catch a chill.

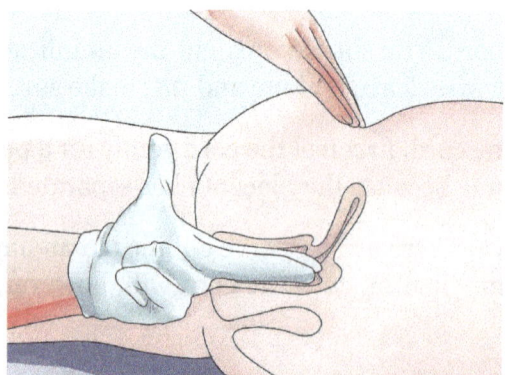

2. Massage the uterus through the abdomen. Sometimes, unexpected deliveries can cause hemorrhaging after delivery. It occurs in up to 18% of all deliveries. To help prevent this, you can firmly massage the uterus. If you see significant blood flow after the placenta is delivered, do the following:

- Place one (*clean*) hand inside the vagina. Place your other hand low on the mother's abdomen. Push down with the hand placed on the abdomen as you push against the uterus from the inside with the other hand.

- You can also make firm, repetitive squeezing movements with on hand on the mother's lower abdomen without placing a hand inside the vagina.

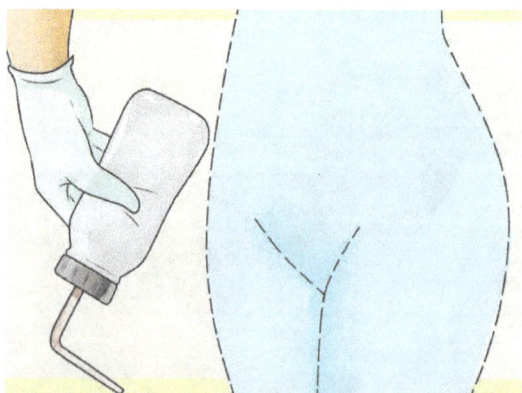

3. Prevent infection while going to the bathroom. Instruct and if necessary help the mother pour warm water over the vagina every time she urinates to keep the area clean. You can use a clean squeeze bottle to do this.

- If she needs to have a bowel movement, have her place a clean pad or washcloth against her vagina while she pushes.

- Help the mother urinate. It is good for her to empty her bladder, but due to blood loss, it may be best to have her urinate in a pan or on a cloth you can move from under her, so she does not have to get up.

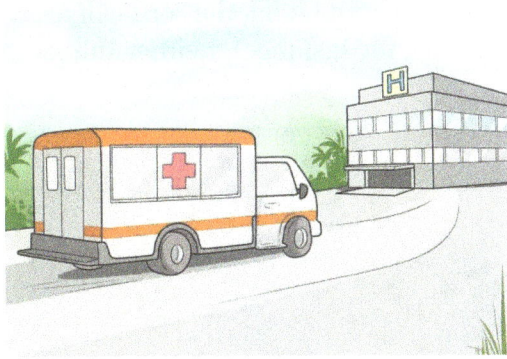

4. Get medical attention as quickly as possible. Once delivery is complete, proceed to the nearest hospital or await the ambulance you called.

How to Cut the Umbilical Cord of a Baby

The umbilical cord is the connection between a mother and her baby. It enters your baby through what eventually becomes their navel, or belly button, and is pretty big, averaging about 50 cm (20 inches) in length and 2 cm (about ¾ inch) in diameter in a full term baby. Blood passes through the umbilical cord from your baby to the placenta and then back to your baby by way of a single vein and two arteries. Your baby's umbilical cord will gradually dry up, become hard stiff tissue, and fall off within 1 to 2 weeks, but as a new parent, you have the option of cutting off the umbilical cord.

Part 1

Clamping and Cutting the Cord at the Hospital

1. Be aware that clamping and cutting the umbilical cord are not necessary. In fact, some new

parents decide to leave the umbilical cord and placenta attached to their baby's navel until it falls off naturally.

- Keeping the umbilical cord on until it falls off naturally can be cumbersome, though. Most parents have the cord cut shortly after birth; they don't feel comfortable with the idea of carrying the placenta with their baby until the umbilical cord separates.

- If you plan to bank your baby's cord blood, the cord will need to be cut. Since the umbilical contains no nerves (like hair, for instance), neither the mother nor the baby will feel the cut.

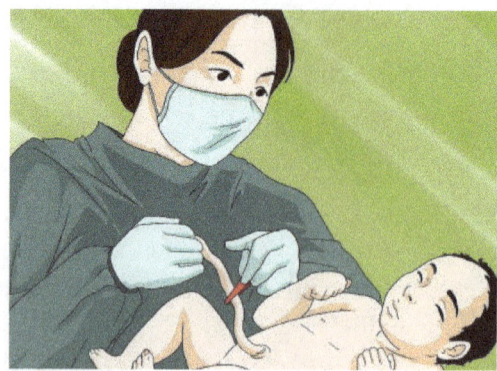

2. Expect your doctor to perform "immediate" clamping within the first moments of your baby's life. This is a common practice, as immediate clamping allows the baby, especially if they are high risk or premature, to be evaluated right after they are born.

3. Keep in mind your doctor may do "delayed" clamping. Recently, there has been a shift to delayed clamping, where the umbilical cord is not clamped until at least 1 to 3 minutes after birth.

- Many physicians feel that delayed clamping is a more natural process, and provides better circulatory support during the baby's transition out of the womb.

- At birth, a significant amount of the baby's blood is still in the placenta and umbilical cord. Delayed clamping allows the baby's circulatory system to recover of much more blood, often as much as ⅓ of the baby's total blood volume.

- Similar to the procedure in immediate clamping, the newborn should be held slightly below the level of the mother to enable some of that blood to return to the baby.

4. Understand the benefits of delayed clamping. In full term infants, babies with delayed clamping had less anemia and iron deficiency during the first 3 to 6 months. However, in some cases, photo-therapy for neonatal jaundice was required.

- Premature infants whose clamping is delayed have a 50% lower chance of an intraventricular hemorrhage, or bleeding into the fluid cavities in their brain.

- Keep in mind that skin-to-skin contact between mother and baby should not be postponed with delayed clamping.

5. Talk to your doctor about which type of clamping you would prefer. Be clear about your expectations for clamping your baby's umbilical cord with your doctor before giving birth.

Part 2

Clamping and Cutting the Cord at Home

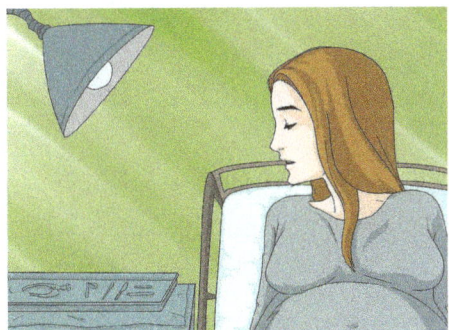

1. Make sure you have access to the right medical supplies. Cutting the cord is a simple procedure that requires:

- An antibacterial solution.

- Sterile surgical gloves, if available.

- A clean cotton pad or (preferably) sterile gauze.

- A sterile clamp or strip of woven umbilical tape.

- A sterile sharp knife or pair of scissors.

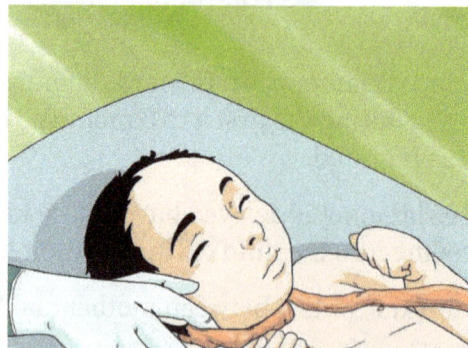

2. If the cord is wrapped around your newborn's neck, slide your finger under the cord. Then, gently pull it over your newborn's head. Take care not to stretch the cord tight.

- With your baby's first breaths in the first few seconds after delivery, your baby's circulation shifts away dramatically from the placenta. In fact, flow of your baby's blood through the placenta usually completely stops within the first 5 to 10 minutes of life.

- You can determine when blood flow through the umbilical cord has stopped when you can no longer detected the umbilical cord's pulse (similar to what the pulse in your wrist or neck feels like).

3. Use sterile plastic clamps or sterile woven umbilical tape to tie off the cord. You can find plastic clamps in bulk online, such as EZ clamp and Umbilicutter, but you may have a hard time purchasing just one clamp.

- While these clamps are very secure, they are bulky and catch easily on clothing.

- If you are using sterile woven umbilical tape, make sure it is at least ⅛ inches wide. You can find this product online in single use lengths.

4. Look for cord rings or cord banders at a medical supply store. These can be slipped over the umbilical cord to tie it off.

- Keep in mind that some brands require additional equipment to place the band on the umbilical cord.

- One type that requires no additional equipment is the AGA umbilical cord ring.

5. Always sterilize any woven materials like silk or a shoelace before using it to tie off the cord. In a pinch, you can use other woven materials like silk, a shoelace or cotton string, but make sure you always boil the material in water first before using it.

- Avoid using thin, strong materials such as dental floss, which could rupture the cord if it is tied too tightly.

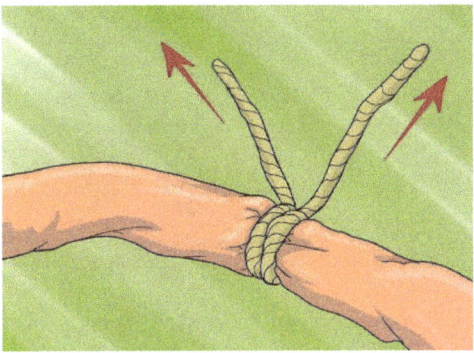

6. If you are using woven material, tie the knots firmly on the umbilical cord. But take care not to rupture the cord by using excessive force.

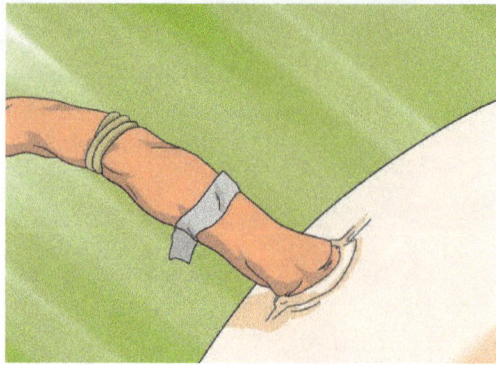

7. If you are using clamps or tape, put the first tie about 5 to 7.5 cm (2 to 3 inches) from the baby. The second tie should be placed further away from the baby, about 2 inches from the first tie.

- Keep in mind that although a pulse in the umbilical cord may stop shortly after delivery, significant bleeding may still occur if the cord is not clamped or tied.

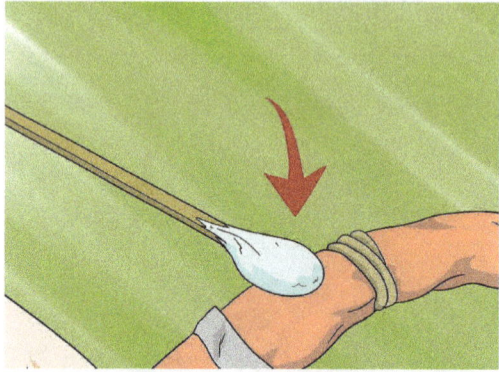

8. Prepare the umbilical cord by swabbing between the clamps or ties with antibacterial solution. You can use betadine or chlorhexidine.

- This step should be done especially if delivery occurs in a public or unhygienic setting.

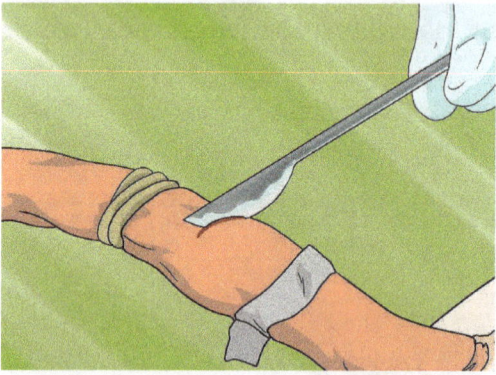

9. Use a sterile, sharp blade such as a scalpel or a strong pair of scissors. The umbilical cord is much tougher than it looks, and will feel like rubber or gristle.

- If the blade or pair of scissors you are using are not sterile, clean them thoroughly with soap and clean water, and then immerse them in alcohol (70% ethanol or isopropyl alcohol) for 2 to 3 minutes.

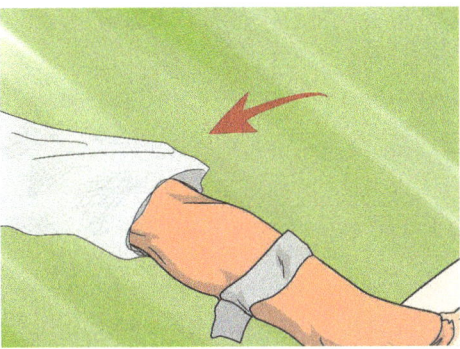

10. Grasp the cord with a piece of gauze. The cord may be slippery so this will ensure you have a firm grip on the cord.

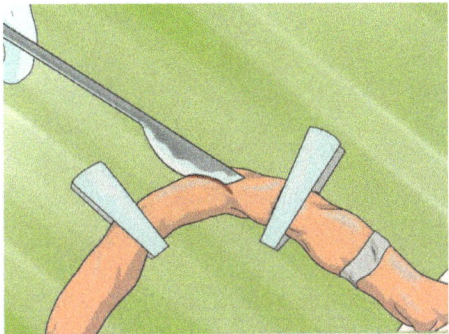

11. Cut cleanly between the ties or clamps. Make sure you hold the cord firmly to ensure the cut is clean.

Part 3

Caring for the Cord Stump

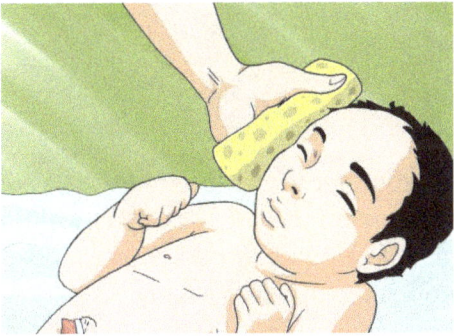

1. Bath the baby within the first six hours of life. Sponge baths can be done for the first few days.

- The newborn baby's risk of hypothermia is more of a concern, especially in the first few days of life, than any issues with the cord stump.

2. Wash your hands with soap and water before and after caring for the stump. Always dry your hands well before touching the stump as you want to keep the cord stump dry, and exposed to air as much as possible.

3. Avoid touching the cord stump or exposing it to unclean substances. While you need to ensure it is not in contact with any dirty or unclean surfaces or substances, you also don't want to cover it tightly with a dressing.

4. Treat the cord stump with an antiseptic. Keep in mind the use of topical antibacterial solutions to reduce the risk of serious infections on the cord stump is still not universally accepted by medical professionals. But umbilical infections can be serious, and many practitioners continue to recommend the use of an antiseptic to keep them clean.

- Effective and easily available antibacterial solutions include triple dye and chlorhexidine. Iodine tincture and povidone-iodine are less effective.

- Alcohol (ethanol and isopropyl alcohol) should be avoided. The antibacterial effect of alcohol is brief and can be harmful to the baby. It can also delay the usual 7-14 days of cord drying and separation by a day or two.

5. Apply the antiseptic daily or with diaper changes for at least 3 days. Only apply it to the cord stump. Try not to leave any of the antiseptic on the skin around the stump.

Part 4

Collecting Cord Blood

1. Be aware of your option as a parent to collect and store your baby's cord blood. You can do this at the time of delivery.

- Long term cord blood frozen storage can be a source of stem cells that may be used for future treatment of your child or another child.

- Currently, the diseases that may benefit from cord blood are limited and rare. However, as medical science advances, other future uses for cord blood are very likely.

2. Keep in mind you can still collect your baby's cord blood even if you use delayed clamping. It is

not true that delayed clamping of the UC removes the option of cord blood banking.

- Even after the transfer of blood from placenta to baby, additional blood can be acquired from the placenta for storage, if desired.

How to Bathe a Newborn

Newborns do not need to be bathed as often as older babies or small children. Their skin can dry out too quickly, and a newborn with the umbilical stump still attached should not have anything more than a sponge bath. When you're bathing a newborn, you need to be extra careful to prevent accidents.

Part 1

Using a Sponge Bath

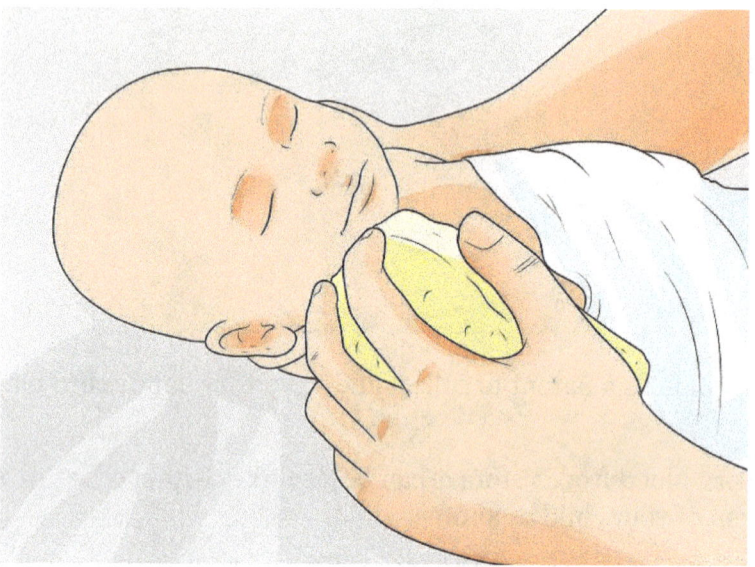

1. Use a sponge bath for the first three weeks. The stump of a newborn's umbilical cord stays attached for up to three weeks. The American Academy of Pediatricians recommends waiting until the stump falls off before submerging a newborn in water. During this time you should stick to sponge baths.

- You do not need to bathe your newborn every day during her first weeks. In fact, too much washing may be harmful to her skin. The face, neck, and diaper area are the areas that truly need washing and can be attended with burp cloths and clean diapers. Do not wash your newborn more than a few times a week.

- Talk to your pediatrician if the stump does not fall off after three weeks. This may be a sign of a larger problem or it may just need to be removed.

2. Gather your supplies. You will need to a variety of supplies ready in order to give your newborn a sponge bath. Make sure you have supplies laid out before you begin the bathing process.

- Find a warm place where there is a flat surface. Aim for a kitchen or bathroom counter. If the room is warm enough, even a blanket laid out on the floor will do.

- You need a soft towel or changing pad for the baby to lie on during the process.

- You'll need a sink or shallow plastic basin to hold the water for the bath.

- You will also need a washcloth, cotton balls, baby soap, baby wipes, and a clean diaper.

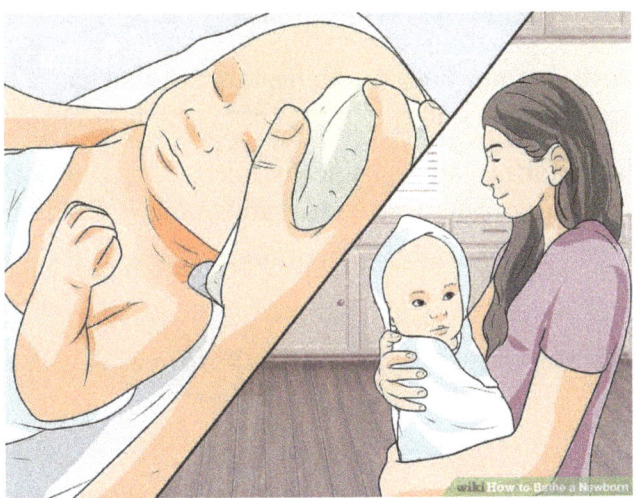

3. Bathe your newborn. Once your supplies are all in one place, you can begin bathing your newborn.

- Always have one hand on your baby. Newborns do not have much control of their movements and you need to keep one hand on your baby to make sure he does not hurt himself by squirming.

- First, undress your baby and wrap him in a towel. Lay him down on his back on a blanket or towel.

- Start with the face. Wet a towel and wring it out. Do not use soap for this part, as you don't want soap getting in your baby's eyes. Gently wipe down the baby's face. Use a damp cotton ball or clean cloth to wipe your baby's eyelids so they're free of crust and residue. Move from the inside to the outside.

- Plain water might be okay when bathing the rest of your baby's body. However, if your baby is dirty or producing a smell, use a baby-safe moisturizing soap. Make sure to wash creases under arms and ears thoroughly, as well as between the fingers and toes.

- Only expose the areas of your baby that you are washing. You want to make sure your newborn stays warm.

Part 2

Bathing a Newborn in a Tub or Sink

1. Choose a tub or sink. Once your newborn's umbilical cord stump has fallen off, you can bathe her in a tub or sink. Make sure you choose a sink or tub that's safe for the baby.

- Free-standing plastic tubs, made specifically for bathing newborns, can be purchased at most baby stores or online. They also sell inflatable tubs that fit inside a bathtub or sink.

- As long as you line a bathtub or sink with a rubber mat to prevent slipping, this can also be a viable option.

- Fill the tub with only 2 to 3 inches of warm water. Keep one hand on your newborn at all times.

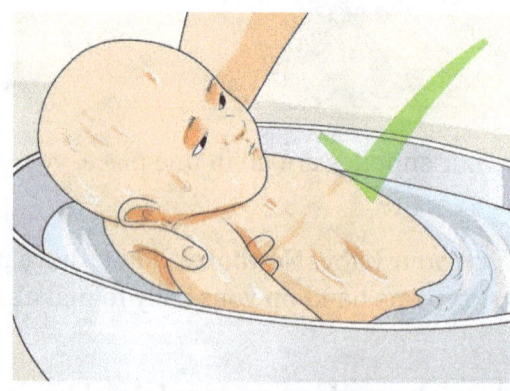

2. Figure out how to hold your newborn in the tub. You want to make sure your baby is secure

and safe in the tub. Figure out to hold him so he's comfortable and does not move around too much.

- Keep a secure hold on your baby, but one that doesn't make him feel uncomfortable.

- Support your baby's head and torso with your arm, using the other hand to wash him. You can do this by wrapping your arm around your baby's back. When the time comes to wash his back and buttocks, shift your baby so he's leaning forward on your arm.

- You can also buy a bath seat at a baby store or online. However, even when using a bath seat, you still need to keep a hand on your baby at all times.

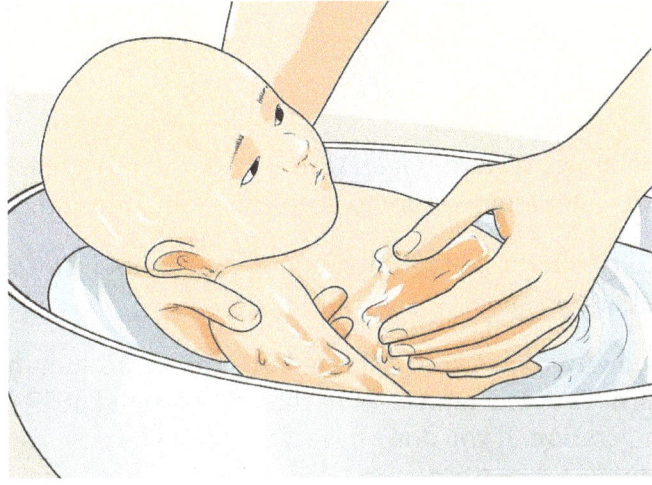

3. Wash the newborn. A newborn's bath should take no longer than 10 or 15 minutes.

- Before putting your baby in the tub, undress her down to her diaper. Wash her face and eyes the same way you would during a sponge bath, with a damp, soap-free cloth and damp cotton balls for the eyelids.

- Once you are done, remove your baby's diaper. If there's feces in the diaper, clean her bottom and genitals before putting her in the bath. When you lower her into the tub, do so feet first.

- You can use your hand, a sponge, or a damp wash cloth to gently clean your baby. You can use baby-safe soap. If your baby's skin is dry, try a moisturizing cleanser.

- You can gently pour water over your baby during the bath to keep her warm.

- Washing your baby's hair might not be necessary. However, if the hair seems dirty, or your baby has a common condition called cradle cap that produces scaly patches on her scalp, it's a good idea to give her hair a quick wash. Gently massage shampoo into the baby's scalp. Rinse the hair with a washcloth or run it under the faucet. Always cup your hand over your baby's forehead to prevent soap from getting in her eyes.

- When you're done washing your baby, remove her from the tub and quickly wrap her in a towel. Gently pat her dry and dress her in clean clothes.

Part 3

Learning Safety Precautions

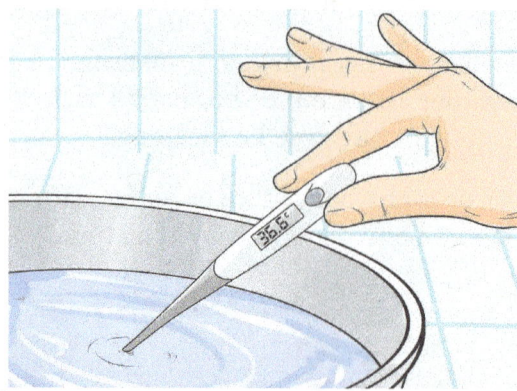

1. Check the water temperature. Water temperature is important to a newborn's well being. Make sure you know the proper water temperature to keep your baby safe and comfortable.

- It's best to put cold water in the tub first and then add hot water. Mix the water well and eliminate any hot or cold spots.

- It might be a good idea to invest in a thermometer to make sure the temperature is a safe level for a newborn. The ideal temperature should be around 98°F (36.6°C). This is around normal body temperature. If you don't have a thermometer, use your elbow instead of your hand to test warmth.

- If your baby has access to water taps during the bath, discourage him from touching them. As he ages, he'll be strong enough to turn the water on and could potentially scald himself.

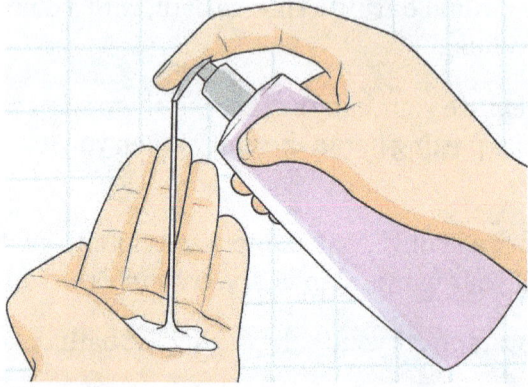

2. Find the right soaps and lotions. While soap is not always necessary when bathing a newborn, if you choose to use soap make sure it's baby safe.

- Never use scented soaps or bubble baths. These can be drying and irritating to a baby's skin.

- Plain water is usually fine. If you feel soap is needed, choose a mild, moisturizing soap specially made for babies as not to dry out a baby's skin.

- Usually, a newborn should not need lotion after a bath. Drying the folds of a baby's skin after each bath prevents rashes well enough. If you end up needing lotion, choose one that's hypoallergenic in case your newborn has allergies you do not know about yet.

3. Never leave a baby unattended in a bathtub. Even if you're just leaving the room for a few seconds, it's extremely dangerous to leave a newborn unattended in a bath.

- Always have everything for your baby's bath ready before putting your baby in the water so you aren't tempted to leave the room to grab something.

- If you absolutely need to leave the room, take your baby out of the tub first. Newborns can drown in only 3 centimetres (1.2 in) of water. Leaving a baby alone, even for a moment, can be disastrous.

- If you are bathing the baby on an elevated surface such as a counter, he can easily fall and get hurt.

Dealing with Post Partum Issues and Challenges

The postpartum stage begins after childbirth and it is a period when the body is recovering. Complications may arise during this stage such as depression and hemorrhage. Midwives provide care for the mother as well as the baby during this period. Postpartum conditions dealt by midwives are best understood in confluence with the major topics listed in the following chapter.

How to Care for Postpartum Bleeding

Postpartum bleeding, or lochia, is a natural although sometimes inconvenient part of recovery from childbirth, and it can last up to a month. The bleeding can be quite heavy in the first few days before tapering off significantly within the week. From there, it is usually more of a light period before reducing further to a light pink discharge (or 'spotting') within the month. By taking care of yourself, taking preventative measures for leaking, and watching for symptoms of more serious conditions, you can make this time much easier to manage so you can focus on your baby.

Part 1

Taking Care of yourself

1. Get plenty of rest. If you start bleeding bright red after having gotten past that state to pink or brown, you need more rest. If you completely soak a pad within an hour, you should call a doctor. While the amount of rest you need will vary from person to person, increased bleeding or decreased mood suggests you should be getting more rest.

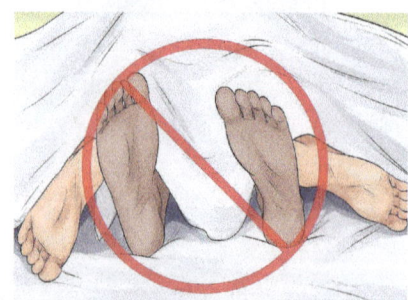

2. Avoid sex for four to six weeks. The main reason for this is that because there are potential

vaginal tears, as well as damage in the uterus, you can get an infection. It will also be uncomfortable immediately after birth to have sex, as you are likely to be sore. You should wait until the bleeding is almost gone before having sex.

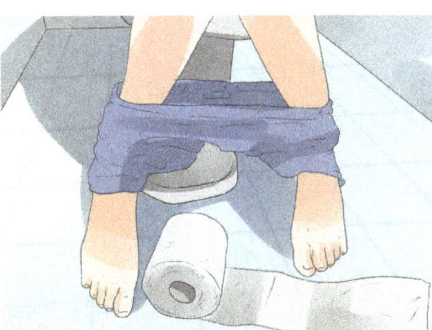

3. Urinate frequently. You may not feel like you need to go, but keeping the bladder somewhat empty will help ease contractions. This will help to decrease pain and bleeding. You should call your doctor if you have the typical symptoms of a urinary tract infection, such as burning urination or a persistent urge to urinate.

4. Get plenty of iron. Iron is important because it helps to replenish your blood count after labor. You should try to get the iron you need from food sources, such as meats, beans and lentils, and certain vegetables such as broccoli or okra. This is because too much iron can cause constipation. You should only take an iron supplement if your doctor recommends it.

Part 2

Protecting Against Leaks

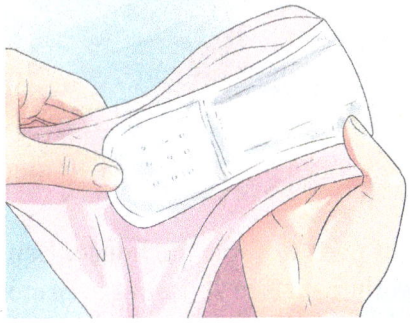

1. Use pads, not tampons. Tampons can increase the chance of infection, and there are plenty of

pads out there that can handle most flows. Consider using overnight or heavy flow pads, especially in the first week or so. You can even use pads regularly meant for urinary incontinence, as they tend to be bigger and more absorbent.

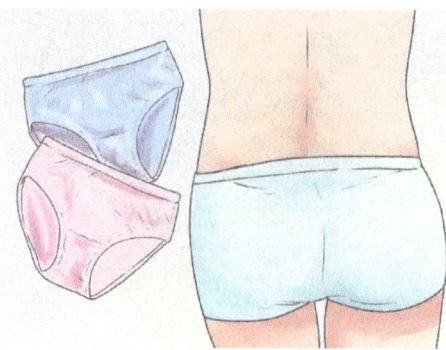

2. Wear disposable delivery underwear. These are mesh underwear that you can wear during the heavy period of postpartum bleeding. You will usually receive some pairs from the hospital. However, you can buy them online as well. They are more convenient than traditional underwear, especially in the first few days after labor, when you'll want to do nothing but rest.

3. Invest in a waterproof mattress pad. This will help protect your mattress during sleep, and will give you some ease about leaks that can occur. If your flow is really heavy or you don't want to stain your sheets, you might want to use a comfortable bed pad that rests on top of the sheets.

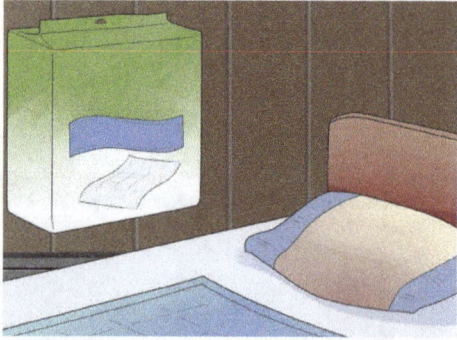

4. Keep a few disposable waterproof pads around the house. Using them when sitting on upholstered furniture, the carpet, or any other surface you want to protect from blood stains. These may not be necessary after the first week or so. Using disposable pads are definitely more convenient, but you can use reusable ones if you want to be more environmentally friendly.

Part 3

Watching for Warning Signs

1. Call a doctor if you pass blood clots bigger than golf balls. While some clots are normal, larger ones should raise concern. This can be a sign of postpartum hemorrhage, which can be fatal if left untreated. Other symptoms include pain in the vaginal region and low blood pressure.

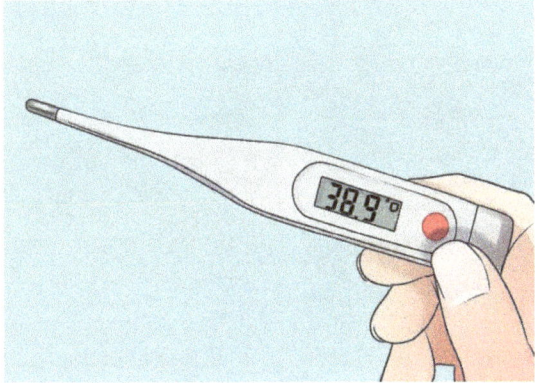

2. Check your temperature if you feel feverish. If you have a fever of over 100.4 degrees, you should check with your doctor. It can be a sign of a serious infection. Fever with any of these other symptoms is especially concerning.

3. Check the smell. If you notice that the vaginal discharge smells significantly different from your

menstrual period, you may need medical attention. Foul-smelling postpartum bleeding may indicate the presence of an infection.

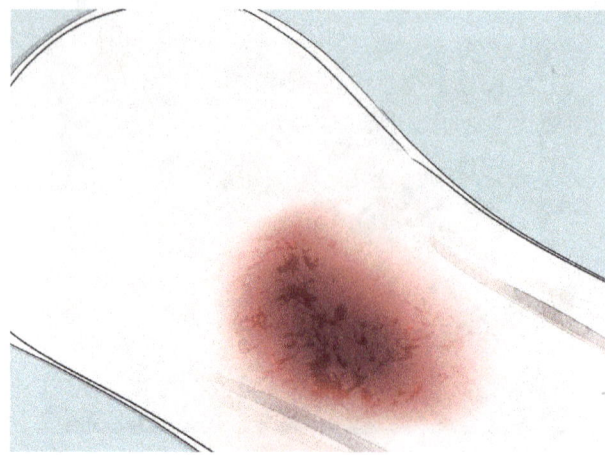

4. Watch the heaviness of the bleeding. If you are soaking a pad once an hour for more than two hours, you should call your doctor. It should be noted that normal moderate to heavy bleeding lasts for the first week or so. While the period may vary some, a return to very heavy bleeding should be looked into.

5. Count the weeks your postpartum bleeding continues. It should typically last two to six weeks. While it is normal for about 15% women to experience bleeding after six weeks, you will still want to talk to your doctor at your post-natal check, especially if the extended time occurs with any other symptoms.

How to Prepare the Breast for Breast Feeding

Breast milk is the best source of nutrition for your baby. It contains exactly what your baby needs for nutrients, energy, and antibodies against illnesses. Your body will prepare your breasts for breastfeeding without you having to do very much. However, there are a few things that you can do to learn what to expect and get organized.

Part 1

Getting Ready to Breastfeed

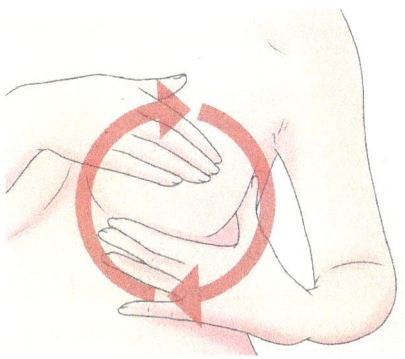

1. Massage, but do not "rough up," your breasts. Massaging your breasts will help you relax and prepare you in case you need to manually express milk for the baby.

- The massage should be gentle and not painful. Start above the breast and stroke with a circular motion while moving towards the nipple. Then move again to the outside of the breast in a different area and repeat, moving towards the nipple. Do this until you have moved around the entire breast.

- Do not "rough up" your nipples by scrubbing them roughly with a towel. This will remove the natural oils that your breast produces and may make them sore.

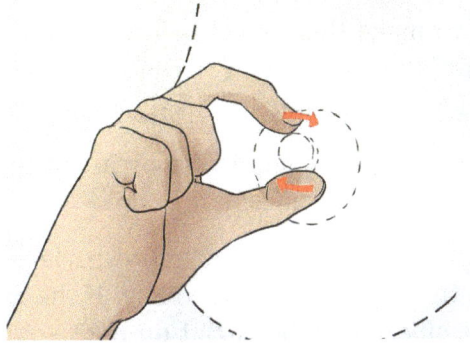

2. Determine whether you have inverted nipples. Some women have inverted, or flat, nipples which appear to have an indentation in the middle. You can determine whether your nipples are inverted using the pinch test:

- Pinch your breast between your thumb and forefinger on the areola, the dark area about an inch above and below the nipple.

- If your nipple becomes erect, it is not inverted. If it retracts into the breast, it is inverted. Women may have one inverted and one protruding nipple.

- The degree of inversion can vary from slight to severe.

- Your doctor will also be able to tell you whether your nipples are inverted or flat.

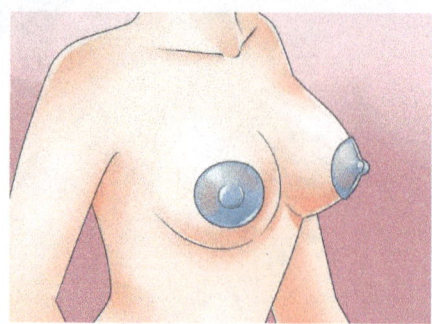

3. Do not worry if you have inverted nipples. Many women with inverted nipples are able to successfully breastfeed without a problem. However, there are devices you can buy and techniques you can learn about to prepare in case your baby has trouble:

- Push your nipples out with breast shells. Breast shells are plastic devices which press on your breast making the nipple pop out. You can prepare your breasts by wearing them before the birth and then after the birth for about 30 minutes before feeding time.

- Use the Hoffman Technique to stretch your nipple and make it easier to pop out. Put both thumbs on either side of your nipple and press into your breast while also spreading your thumbs apart. Work your way around the nipple. Start doing it twice a day and work up to five times per day. Continue doing it after birth.

- Use a breast pump to pull out your nipple right before feeding.

- Try an Evert-It Nipple Enhancer. This device uses suction to pull your nipple out.

- Stimulate your nipples to make them erect before feeding. Massage them between your thumb and forefinger until they protrude. You can also, very briefly, apply a cold compress, but do not numb it. This will make milk less likely to flow.

- As your baby latches on to drink, squeeze your breast or pull the skin back towards your chest. This will help the nipple protrude.

- Try a nipple shield in consultation with a lactation specialist. This is worn over the breast and allows milk to flow through a hole to the baby. If the baby has difficulty gripping the breast in its mouth, the shield may help. But do not use it without professional help to make sure it is done properly.

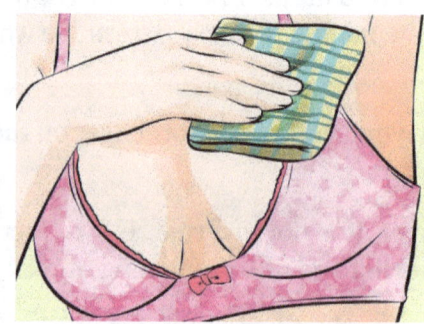

4. Keep your breasts clean, but do not use harsh soaps. Washing your breasts in clear water will be sufficient to keep them clean.

- Lotions and lubricants are not needed unless your nipples are very dry.

- If you have psoriasis or eczema, talk to your doctor about what medications you can use while breastfeeding.

- Wash your hands before breastfeeding or expressing milk.

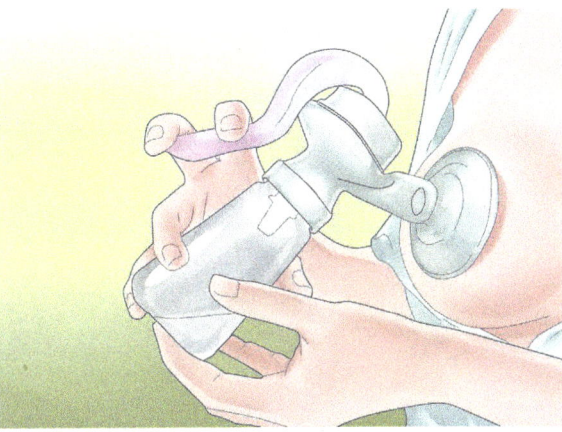

5. Use a breast pump to induce lactation if you are an adoptive mother. Adoptive mothers can often breastfeed by stimulating their breasts to produce milk.

- Stimulate your breasts through pumping every 2-3 hours around the clock before the baby comes.

- Use a Medela Supplemental Nursing System or a Lact-Aid Nurser Training System to feed your baby additional milk while he or she stimulates your body to increase its milk supply.

- The quantity of milk adoptive mothers can produce varies greatly. It may still be necessary to provide some formula.

Part 2

Locating Additional Resources

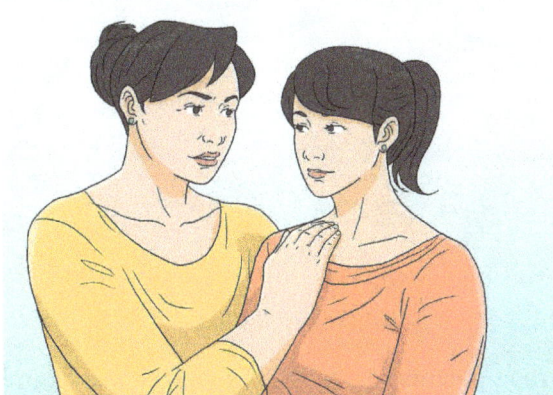

1. Talk to trusted friends and family members who have breastfed. They can provide you with advice and support.

- Breastfeeding difficulties are very common, so chances are you will know people who have had similar problems.

2. Discuss breastfeeding with your doctor. Many maternity wards in hospitals and birthing clinics have staff available to assist new mothers.

- Consult your doctor about any medications, herbal remedies, or supplements you may plan on taking while breastfeeding. Ask your doctor whether they are safe for your baby during breastfeeding.

- If you have had breast surgery or implants, ask your doctor whether it will likely impact your ability to breastfeed.

3. Attend a course on how to breastfeed. You will be able to learn techniques for breastfeeding, including how to hold the baby to encourage it to latch on properly.

- Most courses encourage partners to attend as well so they can learn what to do to be supportive.

- Ask the experts any questions you might have.

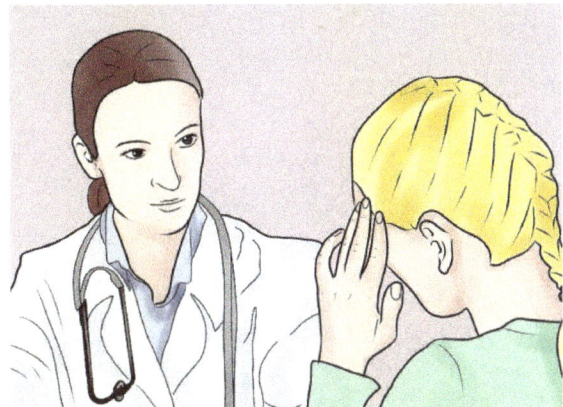

4. Contact a lactation consultant. Even if your baby has not yet arrived, you can meet the consultant, discuss your concerns, and develop a trusting relationship.

- If you need help learning to breastfeed, the expert may be able to come to your home and assist you.

5. Join a support group. Your doctor may be able to suggest a support group in your area. If there isn't one, you may be able to find one online.

- La Leche League International has in-person and online support groups and information sessions in many languages.

How to Lactate

Lactation is the production of milk in female mammary glands, and occurs naturally during pregnancy and post-pregnancy breastfeeding. Women may want to induce lactation if they are planning on adopting a baby or if they agree to be a surrogate nurse for a baby whose biological mother cannot breastfeed. Lactation is governed by pituitary hormones (as opposed to ovarian hormones) and, therefore, any woman can stimulate lactation, regardless of her obstetric or gynecological history. You do not necessarily have to go to a doctor or to take any special medications to start producing your own breast milk. Just follow these instructions for how to induce lactation.

Method 1

Understanding Induced Lactation

1. Understand how induced lactation is possible. Although it may seem surprising, it is indeed possible for women who are not or have not been pregnant to produce breast milk. This is usually undertaken by a mother who wishes to feed her adopted baby.

- The body's production of breast milk is usually triggered by the complex interactions between three hormones - estrogen, progesterone and prolactin - during pregnancy.

- If the production of these hormones can be mimicked through physical stimulation and/or hormone supplements, then breast milk can be produced outside of pregnancy.

- Prolactin (the main hormone involved in milk production) is produced in the pituitary gland, not the ovaries. Therefore, it is possible for women to induce lactation even if their uterus has been removed. However, the induced lactation process is usually more successful in women who have previously been pregnant.

- The induced lactation process can take several months, so it is a good idea to begin the process as soon as you have an idea of your adopted baby's arrival date. Adoptive mothers have the greatest chance of their baby "latching-on" successfully if the baby is younger than three months.

2. Understand the pros and cons. Inducing the production of breast milk is a huge undertaking, so

the pros and cons should be carefully weighed before any final decisions are made.

- Pros: Obviously the main advantage of producing your own breast milk is the benefit it will have for the baby. Breast milk contains important antibodies, proteins, fats and vitamins that will help your baby to grow and gain weight, and fight off infections and disease. In addition, breast feeding is wonderful, intimate way for mother and baby to bond. This is especially true when the baby is adopted, as the bonding process can take time. This is also the most natural method of feeding your baby, and can eliminate the need to use store-bought formulas which may contain chemicals.

- Cons: The major drawbacks of induced lactation mainly involve the time and effort required to be successful. Stimulating the production of milk requires huge dedication and commitment, as breast pumping and stimulation needs to be performed 6 to 12 times a day, including night-time sessions which involve waking up in the early a.m. This process can be painful and uncomfortable on your breasts, and if you're using hormone therapies, you may experience mood swings and disruptions to your menstrual cycle.

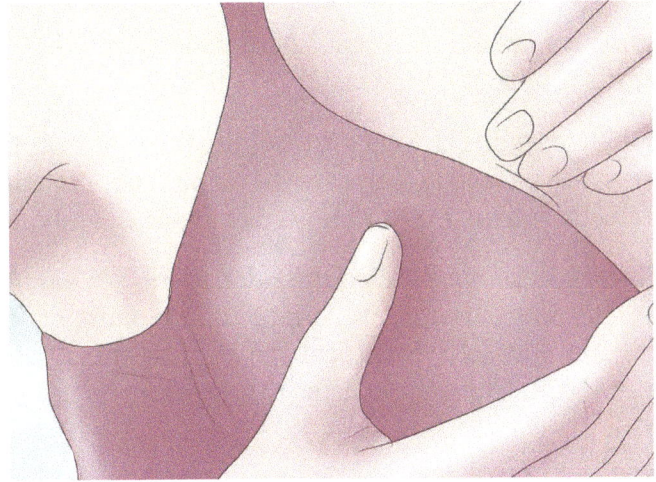

3. Prepare for the changes that will take place in your body. Before you begin the process of inducing lactation, it's important to aware of what will happen to your body, and the possible side effects.

- The side effects of induced lactation will be more severe if you are taking hormones, as you are essentially tricking your body into thinking you are pregnant. You can expect enlarged breasts, swollen or sore nipples and irregular menstruation.

- You will probably experience fatigue and increased hunger, as your body believes it is eating for two. You should increase your calorie intake by about 200 calories per day, but try to make healthy food choices in order to minimize weight gain.

- You may also experience mood swings and periods of depression and anger. This is why it is helpful to have a supportive partner, friend or family member to help you through the process and to remind you of the importance of the end goal. Your sex drive may also be affected by the hormones.

Method 2

Stimulating Milk Production

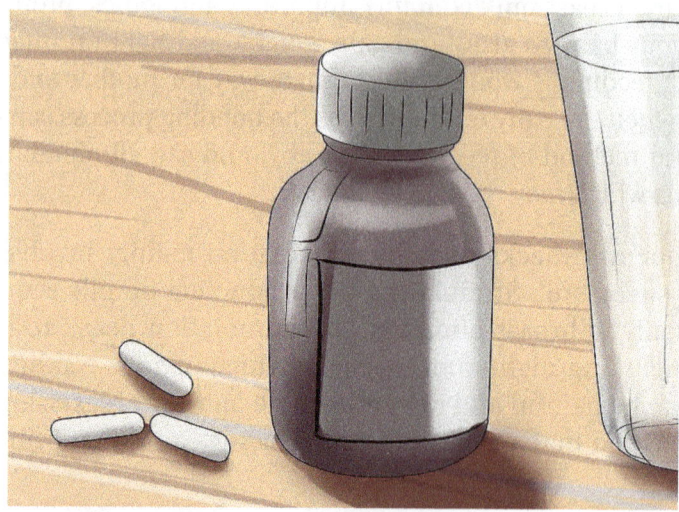

1. Start taking hormones. There are a number of different hormones that can be used to simulate pregnancy and stimulate the production of breast milk.

- The most widely used hormone is domperidone, which suppresses the body's production of dopamine and therefore indirectly increases the amount of prolactin in your system, which is the hormone directly responsible for breast development and the production of milk.

- Sometimes, additional hormones are recommended for use alongside the domperidone, such as estrogen and progesterone. Having higher amounts of these hormones in your system helps to mimic your body's natural state during pregnancy. If you are under the age of 35, you can take these hormones using the estrogen-progesterone combination birth control pill.

- If you have time before the arrival of your adopted child, it is recommended that you begin your "fake pregnancy" six to nine months in advance (however, there are accelerated programs for people with less time). Start taking the three hormones recommended above, following the dosages recommended by a qualified lactation consultant.

- Keep taking the hormones over the course of several months, until approximately six weeks before the baby's arrival. Then you should abruptly stop taking the progesterone and estrogen, thus tricking your body into believing you have given birth.

- Keep taking the domperidone and begin physical stimulation of the breasts using an electric pump or other manual techniques. The milk should start to arrive in as little as a few days, or as long as two weeks. Once it arrives, you should continue taking the domperidone until you achieve a substantial milk supply, or the baby is ready to be weaned.

- Taking hormones without adequate medical supervision can result in serious side-effects. Therefore, it is highly recommended that you set up an appointment with a qualified lactation consultant at a hospital or clinic before you start the process.

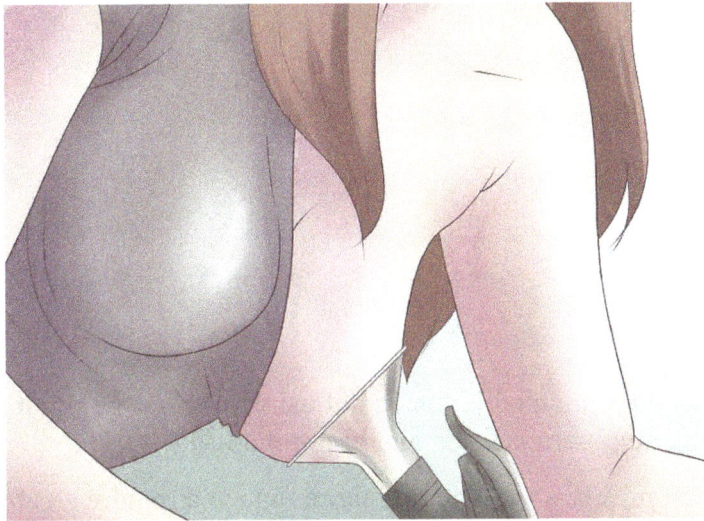

2. Use an electric breast pump. If you are using the hormone method of inducing lactation, you will also need to use a breast pump. However, it is sometimes possible to produce breast milk using the pump alone, although it can take a little longer.

- Physical stimulation of the nipples triggers the release of the prolactin hormone, which aids in the development of the mammary glands and stimulates milk production. It also releases oxytocin, the key hormone necessary for the release, or "let down", of milk.

- The best equipment for the job is a hospital-grade electric breast pump, which allows you to pump both breasts at the same time. These are expensive, but are worth the money if you consider the amount of time you'll spend using them. You can also use hand pumps, however the motorized versions are better at simulating the sucking motions of an infant.

- If you decide to go down the breast pump only route, you will need to begin pumping at least two months before the arrival of the baby. You will need to set a strict schedule, pumping every 2 to 3 hours, for 15 to 20 minutes at a time.

- You will also need to include at least one nighttime pumping session, as your body's natural prolactin levels are highest between 1 am and 5am, so it's important to take advantage of this fact.

- Before you begin pumping, use your hands to to gently massage your breasts and nipples. This will make them erect and ready for pumping. Apply the pump to both breasts simultaneously, doing your best to keep your nipples centered.

- Turn the pump on to a low suction and high speed, as this best mimics the rapid suckling motion of a baby. As you get used to pumping, you can gradually increase to a medium suction, or as high as you can comfortably go without making your nipples sore.

- Don't panic if you're not seeing any milk at first. It can take weeks before you see a single drop. Just stay calm and focused and stick to your schedule - the milk will come.

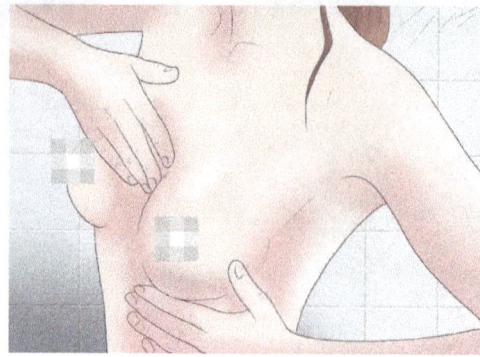

3. Stimulate milk production manually. Instead of using a breast pump, it is possible to induce lactation by hand, using nipple stimulation and breast massage.

- Producing breast milk this way will take more time and require greater effort than the previous two methods, but it is more natural than using hormones and cheaper than buying a breast pump.

- In terms of technique, you will need to use both hands to massage around the entire breast - almost as if you were giving yourself a breast exam. Then you will need to stimulate your nipples and areolas using your fingers and thumbs, massaging them and rolling them between your fingers. Try to press the areolas as you pull the nipples, as this is the motion that best replicates an infant's sucking.

- You will need to do this at least 8 times a day (including one nighttime session) for about 20 minutes at a time. If you feel comfortable with it, you can enlist the help of your partner or a close friend to massage with you. In order to have milk in time for the baby's arrival, you will need to start this process at least two months in advance.

- As you get closer to producing milk, you will need to lean over, so both of your breasts are pointed towards the floor. Gently shake your breasts, as this allows any potential milk to make its way towards the nipples.

- You may find it necessary to purchase a nipple lubricant or balm to protect your nipples from chaffing and becoming sore. However, no matter how sore your nipples become, it's important not to give up. Try to persevere and remember how how glad you will be once your baby arrives.

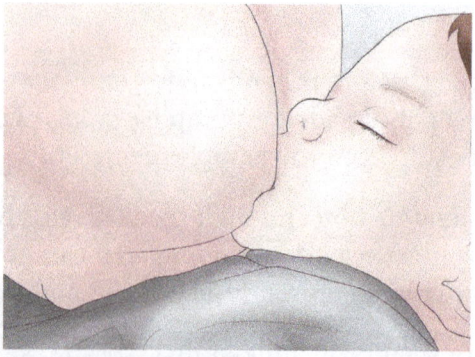

4. Allow your baby to suckle. If your baby has already arrived but you still have not produced any

breast milk, don't worry. Allowing your baby to suckle on your nipple, even if they are not receiving any milk, will help to speed up the process.

- Instead of pumping or manually stimulating your breasts, simply allow your baby to latch on. A baby's natural sucking motion is the best possible way of stimulating the hormones necessary to produce milk. That's because the entire experience - from the feeling of the baby's mouth on your nipple to the suckling sounds your baby makes - feels a lot more real than pumping or manual stimulation.

- In fact, the production of breast milk is as much a psychological process as a physical one. The knowledge that your baby is present and needs milk can be enough to trigger a natural let down response from your body.

- The only issue with this method is that babies can become frustrated if they are attempting to feed but are not receiving any milk. To solve this problem, you can invest in a lactation aid. This is a simple device, consisting of a tube that attaches to the mother's nipple on one end and a bag of formula on the other. In this way, the baby receives food while the nipple is stimulated, eventually allowing the mother to produce her own milk.

- Even if you never achieve a full milk supply, the simple act of breast feeding your baby is an important and irreplaceable bonding experience, which allows you to connect with your adopted child in a special and intimate way. When you look at it this way, any milk you produce is a bonus.

- If your baby has not yet arrived, you can still use the suckling method to induce lactation - you just need to get your partner to do it instead. This requires a huge commitment from both partners, but can be quite effective and can actually create a deeper connection between the two of you. Some couples also do this for erotic reasons, even when there is no baby involved. However, if you are doing it for milk, it is essential that your partner learns the correct latching on and suckling technique, and that you stick to a strict schedule.

Method 3

Increasing the Volume of Milk

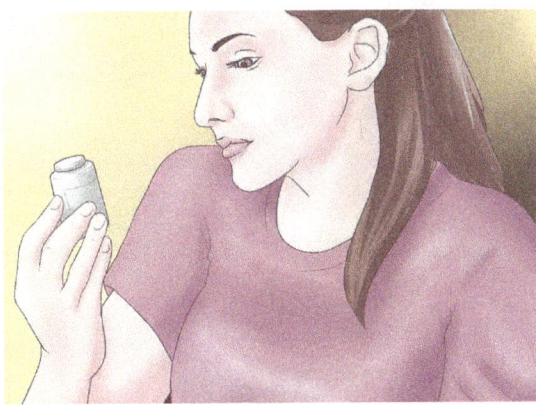

1. Take herbal supplements. Many women recommend herbal supplements to naturally increase the supply of breast. The most popular and effective herbs are fenugreek seed and blessed thistle herb.

- In terms of dosage, it is recommended that you take three capsules of fenugreek seed (containing 390mg per capsule) and three capsules of blessed thistle herb (containing 610mg per capsule) three times a day, with food. You should start taking these supplements as soon as you start pumping milk.

- You can also purchase an herbal tea known as "Mother's Milk", which contains a blend fennel, coriander, fenugreek, blessed thistle and aniseed. It tastes like licorice and can be sweetened with honey or sugar, if desired. It should be drunk up to three times a day, directly before feedings.

- In addition to encouraging increased milk production, this tea may also help to reduce gas and colic symptoms in babies.

2. Drink lots of water. Water is used in the production of breast milk, therefore it is very important to stay hydrated throughout the breast feeding process.

- It is recommended that breast-feeding mothers drink between 6 and 8 glasses of water per day to avoid dehydration. You can also drink herbal teas and eat fruit and veg with a high water content to increase hydration.

- You can tell if you are dehydrated by looking at the color of your urine. It will be very light or straw yellow in color if you are adequately hydrated and will be dark yellow if you are dehydrated.

- It's a good idea to cut back on coffee and other caffeinated drinks while you are breastfeeding, as these are diuretics which cause rapid fluid loss.

3. Eat oatmeal. A common recommendation for breastfeeding mothers is to eat oatmeal in order to increase milk supply.

- There isn't much scientific evidence to explain why, but many breastfeeding moms notice an increase in their milk production on days when they eat oatmeal for breakfast.

- Some theories include the fact that oatmeal contains high levels of iron and helps to reduce cholesterol - both of which are important for healthy milk production.

- Aside from those reasons, oatmeal is a warming comfort food which provides lots of energy - two things that new mothers definitely need.

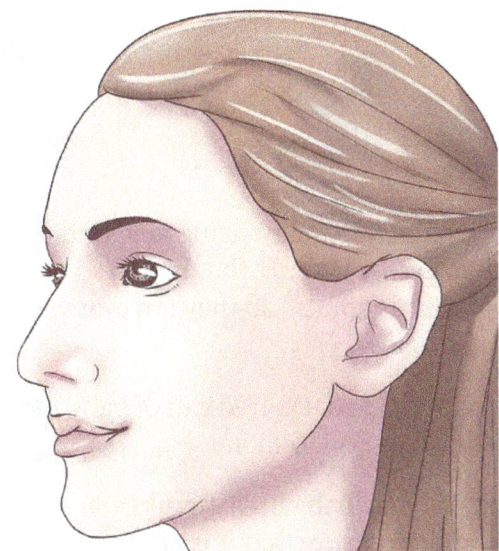

4. Get into the right frame of mind. If your baby has not yet arrived and you are finding it difficult to increase your milk supply, then you may need to work on the psychological side of lactation.

- As you are pumping or manually stimulating your breasts, it's important to focus on the *reason* you are doing it - to feed your baby. This will help your body's natural maternal instincts to kick in and promote milk production and let down.

- If you are having trouble visualizing the need for milk, you can use some props to help you. Hold a photo of the baby you are adopting, watch videos of mothers nursing their babies online, or listen to the sound of a baby suckling. Even holding an article of baby's clothing or a baby blanket can help.

How to Prepare Milk for Baby

Preparing a bottle for your baby is relatively easy, especially once you are used to the process. The procedure will depend on whether you are feeding powdered formula, liquid formula, or breast milk. No matter what you are feeding your baby, you will have to make sure to use good hygiene procedures and store your bottles properly in order to avoid contamination.

Part 1

Maintaining Proper Hygiene While Preparing a Bottle

1. Check the expiration date. If you're using any kind of packaged formula, check the package for the expiration date or use by date. If the date has passed, discard the formula. Babies' immune systems are not as robust as adults', so they are more susceptible to food-borne illnesses that may be present in expired formula.

- If you have an unopened, expired can of baby formula at home, many stores will allow you to return it for a free replacement.

- If you're feeding your baby breast milk, you should always label it with the date that you pumped the milk to ensure that it is not too old to be used. Breast milk can be stored in the refrigerator for up to 24 hours and in the freezer for up to six months.

2. Avoid damaged packaging. As you're shopping for formula, check each container carefully to make sure it is not damaged in any way. Even small defects to the packing can allow harmful bacteria to grow in the formula.

- Although a small dent may not seem like a big deal, it can cause the formula to spoil if the inner layer of the can is damaged.

- If your formula comes in pouches, do not purchase or use any pouch that is swelling or leaking.

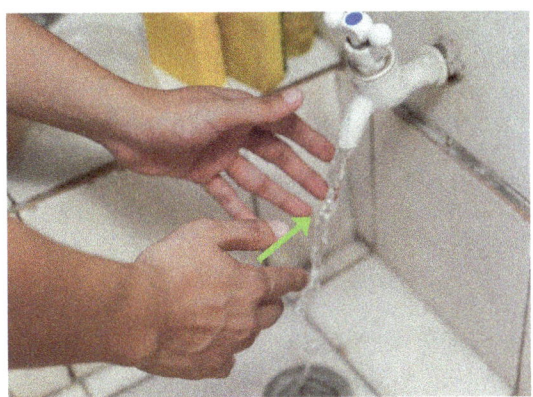

3. Clean your hands and surrounding surfaces. Your hands can carry lots of potentially harmful bacteria, so always wash them thoroughly before handling your baby's bottle. Household surfaces like counter tops can also harbor bacteria, so be sure to clean the surface on which you will be preparing the bottle before you begin.

4. Make sure all bottle components are clean. Before using a bottle or nipple for the first time, sterilize it in boiling water for at least five minutes. You should then thoroughly clean each component using soap and water or in the dishwasher before each subsequent use.

- You can also buy a special sterilizer for cleaning baby bottles. Some experts recommend that you sterilize feeding supplies before each use.

5. Sterilize water used for bottles. If you are using a formula that you need to add water to, it's a

good idea to sterilize the water before mixing the bottle. You can do this by boiling the water for five minutes. Then let the water cool for no more than 30 minutes before mixing the bottle.

- Don't use water that has previously been boiled and cooled.

- Avoid artificially softened water, as it may contain too much sodium.

- Bottled water is not always sterile, so you should boil it just as you would tap water.

- If you use boiled water to make your baby bottles, be sure to let it cool down enough after mixing so that it will not scald your baby. You can check the temperature of the formula by squeezing a small amount on to the inside of your wrist.

- If your bottled water indicates that it is sterile, you do not need to boil water prior to mixing.

Part 2

Preparing a Bottle of Powder Formula

1. Pour sterilized water into the bottle. Start preparing your bottle by pouring the desired amount of sterilized water into a clean bottle. If you are unsure of how much water to add, consult the instructions on the packaging to determine a correct serving size.

- Always add the water before the powder. This will help ensure that you measure properly.

2. Add the stated amount of powder. Consult the formula packaging to determine how much

powder you should add to the water. You should find a ratio of scoops of formula to ounces of water on the packaging. All formulas are different.

- Always use the scoop that was provided with the container of formula to measure out the powder. You do not need to pack the formula into the scoop; simply fill it loosely and level it off using a clean knife or a leveling tool (if one was provided with the formula).

- It is very important that you add the correct amount of powdered formula to your baby's bottle. Adding too much can cause your baby to become dehydrated, and adding too little can cause your baby to become malnourished.

3. Close the bottle and shake. Once you have added both the water and the powder to the bottle, place the nipple, ring, and cap on the bottle. Make sure it is closed securely, and then shake the bottle vigorously. Once the powder has fully dissolved, the bottle is ready to serve or store.

Part 3

Preparing a Bottle of Liquid Formula

1. Determine if the liquid formula is concentrated. There are two different kinds of liquid formula available: concentrated and ready-to-use. Read the packaging carefully in order to determine which type of liquid formula you have. This is very important, as you will need to add water if your formula is concentrated.

2. Shake the formula. Regardless of which type of liquid formula you are using, it's a good idea to shake the container before pouring the formula into the bottle. This will help ensure that the formula is fully mixed and not settled.

3. Pour the desired amount of liquid formula into a bottle. After you have shaken the container thoroughly, open it and pour the desired amount of liquid formula into a clean bottle.

- Remember that if you are using concentrated formula, you will be adding water, so you will want to pour less formula into the bottle. The container should provide instructions regarding how much formula to use for various serving sizes.

- If you do not use the entire container for your bottle, close the container and store it in the refrigerator. Follow the manufacturer's recommendations for storing time.

4. Add sterilized water to concentrated formula. If you are using concentrated formula, you will

need to dilute it with sterilized water before serving it to your baby. All formulas are different, so read the packaging instructions carefully to determine how much water you should add.

- If the formula is labeled as ready to drink or ready-made, do not add water.

5. Close the bottle and shake. Once you have added the formula and the water (for concentrated formula only) to the bottle, attach the nipple, ring, and cap to the bottle. Be sure that everything is securely fastened, and then shake the bottle to mix the contents together. The bottle is now ready to serve or store.

Part 4

Preparing a Bottle of Breast Milk

1. Express the breast milk manually. If you will be feeding your baby breast milk, but will be unable to breastfeed, you will need to express your breast milk ahead of time and store it until feeding time. If you will only be doing this occasionally, you may wish to express your breast milk manually.

- Do this by placing your thumb just above your areola and two fingers slightly below the nipple. Then apply pressure towards your rib cage and roll your fingers towards the nipple.

- You can capture the milk in the bottle you will be using for feeding, or in a separate container. If you will be storing the milk, be sure to keep it in a covered container in the refrigerator.

2. Use a breast pump. If you will be using bottles often, you will probably want to use a breast pump to express your milk. This will make expressing your milk much faster.

- Breast pumps are available in both manual and electric varieties.

- Most breast pumps come with bottles or other containers that can be attached directly to the pump for easy collection.

- Always read the instructions to ensure that you are using your breast pump correctly.

- You may be able to rent a breast pump if you don't want to buy one.

- Be sure to clean the breast pump before using it.

3. Transfer the milk to a clean bottle and close it. If you used a different container to collect the milk than you will be using to feed your baby, pour the milk into the bottle. Then attach the nipple and screw the bottle closed. If you will be storing the bottle, put a cap on it and place it in the refrigerator.

Part 5

Heating a Baby Bottle

1. Decide if you want to heat the bottle. Heating bottles is not necessary, but some parents choose to do it because their babies prefer warm bottles. There is nothing wrong with serving your baby a bottle that is cool or room temperature, as long as the baby will drink it.

- Don't leave formula out of the refrigerator for more than two hours.

- Breast milk can be safely kept at room temperature for up to six hours, although it's best to refrigerate it within four hours.

2. Warm the bottle in a bowl of warm water. If you choose to warm the bottle, one easy way to do it is to place it in a bowl of warm water for several minutes. The water should be very warm, but not hot.

- Place the bottle in the center of the bowl, making sure the height of the water is about the same as the height of the milk or formula.

3. Use a bottle warmer. If you want an even easier way to warm your baby's bottle, you can purchase an electric bottle warmer. To use a bottle warmer, simply place the bottle in the device and turn it on. It will take about four to six minutes to heat the bottle.

- You can also purchase small, battery-operated bottle warmers to use while traveling.

4. Warm the bottle under running water. Another way to warm a bottle is to hold it under the faucet for several minutes. Make sure the water is warm, but not hot enough to scald you.

5. Avoid using the microwave to heat bottles. While it may seem tempting to simply heat your baby's bottle in the microwave, you should avoid doing this at all costs. Microwaves do not heat evenly, so they may create hot spots that can scald your baby's mouth.

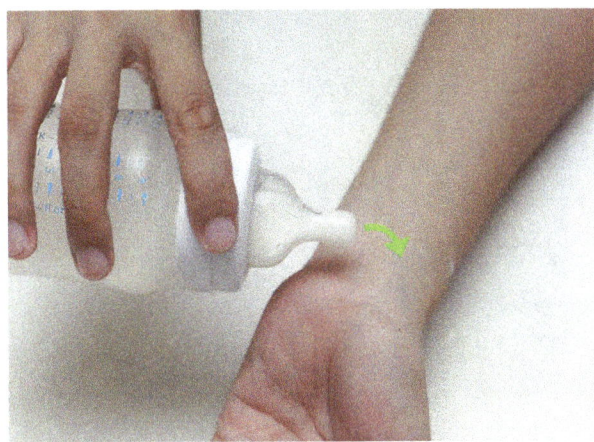

6. Check the temperature before serving. No matter how you decide to heat your bottle, it's always a good idea to confirm that the contents are an appropriate temperature before you give it to your baby. To do so, hold the bottle upside down and sprinkle a few drops of milk onto your wrist. The milk should feel neither cold nor hot.

- If the milk is a comfortable temperature, you can go ahead and give the bottle to your baby.

- If it is too hot, allow it to cool before feeding the baby.

- If the milk feels cold, continue warming the bottle until it is lukewarm.

Part 6

Storing Bottles for Future Feedings

1. Avoid storing whenever possible. The best way to keep bottles free from contaminants is to prepare them on an as-needed basis. If possible, do not mix extra bottles ahead of time and store them for future use.

- If you must store a bottle, store it near the back of the refrigerator, where the temperature remains the coldest.

2. Store breast milk in the refrigerator or freezer. If you need to store bottles of breast milk for future use, you can typically store them in the refrigerator for up to 24 hours. If you will not use the milk within 24 hours, you may freeze it in a plastic container with a lid or a breast milk bag.

- If your baby has been hospitalized, be sure to follow your doctor's recommendations regarding storing breast milk, as it may not be advised.

- If you are using a regular freezer that is attached to a refrigerator, store breast milk frozen for no more than one month. If you are using a deep freezer, you may store it for three to six months. The longer you leave it frozen, the more likely the nutrients in the milk are to degrade, so use it as soon as possible.

- Thaw frozen milk in the refrigerator, or place it in a bowl of warm water. Once it has thawed, do not refreeze it.

- Labeling milk with the date is a good idea, as it will prevent you from accidentally using milk that has been stored for too long.

3. Keep liquid formula in the refrigerator for up the 48 hours. Liquid formula, both concentrated and ready-to-use, can typically be stored in the container in the refrigerator for 24-48 hours. Storage instructions may vary for different brands of formula.

- Always read and follow the storage directions on the container. If the manufacturer recommends storing formula in the refrigerator for a maximum of 24 hours, don't store it for any longer.

4. Find a safe place to store unmixed cans of formula. Extreme heat and cold can degrade baby formula, so try to store your containers of powered formula somewhere where the temperature will consistently be between 55 and 75 degrees Fahrenheit. Keep it away from direct sunlight and heating and cooling vents.

- Once a can of powdered formula has been opened, it's best to use the contents of the can within one month.

5. Travel with unmixed powdered formula. If you will be out when your baby needs to be fed, you can make it easy to prepare a powdered formula bottle on the go. Simply boil and cool your water ahead of time and place it in a sealed bottle. Then measure out the appropriate amount of powdered formula and store this in a separate sterile container. When it's time to feed the baby, empty the powder into the bottle and shake.

- Make sure to wash your hands before mixing the bottle.

- If you will be outside and the weather will be hot, then you may want to place both the bottle and the container of powdered formula in a cooler bag with a small, towel-wrapped ice pack. Remember that you do not want to make the water or formula cold, you just want to prevent it from becoming hot.

- Storing the water and powder separately is preferable to storing pre-mixed powder formula because the powder may separate and clump during storage.

6. Do not store a partially consumed bottle. If your baby doesn't finish a bottle within an hour, throw it out instead of saving it for a future feeding. This applies whether you are feeding breast milk or formula. The bacteria in your baby's mouth can get inside the bottle and grow while the bottle is stored in the refrigerator. This can sicken your baby later on.

How to Bottle feed a Newborn

Bottle feeding your newborn baby is easy once you choose your formula and know when and how to feed your baby. If you want to start bottle feeding your baby but don't know how, just follow these easy steps.

Part 1

Prepare to Bottle Feed your Newborn

1. Choose the right formula. You should choose a formula that is iron-fortified. Though low-iron formulas are available due to the belief that iron makes babies gassy and constipated, this belief has been disproved by studies. The iron-fortified formula will help your baby build strength.

- Consult your pediatrician if you have any concerns about your baby's health, such as thinking your baby may be lactose intolerant because it runs in your family.

- Always check the expiration date on the formula to make sure that you can still use it. Never use expired formula.

2. Sterilize new bottles. To sterilize a new bottle, you simply have to submerge it in boiling water. Just make sure that the bottle is not made of plastic.

3. Prepare your formula. Follow the directions for how to mix your formula. If it's a liquid formula, check to see if it needs to be diluted first. Most formulas come in a powder or concentrate form and they need to be mixed with water. Ready-to-feed formulas are available, but they are more expensive.

- If you're worried about the safety of your tap water and need to dilute your formula, use bottled water.

- Use a clean can opener to open cans of formula. Wash the can opener after every use.

- Always wash your hands before you prepare your formula or feed your baby.

4. Warm your milk -- if the baby likes it warm. There's no health benefit to warming up your milk,

but if your baby likes it, you can do it before it's feeding time. You can heat up the bottle just by placing it in a bowl of warm water or running it under the warm tap.

- *Never use a microwave to heat a bottle of breast milk or formula.* This can create pockets of heat in the milk and may burn your baby.

- You can also buy a bottle heater designed for heating bottles.

Part 2

Bottle feed your Newborn

1. Hold your baby the right way. You'll have to observe your baby to get a sense of whether or not he or she is comfortable. If you hear a lot of loud sucking noises when he or she is drinking, then he or she may be taking in too much air. To help your baby take in less air, hold him or her at a 45-degree angle. Cradle him or her in a semi-upright position and support his or her head.

- Tilt the bottle so the nipple and neck are always filled with milk or formula.

- *Never prop a bottle.* This can cause your baby to choke.

- *Don't feed your baby when he or she is lying down.* He or she can get an ear infection if the formula flows in his or her middle ear.

2. Know how often to feed your baby. In the early weeks of your child's life, you don't need to worry about sticking to a rigid feeding schedule. However, you may start to work out a pattern in the first

month or two. First, just focus on offering the bottle to your baby every two or three hours or when your baby seems hungry.

- Until your baby weights about ten pounds, he or she will typically eat one to three ounces of formula during each feeding.

- Don't force your baby to eat when he or she isn't hungry, and don't force him or her to finish the bottle if he or she doesn't want to. As long as your baby still shows interest in feeding from time to time, there's no need to force it.

- If your baby continues to suck on the bottle when there's nothing left, that means he or she is hungry. Give him a little bit more to eat.

Part 3

Clean up after Feeding

1. Wash your bottles and nipples after you feed your baby. You don't have to sterilize your bottles after the first use. Just wash them in the dishwasher if they're dishwasher safe or just wash them in the sink in warm, soapy water.

- The nipples can also be washed in a sink full of soapy water.

2. Throw out any leftover formula. Don't put away the formula and use it later. Used formula should not be reused because of potential bacteria growth.

How to wake a Baby for Feeding

When you're baby first arrives home, it is important that he or she eats every two to three hours in order to help him or her grow and get needed nourishment. However, you may find that, like most babies, your baby sleeps all the time. If this is the case, you will have to wake him or her up so that you can feed him or her.

Method 1

Waking up your Baby

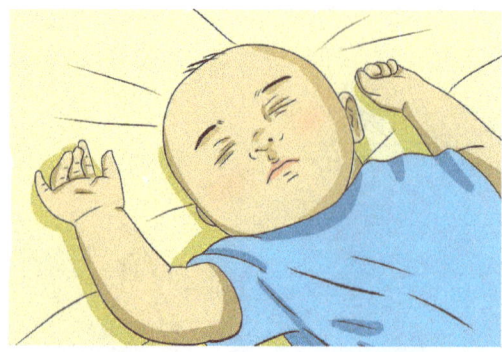

1. Try to wake your baby up when she is sleeping lightly. Like adults, babies can also fall into a lighter or deeper sleep. Your baby's body cycles through these phases of light sleep and deep sleep. Try to only wake your baby up when she is in a light sleep, as this will be easier than waking her when she is sleeping deeply. You can tell when your baby is in a light sleep by looking for these signs:

- Your baby moves her mouth as if sucking.

- Moving her arms and legs.

- Smiling in her sleep.

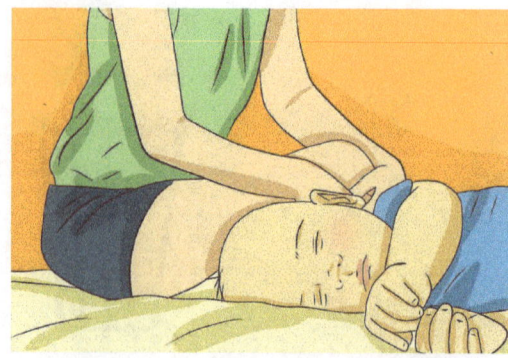

2. Sit beside your baby if she is in a deep sleep. As mentioned above, you should try to avoid waking your baby when she is in a deep sleep. If you want to feed her but see that she is sleeping deeply, you may just want to sit and do some quiet activity near by until she starts showing signs of entering into a light sleeping phase.

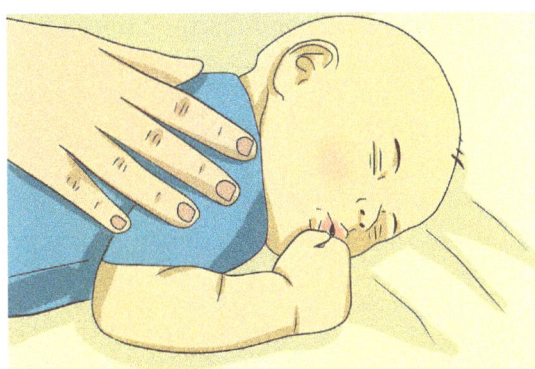

3. Try using light touches to wake your baby up. Skin contact can help to ease your baby into wakefulness. Try removing her blanket or clothes, and gently stroking her arm while she sleeps to help wake her up. Try gently stroking her head or cheek.

- The physical stimulation, as well as a brief exposure to the cold, may be enough to wake him up.

- Skin-to-skin contact helps to calm a stressed baby and prepares him for feeding.

- You can also try dripping a small amount of milk onto your baby's mouth. Some babies will wake up at the taste of milk.

4. Take your baby out of her crib to help wake her up. Taking her out of her crib and holding her in an upright position may be able to help her transition into a light sleep, or even into wakefulness.

- While holding her like this, try singing or talking to help wake her up.

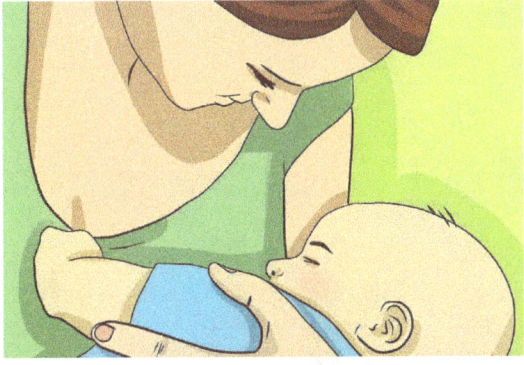

5. Hold your baby in a feeding position. Hold your baby like you are going to feed her, and then run

some milk along her lip. Being in this position and tasting milk may help to wake her up.

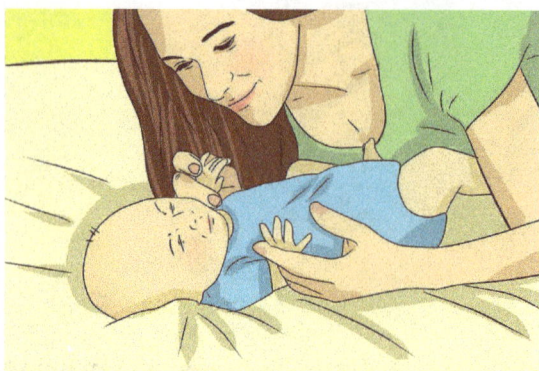

6. Tickle your baby's feet or hands. Try tickling your baby's feet lightly to see if you can wake your baby up that way. You can also try gently blowing on her face or touching her cheek.

- You may find that your baby reflexively turns her head to the side when you stroke her cheek because she thinks it is your breast touching her.

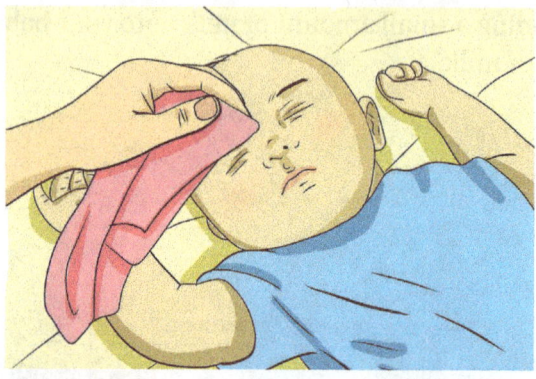

7. Use a cool cloth to wake your baby up. Changes in temperature may help to wake your baby up. You can try getting a washcloth wet with cold water, and then applying the wet part of the cloth to your baby's head, feet, or arms.

- Removing her blanket may also help to wake her up, as she will suddenly be able to feel the cool temperature of the room.

8. Let light into the room that your baby is sleeping in. If your baby is sleeping in a darkened room,

try letting some natural light in by opening the blinds. Your baby's eyes are sensitive to changes in light.

- However, too much light will make your baby want to keep her eyes closed, so try to let just a little light into the room.

9. Make some noise in the room where you baby is sleeping. This does not mean that you should yell or try to bang things to wake her up; try instead to sing or talk with your partner. The sound of your voices may be enough to rouse your baby.

10. Recognize the importance of feeding every two hours. It's important that your baby is fed every 2-3 hours for them to stay healthy and well nourished.

- Their small stomachs can digest food quickly, in about 90 minutes, so you have to make sure that their bellies are not empty, to avoid a fussy, hungry baby.

- Even if your baby is already sleeping, you need to make sure they are fed.

- This is important especially for newborn babies who need to be religiously fed every 2-3 hours, until your baby is ready to set his own feeding pace.

Method 2

Preventing your Baby from Falling Asleep While Eating

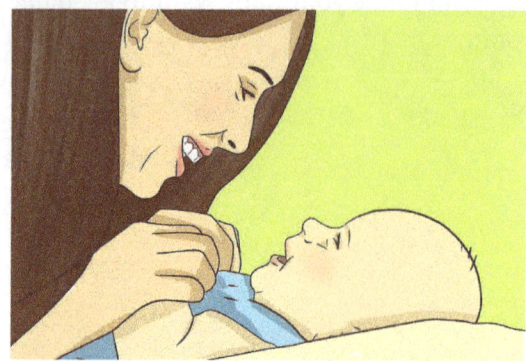

1. Draw your baby's attention when she does start to wake up. Once your baby is awake, you need to try to keep her awake so that you can feed her. Laugh at her, talk to her, and look her in the eyes to keep her attention on you.

- You can also try tickling her.

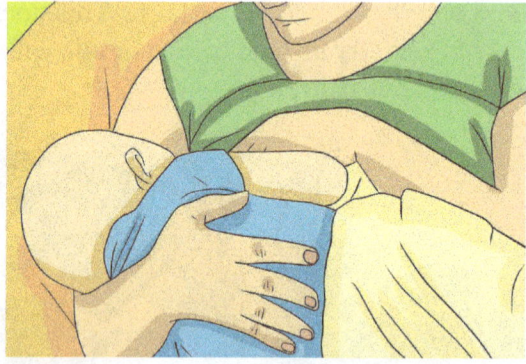

2. Try to feed your baby in a position that she is less inclined to sleep in. When you tuck her up against your body, your warmth and heartbeat can lull your baby back to sleep.

- Instead, hold her with one arm and hold her head with your other hand, keeping her a small distance away from your body heat.

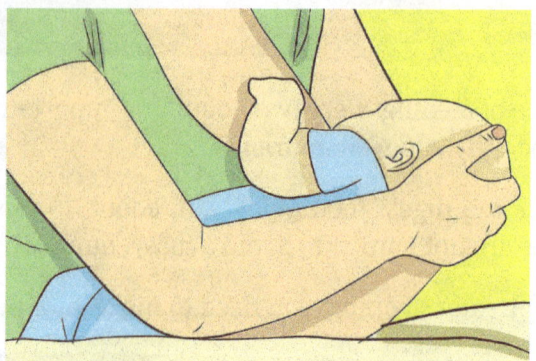

3. Move your baby to the other breast. When you see that your baby is starting to lose interest and

fall back to sleep, try to move her to your other breast. This movement will help to keep her awake and engaged.

- You can also try removing your nipple from your baby's mouth. Moving to release your nipple will help to wake your baby up. It will also help to remind her that she is still hungry. You can also try dropping a little milk on her mouth.

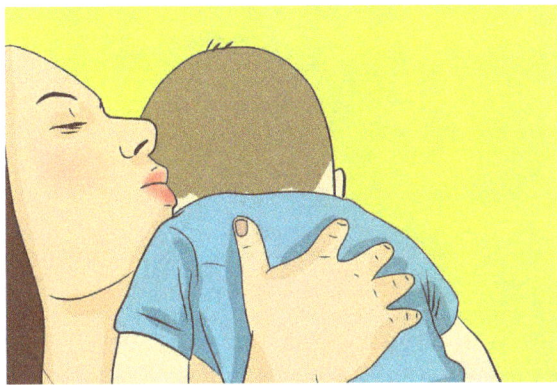

4. Burp your baby. Make a movement like you are going to burp your baby. This movement will help to wake her up, while also helping her to burp. Once she has burped, settle her back down on to your other breast.

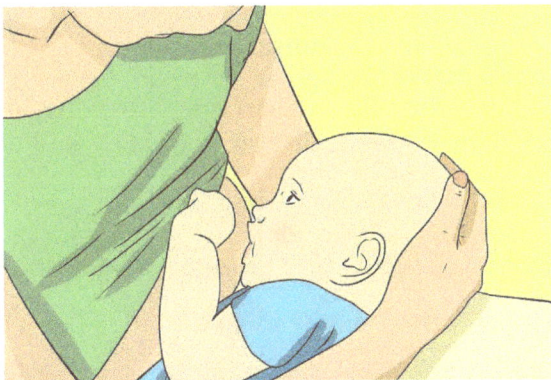

5. Try to give your baby more milk. Changes in the pressure of the milk your baby is receiving can help to keep her awake. You can change how much milk your baby gets by massaging your breast and squeezing the area around your nipple.

- However, do not give your baby too much milk, as she could choke.

How to Formula feed a Premature Baby

Premature babies require special care. You must be extra careful with how you feed your baby. Physicians will determine whether your baby needs tube feeding and when your baby can switch to oral feeding. Once your child can feed normally, breastfeeding and formula feeding are both options.

Part 1

Caring for your Baby in Hospital

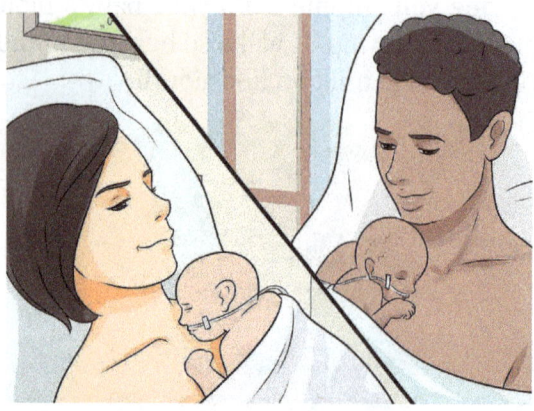

1. Bond with your baby. When your baby is being fed with tubes, you might find it difficult to connect with her. Talk to your nurses about doing kangaroo care, which helps you bond with your baby. With this technique, you hold your unclothed baby (wearing a diaper) against your naked chest. One option is to wear a baggy button down shirt. You then button the shirt up to the child's upper back so that the baby is inside your shirt and the heat is locked in. Alternatively, you can place a blanket on your baby's back so that the heat is trapped.

- Fathers and mothers should both do kangaroo care.

- Kangaroo care can stabilize your baby's heart rate, breathing, and oxygen saturation levels. The care also works to reduce crying and help your baby gain weight.

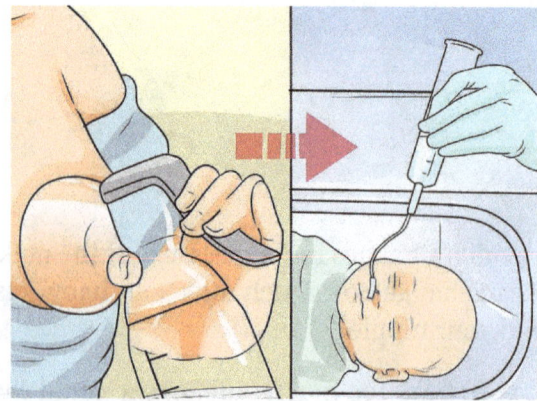

2. Choose whether to express your milk. Premature babies often have difficulty sucking, swallowing, and breathing correctly. This makes breastfeeding and bottle feeding complicated. You can, however, choose to pump your milk and have the doctors feed it to your baby via tubes.

- If you choose not to breastfeed, the hospital might, with your permission, use a donor's milk. There also are formulas available that are designed for premature babies. They have extra fat and protein to help preemies grow. There are also supplements that can be added to pumped breastmilk called human milk fortifier. Most babies born at 34 – 36 weeks gestation can use regular formula or a transitional formula.

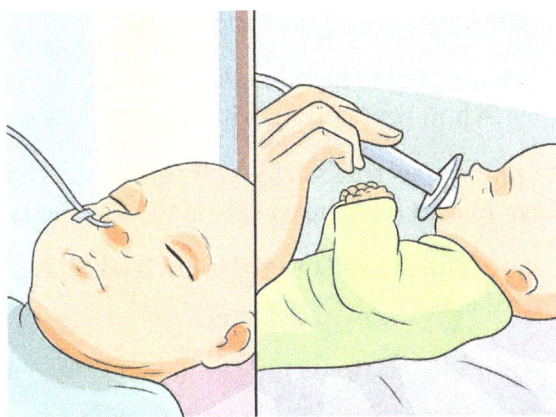

3. Learn how to do tube feedings. Some babies need to be fed through IVs. Others have a tube placed in their mouth or nose that goes to their stomachs. For the latter, some hospitals will allow you to participate in this process.

- The nurses will show you how to put the tube inside the baby and make sure the position is correct. They will instruct how to get your child to suck, which can benefit later breastfeeding or bottle feeding. They also will help you learn how to handle vomit.

- Babies born at 34 weeks or later gestation often can breastfeed or drink from a bottle. Oftentimes, breastfeeding is easier than bottle feeding for premature babies. Preemies can have difficulty stopping the milk flow from a bottle, which can lead to choking or breathing problems.

4. Bottle feed your baby. While your baby is still receiving tube feedings, doctors will encourage you to try bottle feedings when your baby is ready. You will start once a day and gradually increase the number of bottle feedings. Your baby needs to learn how to feed and breathe simultaneously. To bottle feed your baby, do the following:

- Hold the baby in your arms. Cradle him in the crook of your right or left arm so that you are supporting his head. He should almost be sitting, not laying down. You do not want him to choke.

- Position his head so it is leaning forwards and in front of his body. It should not be twisted to the side.

- Keep his arms and hands forward and near the bottle.

- Place the bottle in his mouth. Try to help him suck the nipple. Do not force the bottle down his throat and never leave him propped up with the bottle alone.

- Pull the bottle out after every few sucks. This will reduce the chance of your baby becoming too tired. If his lips turn blue and his heart rate is too low, he is over-exerting himself.

- Do not rush your baby. Preemies need more time to feed as they are learning a new process at a younger than normal age.

Part 2

Planning to Feed your Baby at Home

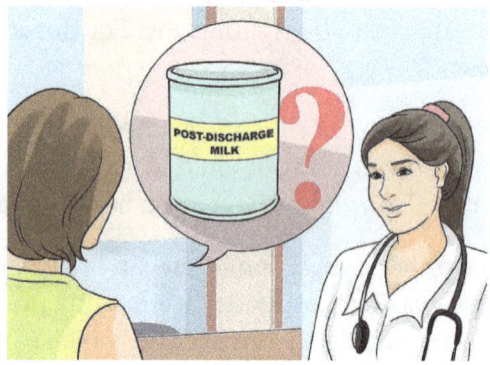

1. Ask your doctor when your baby can switch to formula. While in the hospital, many babies receive either your or a donor's breastmilk or formula via tubes. Upon discharge, the doctor might prescribe a special formula called "post-discharge milk." This formula has more nutrients than ordinary, store-bought formula. Your baby should use this formula until your doctor directs otherwise.

- Larger premature babies often can use normal baby formula that is iron fortified. Your baby should use this formula until she is at least four to six months old.

- Normal formulas are available for purchase at grocery stores, drugstores, and superstores like Target.

- Do not change your formula without consulting your physician.

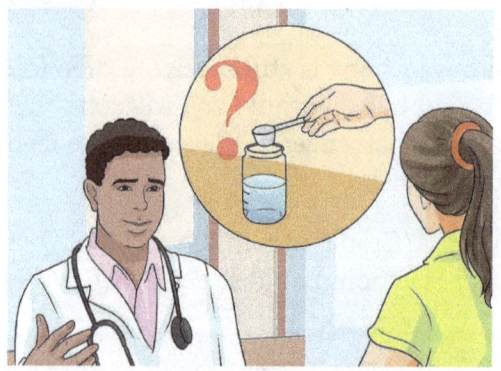

2. Ask the doctor about how much to feed your baby. Generally, newborns should receive 2.5 oz.

(75 ml) of formula per pound (450 g) of body weight each day. Premature babies can have different needs, though. Thus, it is best to have open dialogue with your medical team about feeding amounts. Oftentimes, premature babies drink 2 – 3 oz (60-90 mL) of formula per feeding once home.

3. Create a feeding schedule. Speak with your doctor about how often you should feed your baby once home. If your baby is receiving bottles, how many should he have per day? Many premature babies feed every three to four hours once they are home. They also feed upon wakening.

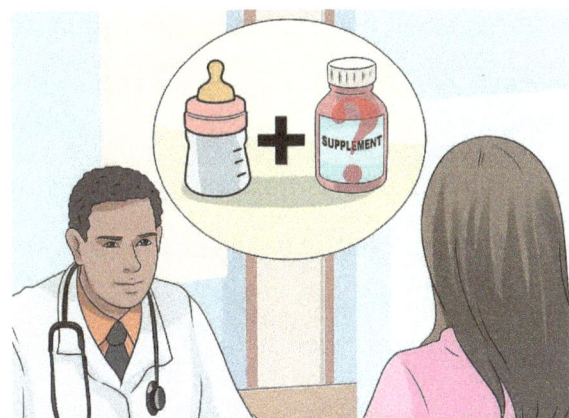

4. Determine whether your baby needs supplements. Preemies who receive formula in the hospital often receive vitamins A, C, and D plus folic acid supplements. When feeding your formula to your baby at home, she likely will need to continue supplements. You can also add the supplements to the formula itself.

- Speak with your doctor about your baby's nutritional needs. Do not implement changes without her approval.

- Your doctor might recommend fortifiers. These give formula or breastmilk added minerals, vitamins, and protein. They help your baby's bone growth.

- Babies taking breastmilk are often prescribed iron supplements also.

- Your doctor also might recommend probiotics to prevent gut infections in your preemie. These nutritional supplements consist of yeast and bacteria.

Part 3

Feeding your Baby Formula

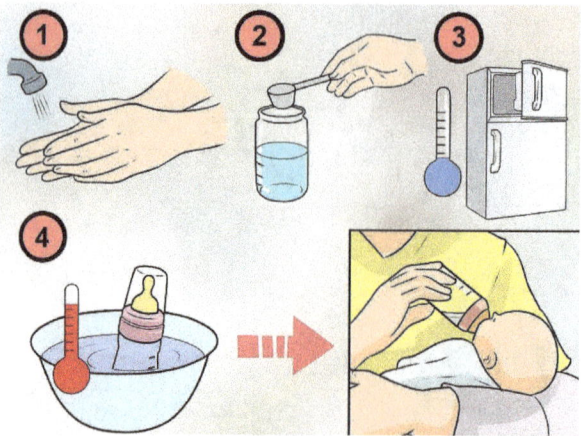

1. Learn how to prepare formulas. There are many different types of formulas. Which type you choose depends largely on what your doctor recommends. Some come in a ready-to-go liquid form. Others are powders that you must mix with water. Still others are concentrated liquids that you must add water to. In every case, follow the instructions on the packaging. Once you have prepared a formula, you should refrigerate it until use and use it within 24 hours.

- It is advisable to make a day's batch all at one time. This will reduce the time you need to spend mixing the formula.

- Wash your hands and any utensils or bottles you use thoroughly. Let bottles dry in the air.

- Keep your formula cool before use but heat it up prior to use. To do so, place it in a container with warm water for five minutes.

- Avoid heating formula in the microwave.

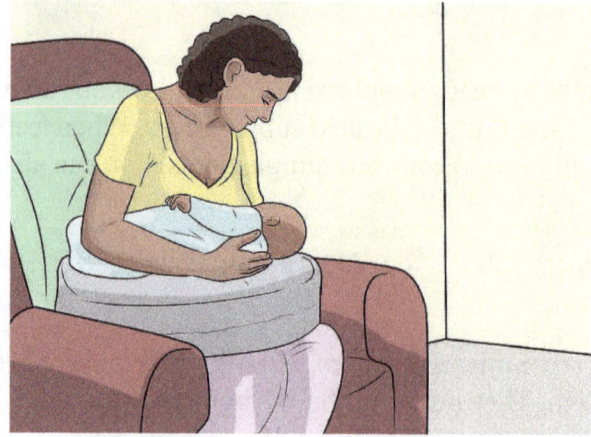

2. Sit in a quiet location. To coax your premature baby to eat, sit in a calm, quiet, and peaceful environment. Avoid harsh sunlight or artificial lighting. Choose a cushioned, supportive chair in which you too will feel comfortable.

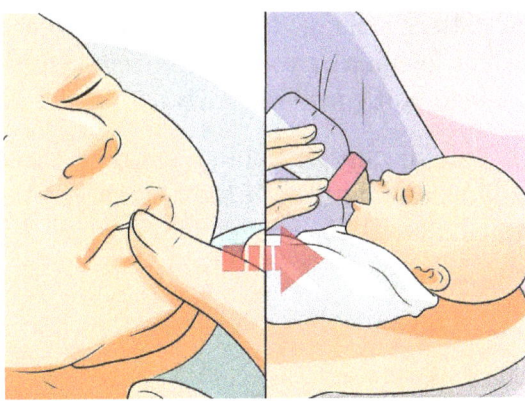

3. Feed your baby. Using the instructions you learned at hospital, hold your baby in his correct position and attempt to feed. Help your baby want to feed by giving your child oral stimulation. To do so, use your finger to gently touch your baby's cheeks, mouth, tongue, and gums. Complete this action before and after you feed. After this process, put the bottle in your baby's mouth.

- Remember that just like in the hospital, feeding can take a longer time with a premature baby. Consider watching a movie (nothing with too loud of sounds) or reading a book.

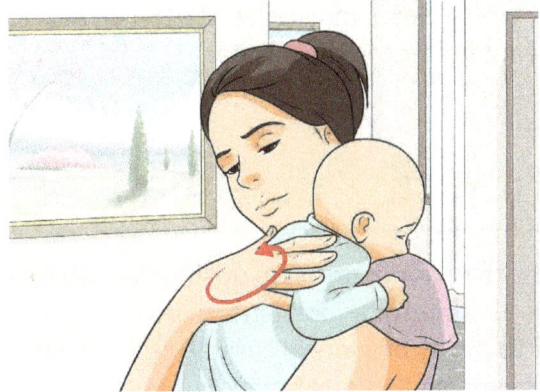

4. Burp your baby. Halfway through the feeding, place the baby upright and over your shoulder. Gently pat her back for one to three minutes. Continue feeding after she has burped. Then at the end of the feeding, burp her again.

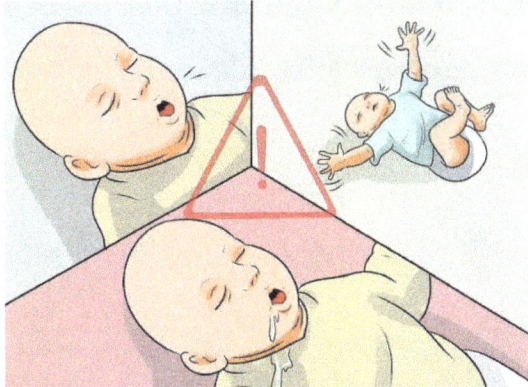

5. Watch for signs of poor feeding. Premature babies' digestive systems are particularly sensitive.

If your baby's stool forms and patterns change for more than two or three days, call your doctor. Your child might need a different formula or you might need to feed more or less often. He also could be developmentally unable to bottle feed regularly.

- Signs of discomfort include hiccups, coughing, gagging, excessive spit up, crying, biting, head turning, turning blue, and fanning of the fingers. If your child exhibits these symptoms, stop feeding immediately. Also, consult your doctor.

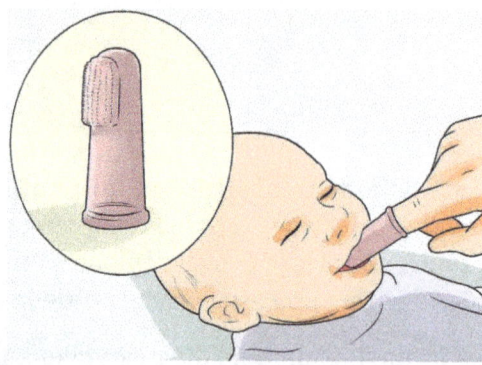

6. Clean your baby's mouth. Even though she might not have teeth, you want to protect her gums. After feeding, wipe her gums with a clean, moistened cloth. You also can purchase an infant toothbrush and use it with warm (not hot or too cold) water.

How to Diagnose Postpartum Bipolar Disorder

Many women are diagnosed with major depression during the postpartum period, or the time after giving birth. This condition is also known as postpartum depression. Yet, a diagnosis of depression alone can prolong symptoms that may be more accurately linked to Bipolar disorder. It's important to diagnose Bipolar disorder early so that treatment can begin right away. Always consult with a mental health expert such as a psychiatrist, psychologist, or therapist to receive a proper diagnosis.

Part 1

Recognizing Worsening Bipolar Symptoms Postpartum

1. Note differences between elation and mania. Some women don't get the "baby blues" but instead

get the "baby pinks." This can include a period of intense elation and feeling overjoyed in the first days of having a baby. While there is nothing clinically wrong with elated feelings, sometimes this elation can change into negative behaviors.

- This period of ecstasy can be followed by feeling irritable. You may notice your behavior becoming very bizarre, such as thinking you has special powers or abilities. You may think you can read your baby's mind or have special abilities related to your baby. You may not feel a need for sleep for several days or may talk excessively. These are manic symptoms.

2. Observe manic behavior. Mania is a part of Bipolar disorder. These behaviors will appear out of the ordinary and affect daily functioning. You may interact with your baby in odd ways or not be able to take care of it. Manic behavior can include:

- Feeling unusually high, jumpy, or wired
- Feeling highly energetic despite not sleeping much
- Having racing thoughts
- Having racing speech
- Impulsivity
- Irritability, feeling "touchy" or sensitive
- Engaging in risky behaviors

3. Look for hypomanic symptoms. Hypomania is a less severe form of mania. This kind of euphoria

can include feeling energetic, productive, and high, yet you can get on with daily activities without disruption. Hypomania may lead to mania or to a depressive episode, so it's important to monitor any changes to your behavior.

- You may notice feeling high to a point that it feels out of the ordinary, but still can function and get on with your day.

- If you are noticing (or someone else notices) odd behavior after giving birth, do not be alone with the baby. Call for help or go to the emergency department.

4. Take note of symptoms of depression. Depression is a part of Bipolar disorder. Depression can affect your mood, behaviors, and activities. You may feel too tired or exhausted to take care of your baby, or feel distant from it. Depression is diagnosed by having a combination of the following symptoms:

- Feeling, low, down, or sad

- Sleeping too much or too little

- Eating too much or too little

- Feeling tired

- Thinking about death or suicide

- Experiencing physical symptoms like muscle fatigue and heaviness, body aches, and brain fog

5. Notice a lack of sleep. Sleep deprivation can trigger symptoms of mania. New mothers may experience a sudden lack of sleep due to their new baby. Especially if you experienced changes in

behavior previously due to lack of sleep, you may also experience negative behaviors as a result of lack of sleep postpartum.

- If mental health problems have arisen due to lack of sleep in the past, be aware of how a lack of sleep affects you now.

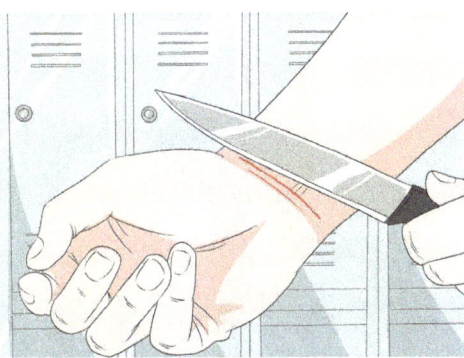

6. Watch for suicidal behaviors. People with Bipolar disorder are at a higher risk for suicide. The risk for suicide is higher when there's a history of drug or alcohol abuse or a personal or family history of suicide. Some warning signs of suicidal behavior include talking about death or suicide, feeling hopeless or helpless, and acting recklessly. For example, you may put yourself and/or the child in danger.

- If you are suicidal, do not be alone with the baby. Remove any dangerous items (such as guns, knives, or other weapons) and remove any pills from the home. Go to the nearest emergency department or ask someone to call emergency services for help.

7. Listen to family and friends who notice behavioral changes. Those with Bipolar disorder often don't recognize that anything is wrong, especially because manic symptoms can feel really good. Many times, Bipolar disorder is identified when a spouse, relative, or friend notices alarming behavioral changes. Be sure to take any comments from loved ones seriously in the postpartum period.

Part 2

Identifying Onset of Symptoms

1. Identify immediate hypomania. While most women experience some degree of euphoria within the first few weeks of childbirth, women who experience hypomania tend to experience it from day one as opposed to day three or four. Hypomania may include a distinct period of euphoria or irri-

table mood for at least three to four days. Unlike mania, the symptoms may not interfere with daily functioning and impairment may not be noticeable. In hypomania, psychotic symptoms (such as hallucinations or delusions) are not present. Ask yourself (or someone close to you) if you've experienced manic or hypomanic symptoms.

- Hypomania is often a precursor to Bipolar disorder and it's important to take these symptoms seriously.

2. Track the onset of symptoms. Bipolar symptoms such as hypomania typically peak within the first few weeks after childbirth. Think about if there was any unusual or strange behavior following the birth of the child, when it started, and if it has continued. Maybe you noticed such behavior, but assumed it was due to stress or life changes.

- Ask yourself when the symptoms began. If hypomanic symptoms started to appear shortly after childbirth, it may be a sign of Bipolar disorder.

3. Look for cycling. People with Bipolar disorder usually cycle through states of mania or hypomania, normalcy, and depression. These cycles typically last around 7 days, and may occur several months apart. Cycling is a key characteristic of Bipolar disorder, so keep an eye out for it in the postpartum period.

- Multiple manic or depressive cycles may occur in a row.

- If your manic or depressive symptoms last for two to three weeks or more, you probably have a different mental health issue.

4. Watch for the emergence of hypomanic symptoms later. Even if postpartum Bipolar disorder is misdiagnosed as postpartum depression, it's unlikely that the Bipolar symptoms will go away

indefinitely. It is likely that Bipolar symptoms may re-emerge within the first year after childbirth. If you had questions or doubts of postpartum Bipolar disorder but did not receive a diagnosis, be sure to check with your mental health provider.

- If symptoms begin to emerge within the first year after giving birth, see a mental health professional. You may wish to recount events or behaviors right after childbirth and how they are similar or different to your current symptoms.

Part 3

Assessing for Bipolar Disorder in the Family

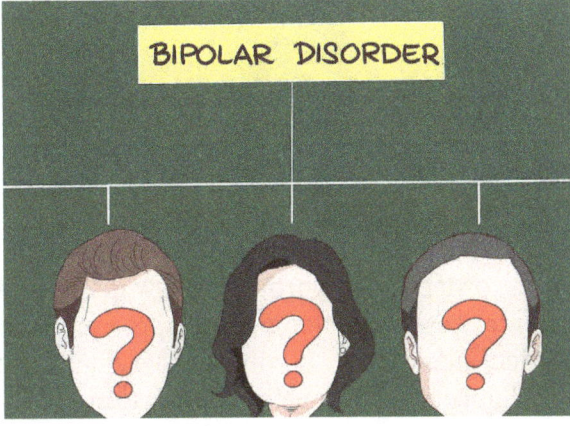

1. Ask about a family history of Bipolar disorder. Bipolar disorder tends to run in families. There's a higher risk of developing Bipolar disorder if a parent or sibling has Bipolar disorder. Ask questions about family mental health and any history of Bipolar disorder.

- This could include grandparents or cousins, aunts, and uncles as well.

- If you have a family history of Bipolar disorder, it does not mean that you will have Bipolar disorder. Most people with a family history will not develop Bipolar disorder. It just increases the risk the having Bipolar disorder.

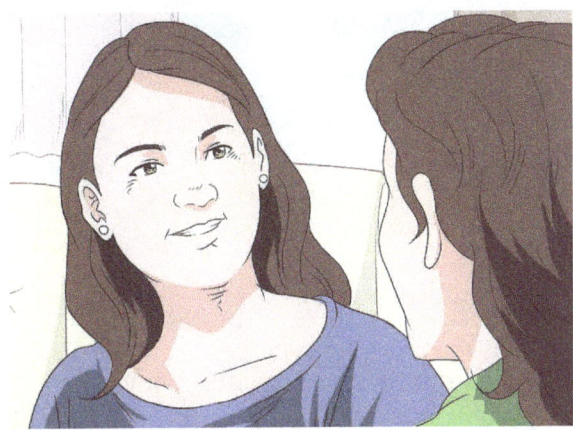

2. Ask about family birth experiences. It may be helpful to gather information about how other women in your family have experienced the postpartum phase. Ask aunts, cousins, sisters, and

other members of your family about their postpartum experiences. You may also ask the fathers and men of the family to recount what it was like for the women postpartum. If hypomania is common in the family, it may increase your risk of postpartum Bipolar disorder.

- It may be sensitive to ask these questions to the family. You can say, "My (or my wife's) behavior has changed a bit since giving birth. Did something similar happen to you or your wife? What was that like?"

3. Screen for previous Bipolar disorder. It's important for new moms to discuss any previous history of Bipolar disorder. Any mental health problems should be discussed with the provider, including depression, Bipolar disorder, anxiety, etc. If you've experienced previous episodes of Bipolar disorder, it can increase your chance of experiencing postpartum Bipolar disorder.

- Having a manic episode or previous diagnosis of Bipolar disorder should be clearly communicated with a medical or psychological professional. Discuss all mental health concerns prior to delivery if possible.

Part 4

Diagnosing Bipolar Disorder Professionally

1. Make an appointment with a mental health provider. Only a professional can diagnose Bipolar disorder. This includes a psychiatrist, psychologist, therapist, or general practitioner trained in mental health. It's important to receive a diagnosis of Bipolar disorder in order to treat the symptoms. Without treatment, Bipolar disorder tends to get worse and symptoms become more

severe. There are also different types of Bipolar disorder. A mental health professional will help you determine which type of Bipolar disorder is present, which will affect treatment.

- Treatment of Bipolar disorder includes therapy, medication, lifestyle changes and social support.

- Most people work with a therapist and a psychiatrist.

2. Monitor stressors. Stress can trigger Bipolar disorder in people who are genetically vulnerable. Giving birth and becoming immediately responsible for a life is a major stressor, and this experience may trigger symptoms of Bipolar disorder. Be aware of how you generally handle stress and what ways you cope.

- Be aware of any other stressors you are experiencing, which may include moving, the loss of a loved one, or getting married. Find ways to cope with this stress, such as engaging in relaxation exercises. Check out How to Relax for tips on relaxation.

3.Discuss symptoms of Bipolar I Disorder. Bipolar I disorder is characterized by at least one manic episode. This manic episode can cause significant impairment and changes to functioning, which may require hospitalization. Sometimes the mania may include psychotic symptoms, such as delusions or hallucinations. Either before or after the manic episode, you experience either hypomanic of major depressive episodes.

- The mania may include a period of at least one week of excessive energy without the need for sleep. Other symptoms may include rapid speech, abnormally elevated mood with impaired judgment, reckless spending, and elevated sexuality.

4. Talk about Bipolar II Disorder. Bipolar II disorder includes a pattern of depressive episodes and hypomanic episodes. The hypomanic episodes are not as severe as the manic episodes experienced in Bipolar I disorder. You may not need immediate hospitalization, but the hypomania may affect functioning and daily living. Hypomanic episodes must last at least four days and depressive episodes must last at least two weeks.

- The hypomanic symptoms are less severe than manic symptoms, yet still may include irritability, inflated self-esteem, distractibility, talkativeness, and racing thoughts.

5. Discuss Bipolar Disorder NOS. Bipolar disorder NOS is diagnosed when symptoms are similar to Bipolar I or Bipolar II disorder, but do not meet the criteria for diagnosis. The symptoms may not last long enough or be severe enough for diagnosis. Yet, you clearly exhibit symptoms in line with an experience of Bipolar disorder.

- Bipolar disorder NOS may be considered during postpartum, especially because symptoms may not exactly express as Bipolar disorder or meet the time frames for a Bipolar I or Bipolar II diagnosis.

How to Massage a Newborn Baby

Baby massage has long been a common part of infant care in many parts of the world, and is becoming increasingly popular worldwide. Infant massages can begin as early as ten days after birth (with a pediatrician's input), and proponents contend that they promote better sleep, improve motor skills, soothe colic, and possibly boost the immune system. While medical research backing up such claims is limited at best (with the possible exception of premature infants), there is no harm in trying gentle massage with a typical baby. It can also be a great way for parents and baby to enhance the bonding experience, and can easily be incorporated into the daily routine of baby care.

Method 1

Massaging from Top to Bottom

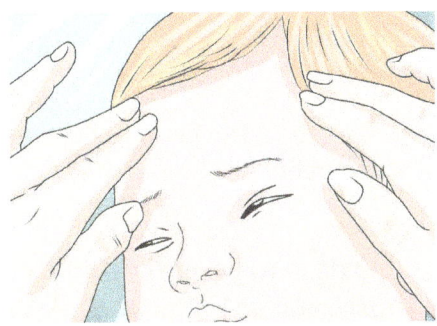

1. Start at your baby's head. With both thumbs at the center of your baby's forehead, begin gently pushing outward. Continue to massage different facial parts. Using your thumbs, make small circle motions over the cheeks, mouth area and jaw.

- You can try "walking" your fingers across the baby's forehead and cheeks, or gently pulling the lips into a smile with your thumbs.

- Massaging too close to the eyes or nose may cause greater discomfort, rather than enjoyment, in a newborn.

- There's no rule against reversing the order by finishing with the head massage. For some babies, in fact, starting with the legs and feet may help ease the transition from play time to calm time.

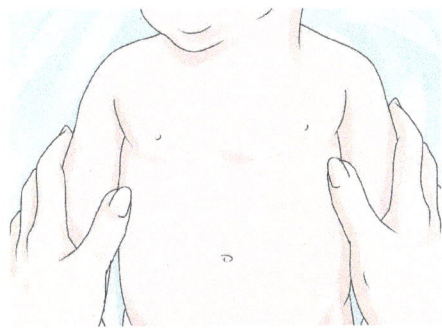

2. Move on to the upper limbs. Gently massage each of the baby's arms in your hands. Incorporate the hands into this by opening and massaging each finger individually.

- Try a milking massage on your baby's arms and legs. Make a loose C-shape with your thumb and forefinger around your baby's arm or leg. Very gently pull downward toward the foot or hand, in a motion similar to milking a cow, and repeat it several times.

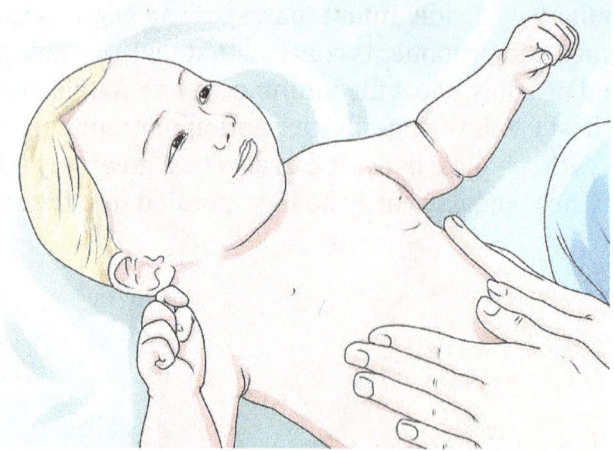

3. Massage the chest and stomach. Start from the center chest outward, smoothing over the skin as if gently flattening the pages of an open book. Then, mimic the digestive process by rubbing the stomach in a clockwise motion.

- You can also try using your hands to roll over the tummy from right to left, back and forth several times to cover the entire area.

- Some people believe that massaging away from the heart has a soothing effect, while going toward the heart can help invigorate a baby for play time.

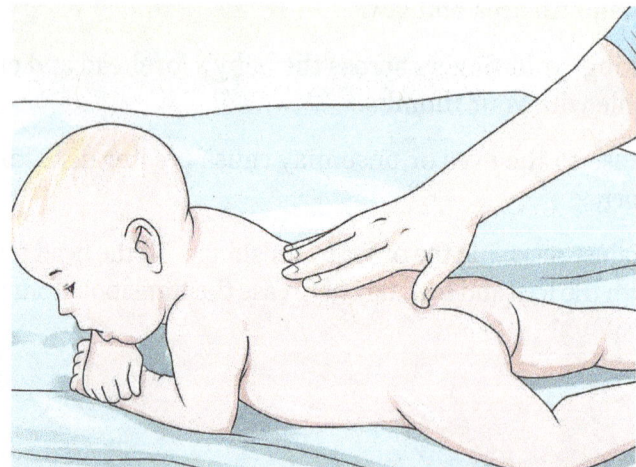

4. Switch over to the baby's back. Gently turn the baby over to access the back, making sure to support the head and neck the entire time. As with the chest, smooth your hands from the center of the back outward. You can also try stroking from side to side before progressing to an up and down motion.

- Don't grip and knead the shoulders as you might with an adult. Use gentle, circular motions to massage the baby's shoulders and lower back.

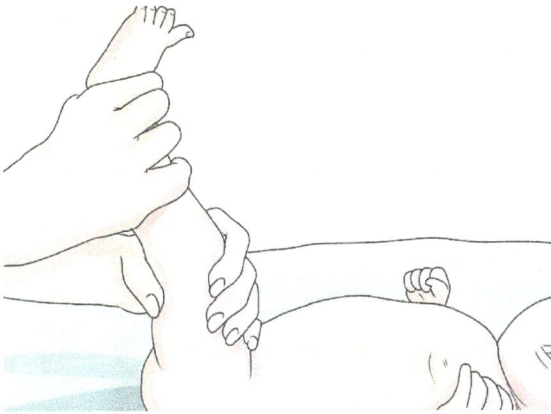

5. Finish with the legs and feet. Return the baby to a face up position. Roll each leg between your hands in a gentle motion. Include the feet and toes.

- Consider the "milking" technique for the legs as well. Encircle the baby's thigh with your thumb and finger, and work your way down the leg several times. Then, rub the baby's feet with your thumbs and curl and uncurl the toes.

- You can also try gently flexing each knee by slightly bending and straightening them several times. If the baby resists, don't force the knees to bend or straighten.

6. Give a rolling massage a try as well. Many babies enjoy the sensation of having their arms and legs "rolled" by loving hands. Gently roll your hands back and forth over one arm or leg at a time, as if you were rolling out dough on a pastry board. The arm or leg will lightly rock back and forth over the towel or blanket beneath your baby.

Method 2

Choosing the Right Time to Massage

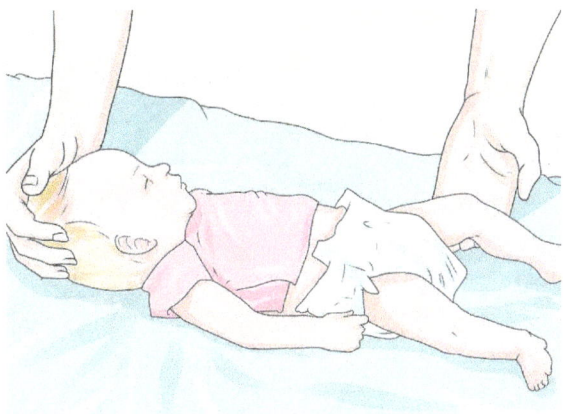

1. Start the massages early in the baby's life. Most babies can be massaged starting at around ten days to two weeks of age. Always consult your infant's doctor for guidance specific to your baby, however.

- While the evidence is limited regarding the overall benefits of infant massage, babies born prematurely do seem to gain weight more readily when massaged regularly, especially if food-based massage oils are used.

- The sooner you begin the massage process, the more natural the experience will be for your baby.

2. Massage a baby in between feedings. Try to avoid massaging a baby with a full tummy. Massaging a full stomach could lead to discomfort, fussiness, or spitting up. Ideally, try to do the massage at least 45 minutes after a feeding.

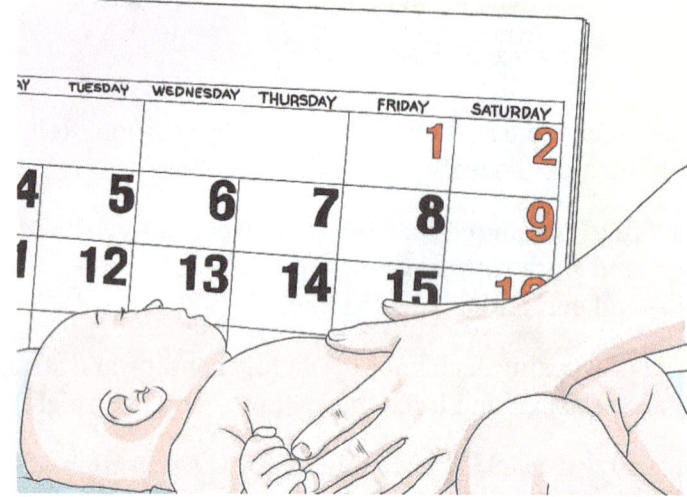

3. Create a routine. Your baby may be more responsive to massage sessions if you schedule them close to the same time daily. One of the best times for your baby may be a little while after the last feeding for the night. Massage can help stimulate digestion and promote a state of relaxation that may assist with a sounder sleep. (Although, with a newborn, it still probably won't last too long!)

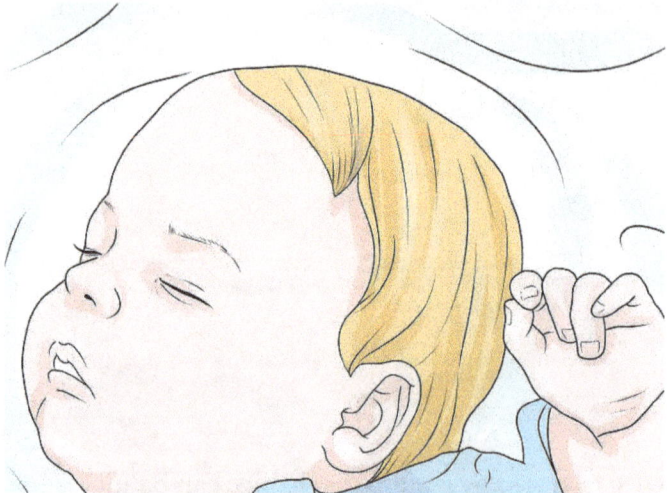

4. Slowly increase the massage duration. Initially, a five-minute massage should be sufficient to get your baby used to the feeling and process. Slowly increase the duration of the massage sessions until you get up to a half hour or so. There's no need to go for this long, of course.

5. Know when it's time to stop a massage. If the baby shows signs of discomfort or displeasure, like restlessness, straining, or crying, end the massage session. If this is a recurring issue, consider whether you may need to make adjustments to your technique.

- That said, it may just be the case that your baby doesn't like massages. If so, remember that there is no definitive medical evidence that infant massage is necessary or undeniably beneficial.

- Back arching is usually a sign that your baby is being over-stimulated. If your baby is not responding in a relaxed manner, you should end the session and try again later.

Method 3

Creating the Proper Environment

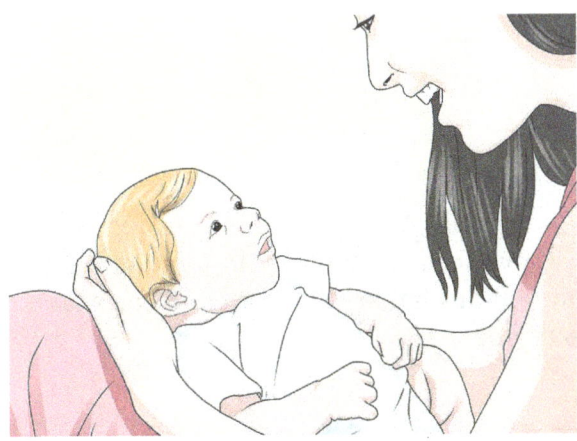

1. Make comfort a priority for both of you. Sit wherever you and your baby will be most comfortable. You can sit on a bed with your baby placed between your legs. If using the floor, place a comfy blanket under you and your baby. Your baby can also lie across your lap rather than between your legs. Just make sure the newborn's head and neck are supported at all times.

- Make sure that the room is set at an adequate temperature to keep your baby warm. Your baby will not respond well to a massage session if the room is chilly.

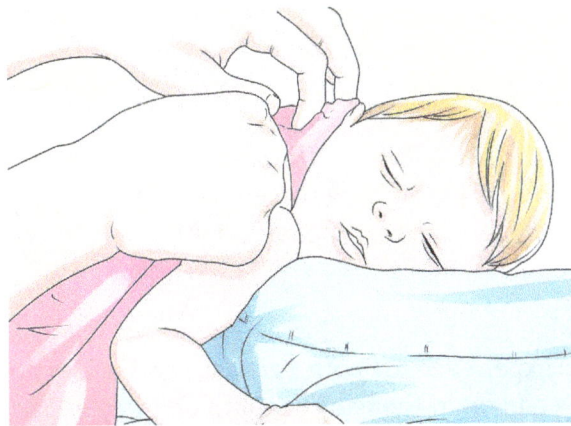

2. Undress your baby down to only a diaper. This will give you easier access to the baby's various

body parts. Also, skin-to-skin touch promotes better comfort and bonding. Keep a warm blanket nearby in case the baby gets chilly. You can keep your baby covered with the blanket and expose only the area you are working on.

- You can massage your baby with the diaper removed as well, so long as you are prepared and willing to deal with a potential mess.

3. Play soft music or sing softly. Recorded music can help set the mood, but live singing (from you) is even better. Not only will this help relax your baby; the sound of your voice will also help strengthen the bond between you.

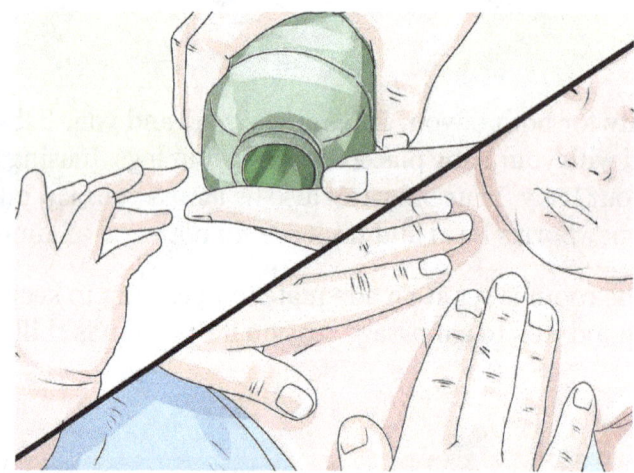

4. Warm any oils that you plan to use. Rub the (low-odor, edible) massage oil between your palms before applying it to your baby's skin. Nothing will end a session quicker than some cold oil placed on your baby's chest. If you are going to incorporate oil into the session, remember to protect your bedding and clothing with a towel.

- Use a low-odor, edible massage oil. Massage oil is not necessary, but many parents find that it improves the experience for both parties. Try, for instance, olive oil or avocado oil, since some of it may end up in the baby's mouth one way or another.

- Avoid inedible or non-digestible oils like mineral oil or baby oil.

- Avoid using oils on your baby's face or head during a massage. This will help limit ingestion and the possibility of getting oil in the infant's eyes.

- Test the oil on a small area of your baby's skin a day prior to using it for massage purposes. If your baby has a reaction to the oil, don't use it.

Method 4

Improving your Technique

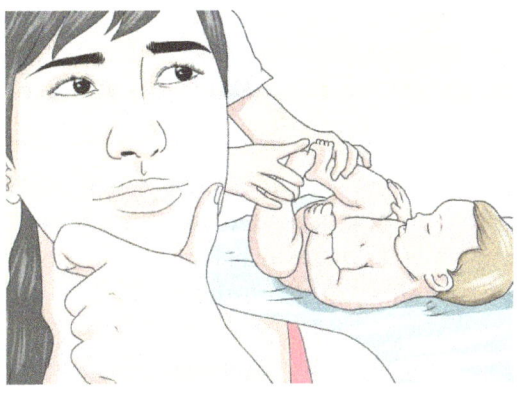

1. Learn about the normal reflexes of a newborn baby. By understanding these typical reflex responses, you will be able to calmly incorporate them into your massage routine.

- For instance, when you touch the cheek, your baby's head will usually turn towards that touch.

- Or, if you stroke the sole of a foot, your baby's toes will curl. The same is true if you stroke the palm of a hand.

- If you turn the infant's head to one side, the baby's body will normally arch away. These are common reactions that almost all babies have when touched.

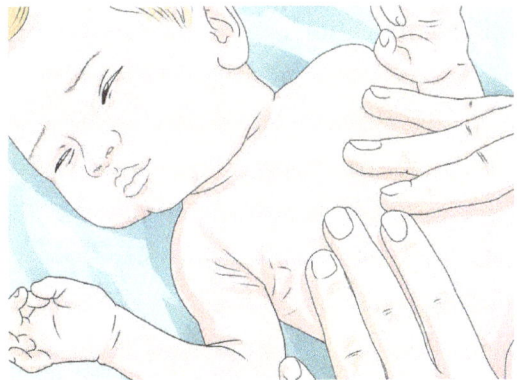

2. Discover which massage strokes work best for your baby. As long as you work slowly and gently, you don't have to worry about hurting your baby as you figure out which strokes provide the best results. Just remember, all strokes should be done with a slow, lightly pressured touch.

- Start with very gentle strokes and gradually build up the pressure a little at a time. A somewhat firmer stroke may in fact help prevent tickling.

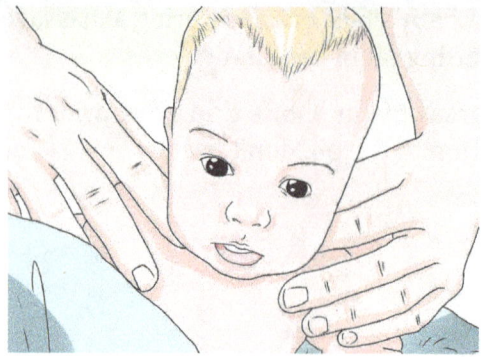

3. Quit using strokes that prove ineffective. For instance, you can try kneading the shoulders lightly, but only if the baby accepts it. More often than not, you'll probably find that the baby dislikes this maneuver; if so, stop kneading.

- As another example, some infant massage advocates say that an upward stroke will stimulate the nervous system, while a downward stroke will result in a calming effect. That said, use your own experience as your primary guide.

How to Recognize Symptoms of a Postpartum Hemorrhage

Postpartum hemorrhage is defined as abnormal amounts of bleeding from the vagina post-delivery. This bleeding can occur within 24 hours after delivery or after a few days. PPH is a leading cause of women post-delivery today, and results in 8% of the deaths among women after delivery. The PPH mortality figures are much higher in under-developed and developing nations. However, it is normal to have some amount of bleeding (known as lochia) after you have delivered your baby. This bleeding often lasts for a few weeks. It is important to learn how to differentiate PPH from lochia early on, in order to avoid complications.

Method 1

Recognizing High Risk Situations

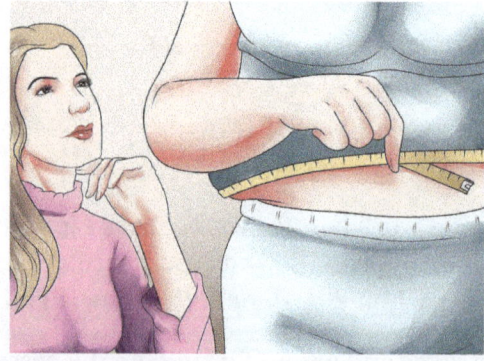

1. Know which conditions can cause a PPH. Several conditions that occur before, during, or after

delivery can result in the precipitation of PPH. Some of these conditions require close monitoring of the woman during and after delivery to rule out PPH. It is important to know about these conditions, as they increase a woman's chances of suffering from this condition.

- Placenta Previa, placental abruption, retained placenta, and other placental abnormalities

- Multiple pregnancies

- Pre-eclampsia or increased blood pressure during pregnancy

- History of PPH in a previous delivery

- Obesity

- Uterine abnormalities

- Anemia

- Emergency caesarean section

- Bleeding during pregnancy

- Long lasting labour more than 12 hours

- Baby's birth weight above 4 kgs

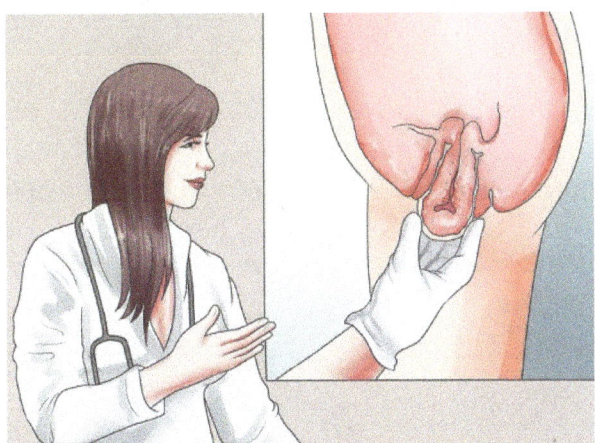

2. Understand that uterine atony is a cause of major blood loss. Postpartum hemorrhage, or blood loss after giving birth, is one of the world's leading causes of maternal death, even after safe delivery. There are several reasons why excessive bleeding of more than 500 ml after delivery of the baby occurs. One of this is called uterine atony.

- Uterine atony is when the uterus of the mother (the part of the female reproductive system that housed the baby) is having difficulties in going back to its original state.

- The uterus remains lose, hollow and non-contracting when it should be firm and contracting. This makes the passage of blood easier and faster, contributing to postpartum hemorrhage.

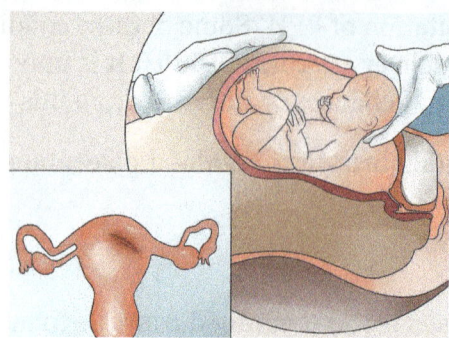

3. Know that trauma during childbirth can lead to a postpartum hemorrhage. Another reason why excessive bleeding occurs is when trauma or injury occurs as the baby exits the body.

- Trauma may be in the form of cuts, which can be caused by using assistive devices during delivery

- Alternatively, lacerations can occur when the baby is larger than average and is coming out rapidly. This may cause a tear in the vaginal opening.

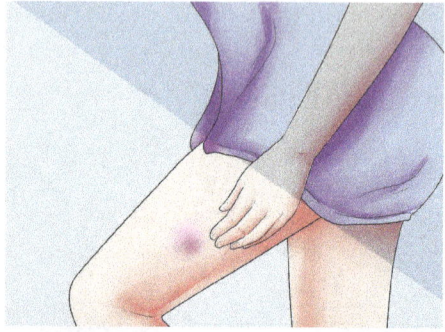

4. Understand that sometimes the blood does not flow out of the woman's body. Bleeding caused by PPH will not always flow out of the body. At times, bleeding occurs internally and if there's no outlet for the blood it will move toward the small crevices found in between bodily tissues and will form what is called a haematoma.

Method 2

Recognizing Bleeding Associated with PPH

1. Keep track of the quantity of blood. The type of bleeding that occurs immediately after delivery,

within 24 hours of delivery, or a few days after delivery is crucial to help rule out a PPH. The most important parameter for this purpose is the quantity of the bleeding.

- Any bleeding above 500 ml after a vaginal delivery and above 1000 ml after a caesarean section is considered as a PPH.

- In addition, bleeding that exceeds 1000 ml is labeled as severe PPH and requires immediate medical intervention, especially if there are additional risk factors.

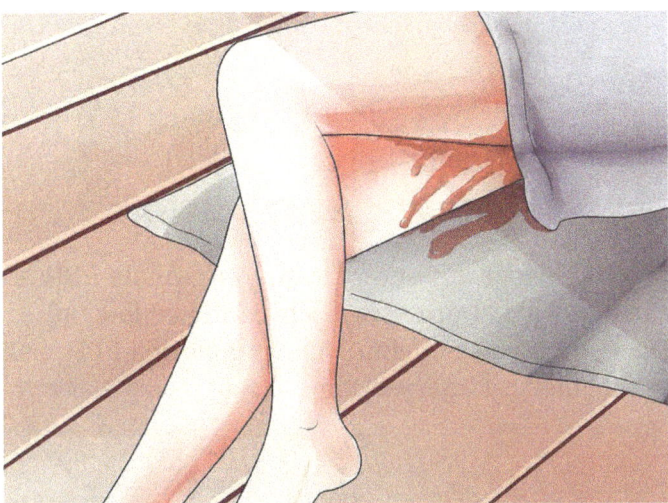

2. Look at the flow and texture of the blood. PPH is generally continuous in flow and is profuse, with or without several large clots. However, clots are much more common in a PPH that develops after a few days of delivery, and this type of bleeding may also be more gradual in flow.

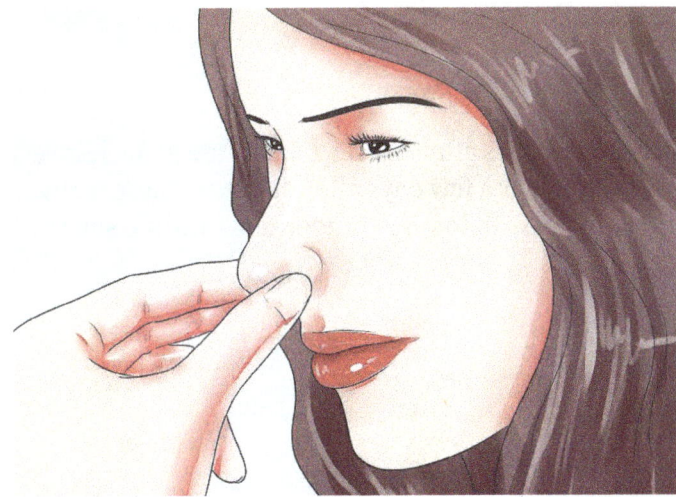

3. Know that the blood's odor may help you determine whether or not there is a PPH. Some additional characteristics that can help differentiate a PPH from normal post-delivery bleeding or lochia (vaginal discharge consisting of blood, tissue from the lining of the uterus and bacteria) are its odor and flow. Suspect a PPH if your lochia has an offensive smell, or if your flow suddenly increases after delivery.

Method 3

Recognizing Accessory Symptoms

1. Seek medical help if you recognize any severe symptoms. Acute PPH is often accompanied by signs of shock such as reduced blood pressure, tachycardia or low pulse rate, fever, rigors, and faintness or collapse. These are the most definite indications of a PPH, but also the most dangerous. They require immediate medical intervention.

2. Watch for signs that occur a few days after delivery. There are some less severe yet dangerous signs of a secondary PPH that tend to occur a few days after delivery. These include fever, abdominal pain, painful urination, general weakness, abdominal tenderness over the suprapubic area and adnexae.

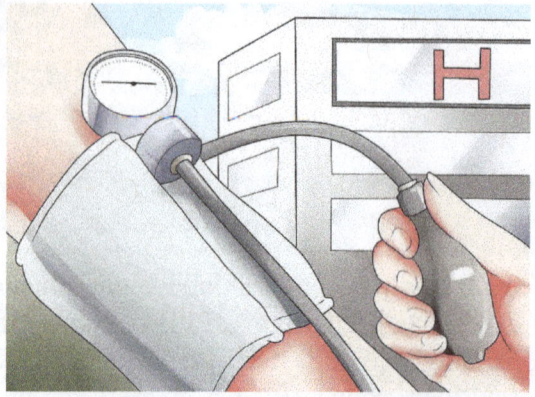

3. Go to the hospital if you see these warning signs. PPH is a medical emergency and requires

immediate hospitalization and measures to stop the bleeding. Hence, it isn't a condition that can be ignored. If you experience any of the following symptoms after delivery, contact your OB immediately, as you could be developing shock.

- Low blood pressure

- Low pulse rate

- Oliguria or reduced urine

- Sudden and continuous vaginal bleeding or passing of large clots

- Fainting

- Rigors

- Fever

- Abdominal pain

Method 4

Creating a Nurse Care Plan (for Nurses and Doctors)

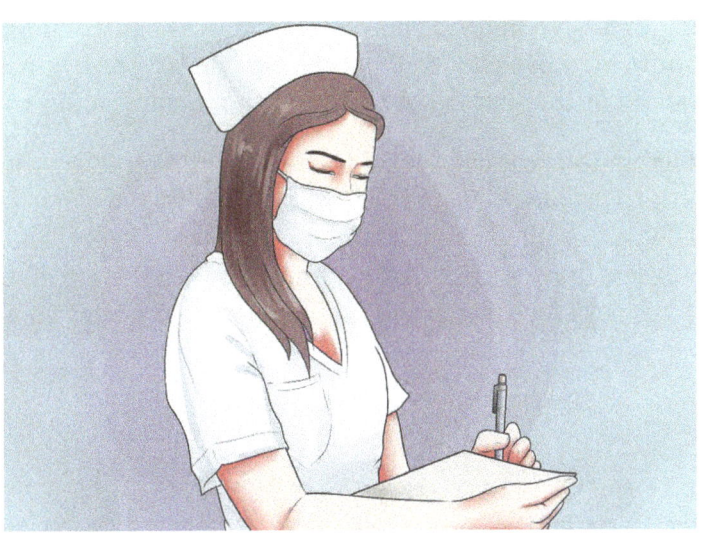

1. Understand what a nurse care plan is. The most important thing for decreasing the occurrence of death after childbirth is the ability to catch the signs of bleeding early in its course and pinpoint its cause. Quickly identifying the cause of the bleeding allows for faster intervention.

- A nursing care plan is a very useful tool in doing just that. There are five steps in the nursing care plan. These steps are assessment, diagnosis, planning, intervention and evaluation.

- In order to make a nursing care plan on postpartum hemorrhage, it is important to know what to look for and what to do in each of these steps.

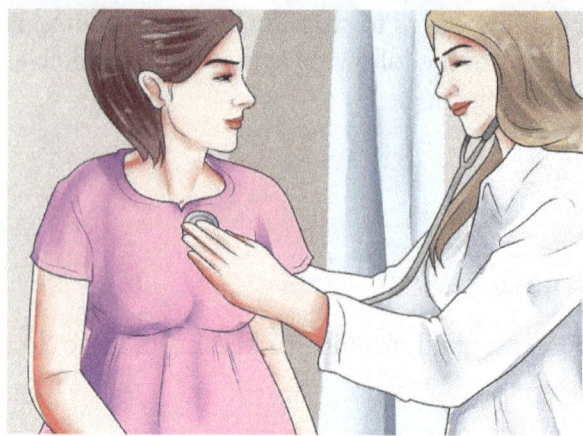

2. Pay close attention to mothers who are predisposed to developing a postpartum hemorrhage. Before carrying out an assessment, it is important to take note of the mother's history. There are several predisposing factors that make the mother more prone to postpartum hemorrhage, as all women who had just given birth are prone to excessive blood loss. If one or more of the following are present in the mother, assessment should be done at least every 15 minutes during and following delivery until the mother is not showing any signs of bleeding.

- These predisposing factors include a distended uterus caused by carrying a large infant inside or having excessive fluid in the placenta (the sac surrounding the infant), having given birth to more than five children, rapid labor, prolonged labor, utilization of assistive devices, a caesarean birth, removal of the placenta manually and an inverted uterus.

- Predisposing factors to excessive bleeding also include mothers who have suffered from conditions such as placenta previa, placenta accreta, utilizing drugs such as oxytocin, prostaglandins, tocolytics, or magnesium sulfate, underwent general anesthesia, if the mother has clotting disorders, have suffered from hemorrhage in the previous childbirth, has uterine fibroids, or has suffered from bacterial infection of the fetal membranes (chorioamnionitis).

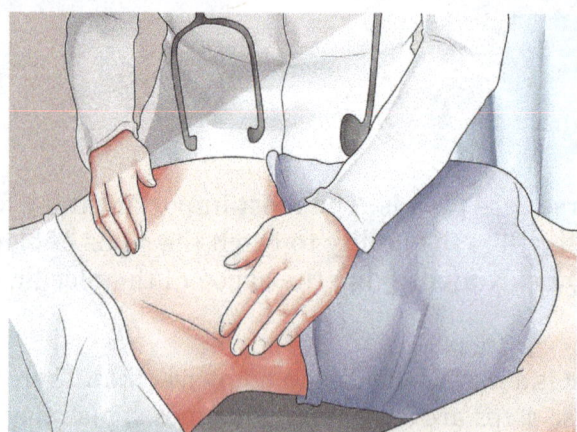

3. Evaluate the mother's condition frequently. In assessing the mother, there are certain physical aspects that need to be checked regularly to determine if there is an ongoing postpartum hemorrhage and also to help determine the cause. These physical aspects include:

- The fundus (the top part of the uterus opposite the cervix), the bladder, the amount of lochia (the fluid coming out of the vagina that is composed of blood, mucus, and tissue from the uterus), the four vital signs (temperature, pulse rate, respiratory rate and blood pressure) and skin color.

- When assessing these areas, it is important to note what to look out for. Follow the steps below for more info.

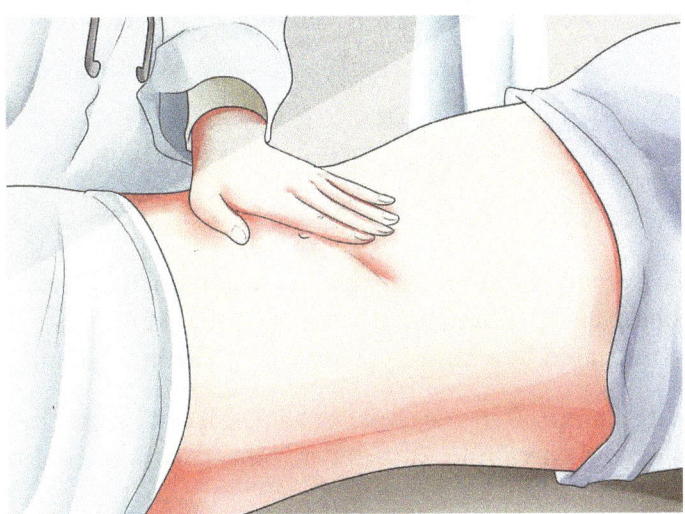

4. Monitor the fundus. it is important to check for the consistency and the location pf the fundus. Normally, the fundus should feel firm upon palpation and the level will be inclined towards the umbilical (belly button) area. Any changes to this - for example if the fundus feels soft or is difficult to locate - could be indicative of postpartum hemorrhage.

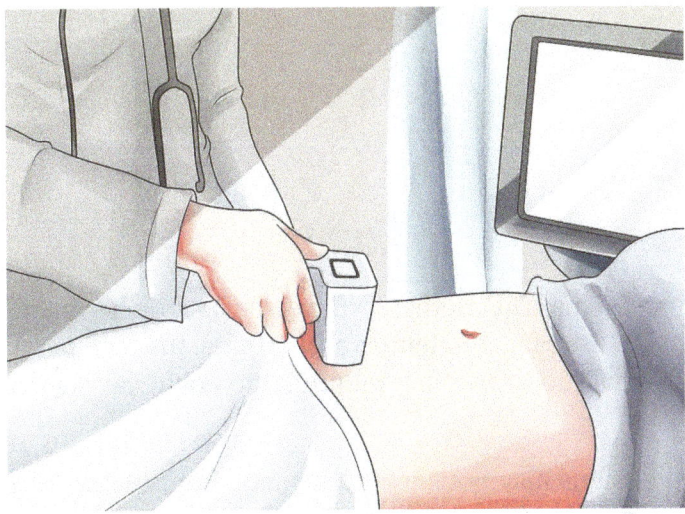

5. Look at the bladder. There might be instances when the bladder is causing the hemorrhaging and this is indicated by the fundus being displaced above the umbilical (belly button) area.

- Let the mother urinate and if after urinating the bleeding goes away, then it is the bladder causing the displacement of the uterus.

6. Assess the lochia. In assessing the amount of discharge coming out from the vagina, it is important to weigh the pads being used before and after in order to get accurate documentation. Excessive bleeding should be indicated by saturation of one pad within fifteen minutes.

- Sometimes, the discharge often goes unnoticed and it can be checked by asking the mother to turn on her side and check underneath her, especially in the buttocks area.

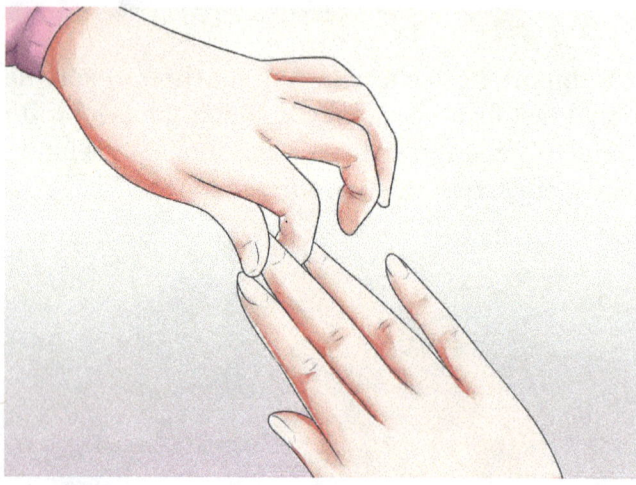

7. Check the mother's vital signs. The mother's vital signs include her blood pressure, respiratory rate (number of breaths), pulse rate, and temperature. In postpartum hemorrhage, the pulse rate should be lower than normal (60 to 100 in a minute), but could vary depending on the mother's previous pulse rate.

- However, the vital signs may not show abnormality until later the mother is already suffering from excessive blood loss. Therefore, you should assess any deviation from what is normally expected with adequate blood volume, such as warm, dry skin and pink lips and mucous membranes.

- The nails can also be inspected by pinching and releasing them. There should only be a there second interval for the color of the nail bed to return to pink.

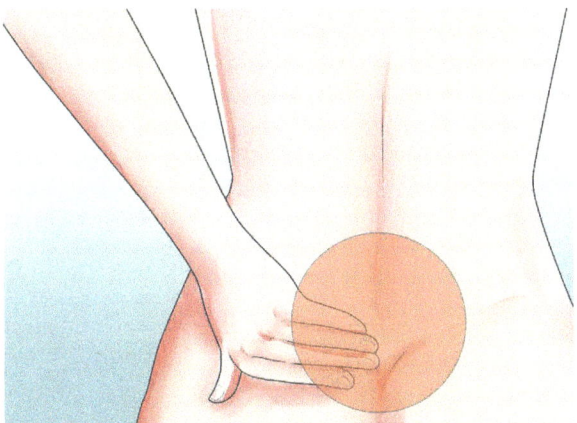

8. Understand that trauma could lead to excessive bleeding. If any of these changes have been assessed, the mother could be suffering from postpartum hemorrhage caused by the uterus failing to contract and getting back into its original shape. However, if the uterus has been assessed and it was found to be contracted and not dislocated, and yet there is still excessive bleeding, this could be due to trauma. In assessing for trauma, pain and external color of the vagina have to be considered.

- Pain: The mother will be experiencing deep, severe pelvic pain or rectal pain. This can be indicative of internal bleeding.

- External vaginal orifice: there will be bulging masses and skin discoloration (usually purplish to bluish black hue). This can also be indicative of internal bleeding.

- If the laceration or wound is found outside, it can be easily assessed upon visual inspection, especially if done under proper lighting.

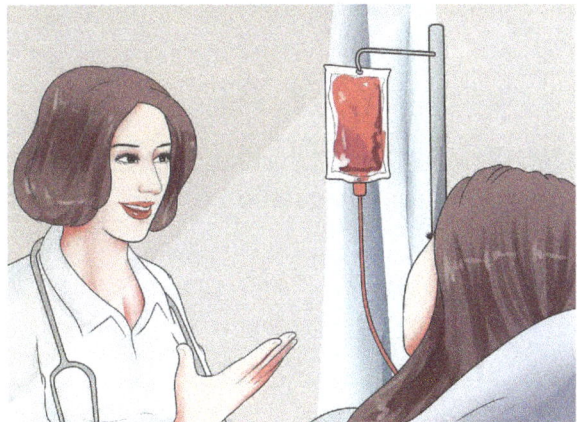

9. Notify other healthcare providers. If there is considerable blood loss and the cause have been determined, the next step in the nursing care plan has already been accounted for, which is the diagnosis.

- Upon confirmation of the diagnosis of postpartum hemorrhage, the first step in planning is always to inform the physician and other healthcare providers involved in the care of the mother as the nurse cannot use client-centered goals.

- The nurse's key roles in this kind of complication is to monitor the mother, implement ways to minimize blood loss and replace it, and to report right away if there are any significant changes in the previously noted condition and if the response from the mother is not what is desired.

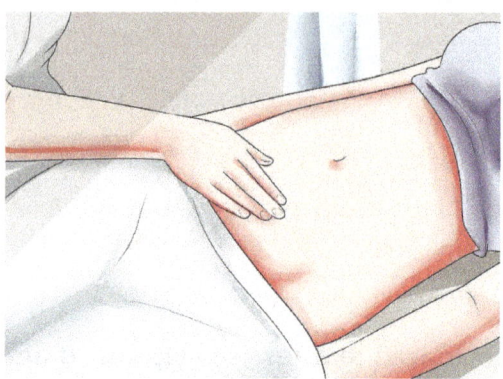

10. Massage the mother's uterus and keep track of blood loss. Nursing interventions appropriate for postpartum hemorrhage will be to continuously monitor the vital signs and the output via weighing blood soaked pads and linens. Massaging the uterus will also aid in getting it to contract and become firm again. Notifying the physicians or midwives when there is still bleeding (even during the massage) is important as well.

11. Regulate the mother's blood levels. The nurse should have already notified the blood bank in case there is a need for blood transfusion. Regulation of intravenous flow is also the nurse's responsibility.

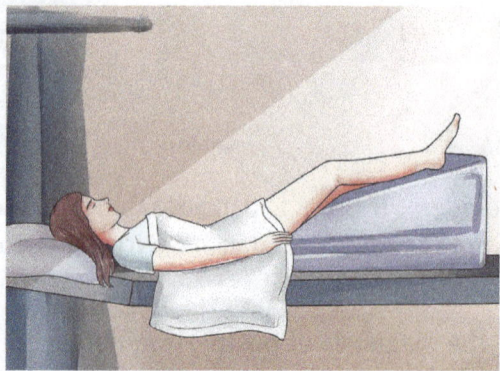

12. Put the mother in the Trendelenburg position. The mother should also be positioned in what

is called a modified Trendelenburg, where the legs are elevated by least 10 degrees and at most 30 degrees. The body is horizontal and the head elevated a little bit as well.

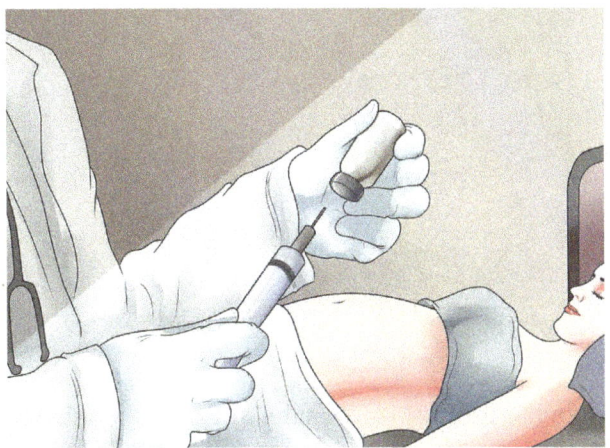

13. Give the mother medications. The mother will usually be on a number of medications, such as oxytocin and Methergine, and the nurse should be able to determine the side effects of these medications, as they could also be life threatening to the mother.

- Oxytocin is mainly used for labor induction and is safe to be given during labor; however it is also utilized after delivery. The action of the drug is to facilitate the contraction of the smooth muscles of the uterus. It is usually given through an intramuscular (usually in the upper arm) injection with a dose of 0.2 mg given every 2 to 4 hour with a maximum of 5 doses after delivery. Oxytocin has an antidiuretic effect, which means that it will inhibit urination.

- Methergine is a drug that is never given before labor, but can be given afterwards. This is because the action of Methergine is to promote sustained uterine contractions, and will therefore cause a decrease in the oxygen consumption of a baby still inside the uterus. Methergine is also given by injection intramuscularly with a dose of 0.2 mg every 2 to 4 hours. Methergine's side effect is an increase in the body's blood pressure. It should be noted if the blood pressure spikes up more than normal.

14. Monitor the mother's breathing. The nurse should be aware of any buildup of fluids inside the

body by consistently listening to breath sounds. This is done in order to identify any fluid in the lungs.

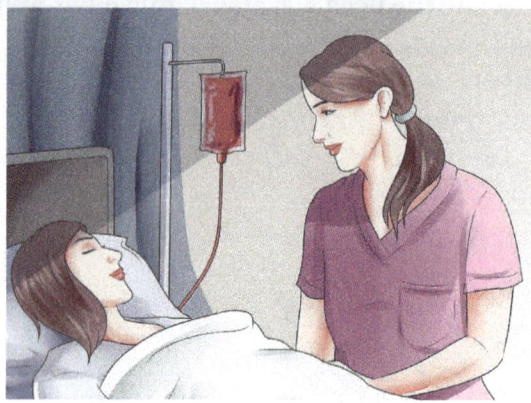

15. Evaluate the mother when the mother is in a safer state. The final step in the nursing process is evaluation. Like the assessment, the areas of concern in a mother suffering from excessive bleeding will be checked.

- The location of the uterus should be midline, with the umbilicus as the center. The uterus should be firm upon palpation.

- The mother should not be changing pads as often (using only one pad every hour or so) and there should be no leakage of blood or fluids found on her bed sheets.

- The mother's vital signs should have returned to her normal, pre-delivery vital signs.

- She will not have clammy or cold skin and her lips should be pinkish in color.

- Because she is no longer expelling fluids in bulk, her urine output should return to 30 ml to 60 ml every hour. This shows that there are enough fluids inside her body for adequate circulation.

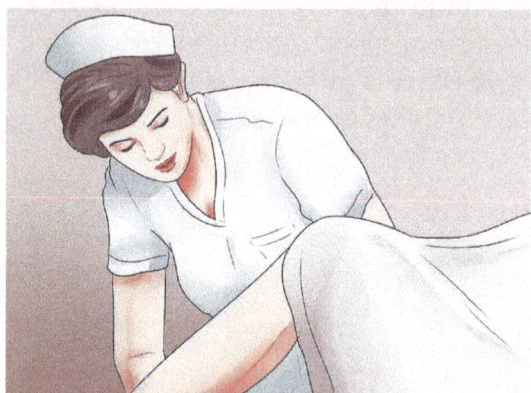

16. Check on any open wounds the mother may have sustained. If her bleeding was due to trauma, any open wounds will have been sutured by the physician. These wounds will need consistent monitoring to ensure that they don't re-open.

- There should be no more severe pain, although there may be some local pain coming from the sutured wound.

- If there was blood pooling inside the mother's muscles or tissues, the treatment should have eradicated the purplish or black bluish coloring on the skin.

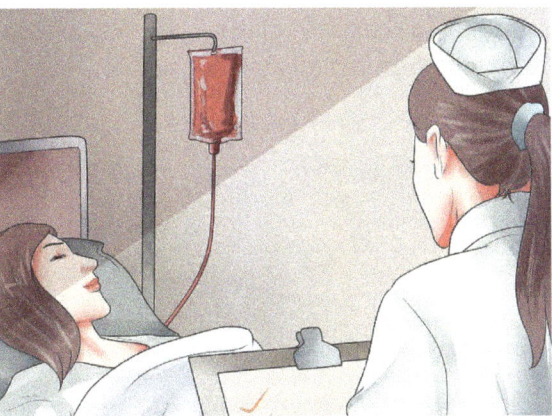

17. Check for side effects of the medications. The medications that were aforementioned should be routinely checked for any side effects, until the use of the medications is discontinued. Even though managing postpartum hemorrhage is done in cooperation with the physician, the nurse will be able to gauge the effectiveness of the interventions by a consistent improvement in the condition of the mother.

How to Eliminate Postpartum Hemorrhage

Postpartum Hemorrhage, or PPH, is medically defined as blood loss greater than 500ml after vaginal delivery, and 1000ml after cesarean delivery. It has been stated than PPH is the leading cause of maternal morbidity and mortality. Hence, it is a serious condition that requires prompt management and optimal treatment.

Method 1

Managing PPH

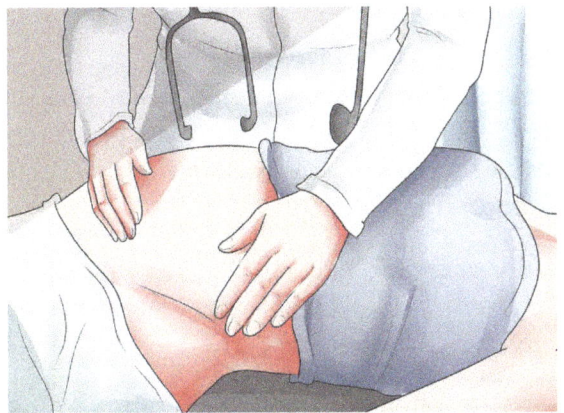

1. Perform a uterine massage. The first step in managing this condition is a technique called

bimanual uterine massage which is performed to try to stimulate the uterus to regain its tone. At the same time, administration of uterotonics (like oxytocin) should be carried out.

- Uterine massage should only be carried out by a physician. It involves elevating the uterus, by pressing on the fundus both internally (with one hand) and externally (with the other).

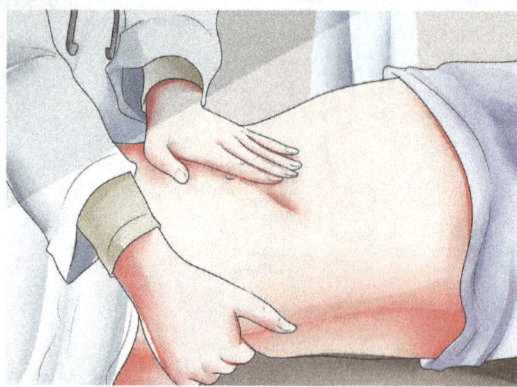

2. Try bimanual compression if the massage does not work. If uterine massage fails to give the uterus some degree of "tone", bimanual compression should be applied. This is a similar maneuver to the uterine massage, with a more aggressive approach.

- With bimanual compression, a firm pressure is applied by the physician with both hands (which are in similar positions as in uterine massage) in order to evoke a response from the uterine musculature.

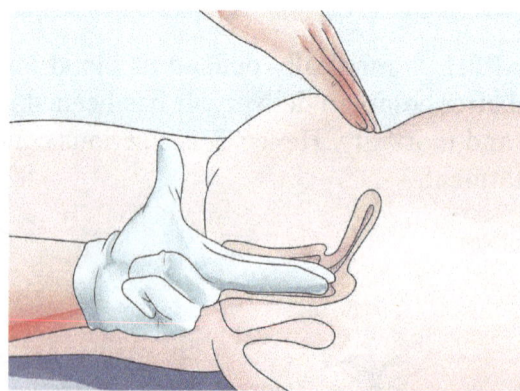

3. Manually explore the uterine cavity if bimanual compression does not produce results. Manual exploration of the uterine cavity is carried out by the physician, to try to find the cause of PPH. Exploration of the uterine cavity should be performed in the operating room, in more sterile conditions, to minimize chances of contracting an infection.

- The exploration may reveal some defects in the muscular wall of the uterus, as well as hematomas, or even uterine rupture, which can be seen if the patient had previous cesarean delivery or uterine surgery.

- If any of these disorders are found during the exploration by the physician, operative intervention will be necessary.

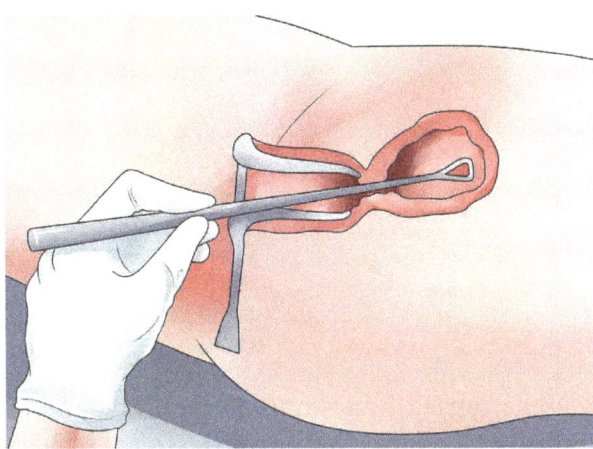

4. Remove any fragments found in the uterus. During a manual examination, placental fragments that were retained in the uterus during birth may be discovered.

- Removal of these fragments is essential in eliminating PPH, since they can be recognized as the source of bleeding.

- Manual removal of these fragments or curettage are procedures by which these fragments are removed. Curettage comprises surgical "scraping" of these fragments, with the use of a scoop.

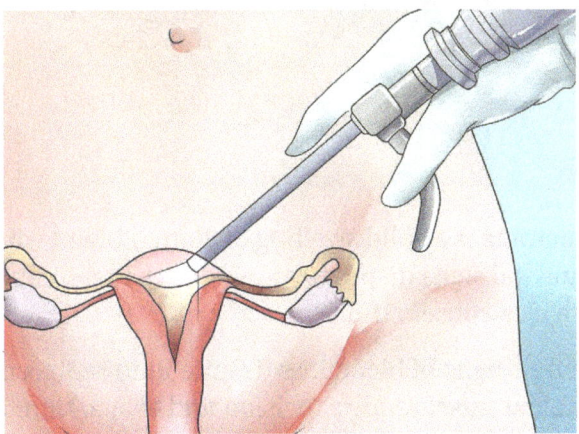

5. Use surgical methods to combat the PPH. In such cases, a laparotomy is performed to efficiently control and stop the bleeding, by promptly identifying the source of hemorrhage. Laparotomy is a procedure carried out via a large incision on the abdominal wall, in order to gain direct access into the abdomen and uterus.

- Depending on the findings, surgical suturing, ligation of blood vessels, and in severe cases, hysterectomy, are procedures that are indicated in PPH.

- Suturing and ligation include management of the arterial supply to the uterus and the abdominal cavity. Closing these arteries may effectively reduce and eliminate PPH.

- Hysterectomy is performed only if these surgical procedures fail, and the patient is not hemodynamically stable.

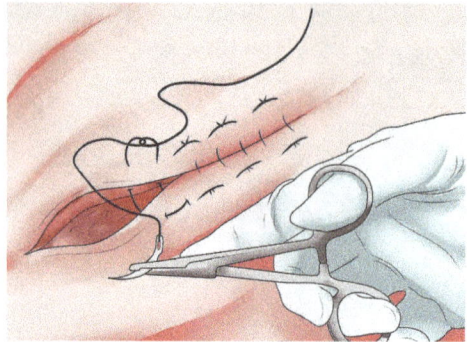

6. Use sutures to repair wounds caused by trauma. Lacerations and hematomas resulting from birth trauma can cause significant blood loss that can be lessened by hemostasis and timely repair. Sutures should be done if direct pressure does not stop the bleeding.

- Episiotomy increases blood loss and the risk of anal sphincter tears, and this procedure should be avoided unless urgent delivery is necessary and the perineum is thought to be a limiting factor.

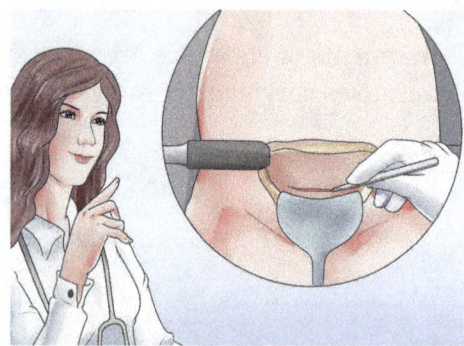

7. Treat hematomas. A hematoma is a solid swelling of clotted blood within the tissue. It can present as pain or as a change in vital signs disproportionate to the amount of blood loss. Small hematomas can be managed with close observation.

- Patients with persistent signs of blood loss despite fluid replacement, as well as those with large or enlarging hematomas, require incision and evacuation of the clot.

- The involved area should be irrigated and the bleeding vessels ligated.

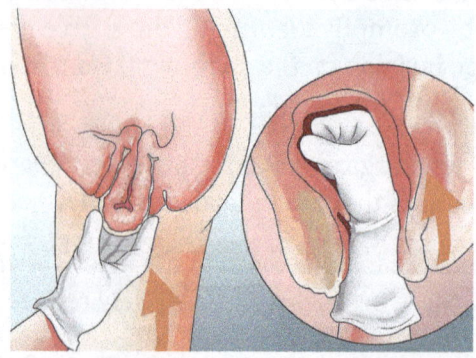

8. Revert the uterus in case of uterine inversion. Uterine inversion is rare, occurring in 0.05 percent

of deliveries. The inverted uterus usually appears as a bluish-gray mass protruding from the vagina.

- Every attempt should be made to replace the uterus quickly. Once the uterus is reverted, uterotonic agents should be given to promote uterine tone and to prevent recurrence.

- If initial attempts to replace the uterus fail or a cervical contraction ring develops, administration of magnesium sulfate, terbutaline (Brethine), nitroglycerin, or general anesthesia may allow sufficient uterine relaxation for manipulation.

- If these methods fail, the uterus will need to be replaced surgically.

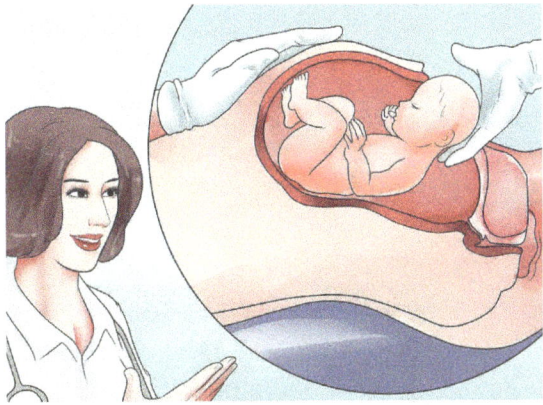

9. Consider a cesarean delivery in the case of a uterine rupture. Although rare in an unscarred uterus, clinically significant uterine rupture occurs in 0.6 to 0.7 percent of vaginal births, after a cesarean delivery in women with a low transverse or unknown uterine scar.

- The risk increases significantly with previous classical incisions or uterine surgeries, and to a lesser extent with shorter intervals between pregnancies or a history of multiple cesarean deliveries, particularly in women with no previous vaginal deliveries.

- Before delivery, the primary sign of uterine rupture is decrease in fetal heart rate (bradycardia). Vaginal bleeding, abdominal tenderness, maternal tachycardia (increased heart rate in mother), circulatory collapse, or increasing abdominal girth are also signs of uterine rupture. Symptomatic uterine rupture requires surgical repair of the defect or a hysterectomy.

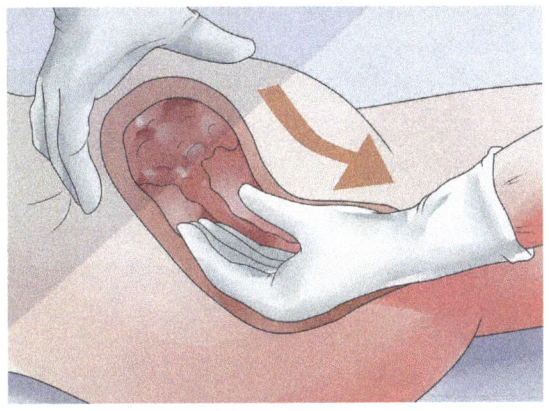

10. Treat tissue retention. Classic signs of placental separation include a small gush of blood with

lengthening of the umbilical cord and a slight rise of the uterus in the pelvis. The mean time from delivery until placental expulsion is eight to nine minutes. Longer intervals are associated with an increased risk of postpartum hemorrhage, with rates doubling after 10 minutes.

- Retained placenta (i.e., failure of the placenta to deliver within 30 minutes after birth) occurs in less than 3 percent of vaginal deliveries. One management option is to inject the umbilical vein with 20 mL of a solution of 0.9 percent saline and 20 units of oxytocin. This significantly reduces the need for manual removal of the placenta compared with injecting saline alone.

- Alternatively, physicians may proceed directly to manual removal of the placenta, using appropriate analgesia. If the tissue plane between the uterine wall and placenta cannot be developed through blunt dissection with the edge of the gloved hand, invasive placenta should be considered.

Method 2

Using Medications to Stop PPH

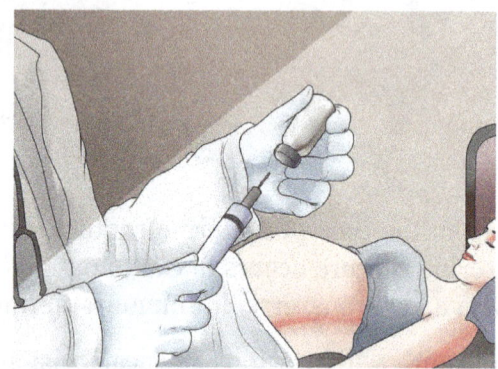

1. Consider the use of oxytocin. Oxytocin stimulates the upper segment of the uterine myometrium to contract rhythmically, which constricts spiral arteries and decreases blood flow through the uterus. Oxytocin is an effective first-line treatment for postpartum hemorrhage.

- 10 international units (IU) should be injected intramuscularly, or 20 IU in 1 L of saline may be infused at a rate of 250 mL per hour.

- As much as 500 mL can be infused over 10 minutes without complications.

2. Give the mother ergot alkaloids. Methylergonovine (Methergine) and ergometrine are ergot

alkaloids that cause generalized smooth muscle contraction in which the upper and lower segments of the uterus contract.

- However, these ergot alkaloid agents raise blood pressure, hence they are contraindicated in women with hypertension. Other adverse effects include nausea and vomiting.

- A typical dose of methylergonovine, 0.2 mg administered intramuscularly, may be repeated as required at intervals of two to four hours.

3. Give the mother prostaglandins. Prostaglandins enhance uterine contractility and cause vasoconstriction. The prostaglandin most commonly used is 15-methyl prostaglandin F2a, or carboprost (Hemabate). Misoprostol is another prostaglandin that increases uterine tone and decreases postpartum bleeding.

- Misoprostol is effective in the treatment of postpartum hemorrhage, but side effects may limit its use.

- It can be administered sublingually, orally, vaginally, and rectally. Doses range from 200 to 1,000 mcg; the dose recommended by FIGO is 1,000 mcg administered rectally.

Method 3

Preventing PPH

1. Discuss your patient's medical history. Risk factors for postpartum hemorrhage include a prolonged third stage of labor, multiple delivery, episiotomy, fetal macrosomia (large baby), and history of postpartum hemorrhage.

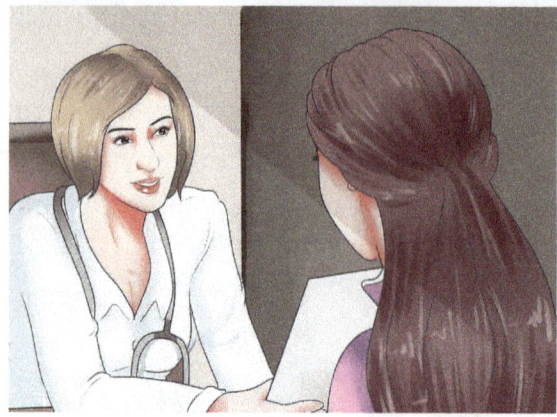

2. Actively manage your patient. Active management, which involves administering a uterotonic drug with or soon after the delivery of the first shoulder and using controlled cord traction and uterine massage after delivery of the placenta can decrease the risk of postpartum hemorrhage and shorten the third stage of labor with no significant increase in the risk of retained placenta.

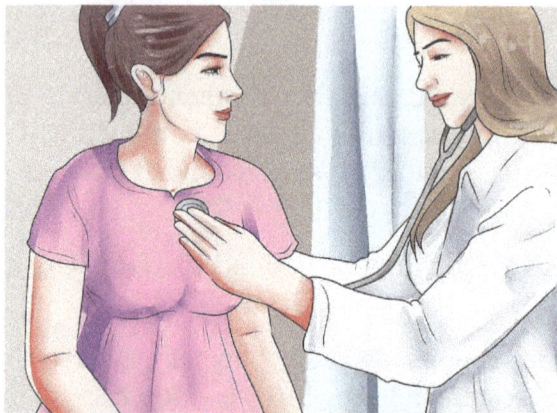

3. Reexamine your patient regularly. Reexamination of the patient's vital signs and vaginal flow before leaving the delivery area may help detect slow, steady bleeding.

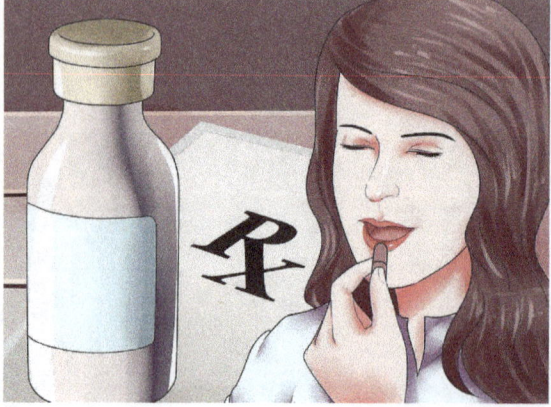

4. Consider giving your patient oxytocin to reduce her chances of developing PPH. Prophylactic administration of oxytocin (Pitocin) reduces rates of postpartum hemorrhage by 40 percent. This reduction also occurs if oxytocin is given after placental delivery.

How to Care for your New Baby

Congratulations on entering into this wonderful new experience! Your new baby will be so small and completely dependent on you, which will probably make you feel equally responsible, determined, and terrified. Don't panic! Read below for some basic guidelines for taking care of your new baby, as well as links to helpful resources.

Method 1

Handling your Newborn

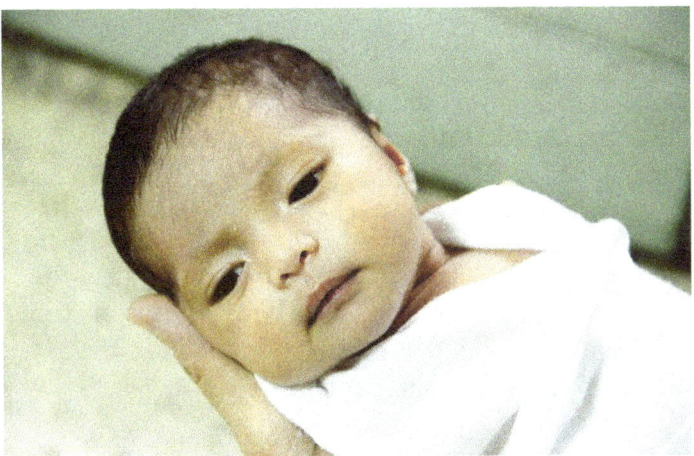

1. Support your baby's head. When you pick your baby up, be sure that you are supporting the head and neck. Babies have little muscle development in this area and if they do not have support when lifted, they can become seriously injured. Lift them delicately and cradle their head as you do so.

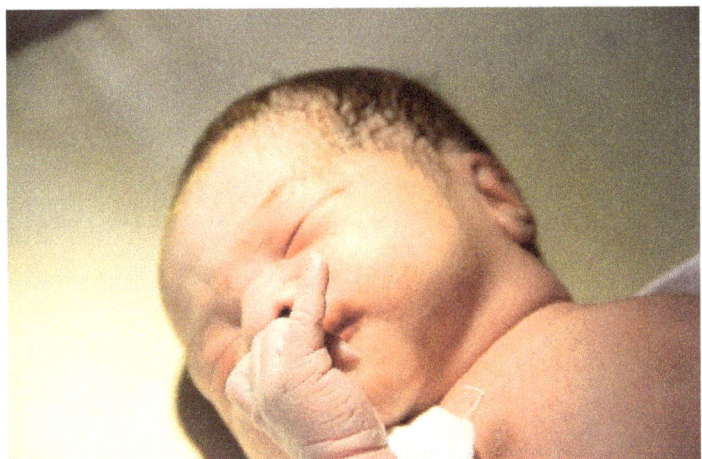

2. Don't worry too much about the soft spot. Babies skulls will not fully close until they are roughly a year and a half to two years old. Until then, you will notice that there are soft spots on their head. Don't worry too much, however. The membrane that covers these spots is very tough and your baby will be perfectly safe. You can touch these areas or comb the baby's hair without causing any harm.

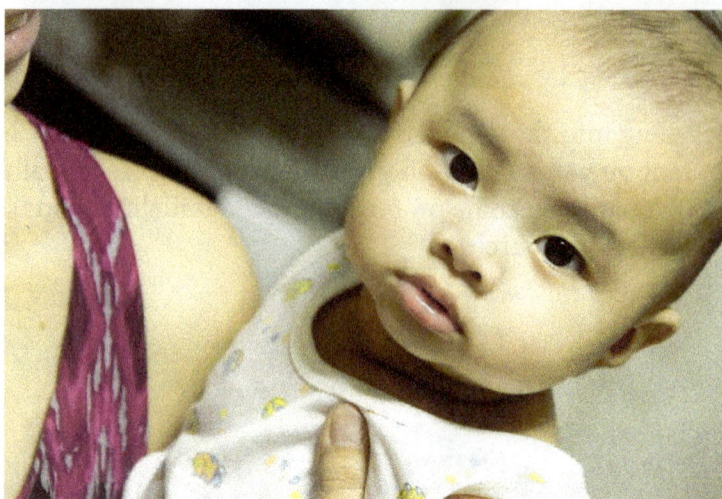

3. Don't ever shake your baby. Do not, under any circumstances, shake your baby. This will easily cause serious brain damage, spinal damage, or even kill your baby. You should not even shake them as a part of play until they have developed the muscles necessary to support this.

- If you are angry with your baby (which may very well happen, they cry a lot) and you are concerned that you feel the need to shake the baby or do something violent to make it be quiet, please seek help. Ask a friend or parent to watch the baby or give you advice until you calm down. Sleep deprivation is a harsh mistress.

Method 2

Feeding your Baby

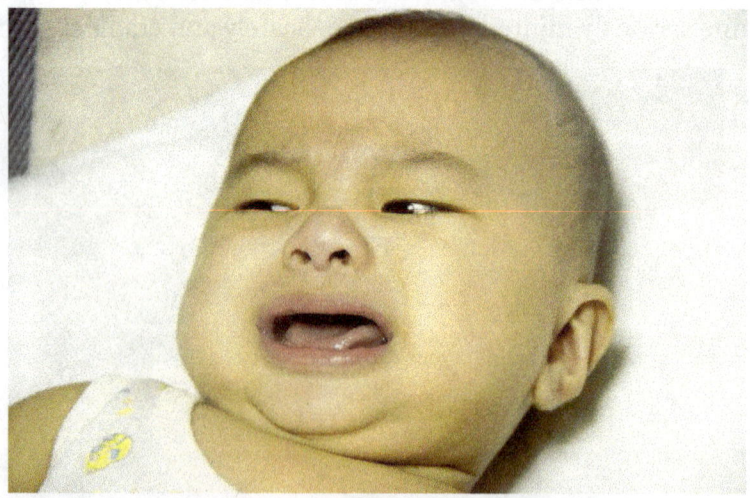

1. Understand when to feed your baby. Your baby will generally let you know when they need to be fed. Expect crying. With time you may come to be able to hear the difference between the cries and know which means hunger and which means bedtime and so on. How often they eat will depend on what they are eating, how much of it they are eating, and their own individual metabolism.

- Older babies will often give an indication when they are hungry, such as hand movements.

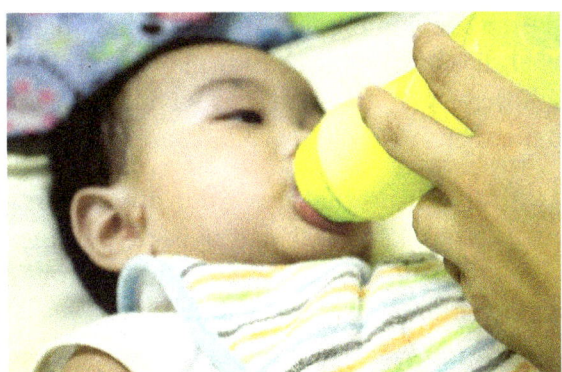

2. Be conscious of what to feed your baby. Infants will need to drink milk, either from formula or breast milk. Try not to give them anything other than this, as it will likely make them sick or lead them to choke. They can eat baby food once they reach a few months old and as they start to get teeth you can introduce more solid foods.

- Breast milk has been shown to be much healthier for your baby than formula, as it will provide not only the nutrients your baby needs but will also temporarily pass on many of your immunities to your baby.

3. Know how to feed your baby. You will need to choose between bottles or breastfeeding. No matter which method you choose, you will need to ensure that you are doing it correctly in order to prevent your baby from getting an infection and to help decrease the likelihood of spitting up.

- If bottle feeding, you will need to decide between a variety of bottle types. You may wish to purchase simple, more cost-effective bottles or you may wish to purchase more complex ones. Bottle liners can be purchased if you want to reduce the amount of washing you'll be doing, but you'll make more garbage in exchange.

- Breastfeeding is incredibly simple. Women were born to do it, after all! Be sure that you are keeping your nipple clean and free of any infections. Consult with your doctor if you are taking any medications and check labels on over-the-counter drugs. You will also want to eat as healthfully as possible, since you will be sharing those nutrients with your baby!

- While there are a variety of acceptable feeding positions for either method, you may want to feed with the baby in an upright position, as this will help prevent spit up.

4. Prepare for spit up. Babies stomach muscles are very weak in the beginning. So weak that

sometimes they have a hard time keeping food in there! Don't worry, this is very normal...it's just messy. Prepare for spit up by always having rags handy in order to clean up the mess, keeping a bib on your baby when they're a little bigger, and generally having a rag placed in front of your mouth any time you intend to burp them or move them around soon after eating.

- You will want to watch for spit up that is a color other than white or clear (red, yellow, green, and brown, for example) as these can be signs of illness. If you see this, take the baby to the doctor. Similarly, spitting up very forcefully or your baby not gaining weight are signs that would warrant a doctor's visit.

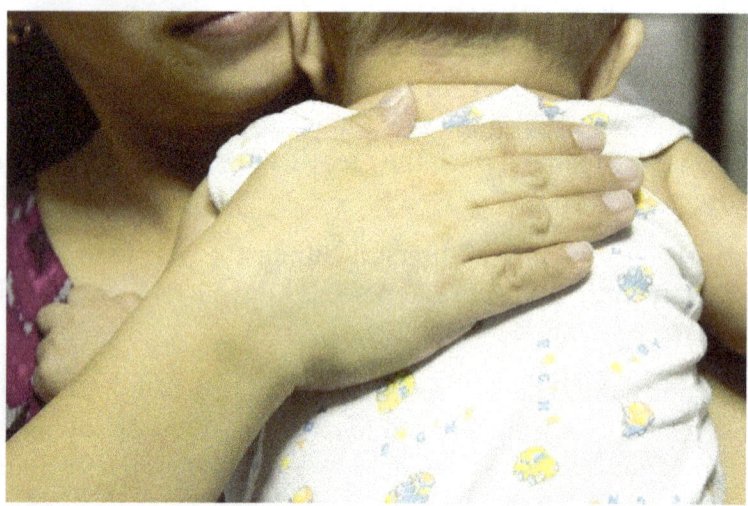

5. Burp your baby. After your baby has eaten, you will want to burp them. They can easily swallow too much air while eating and the bubbles in their stomach will make them cranky and uncomfortable. Lay your baby so that they are slightly over your shoulder and then firmly pat their back. This will help release the air and make your baby very happy.

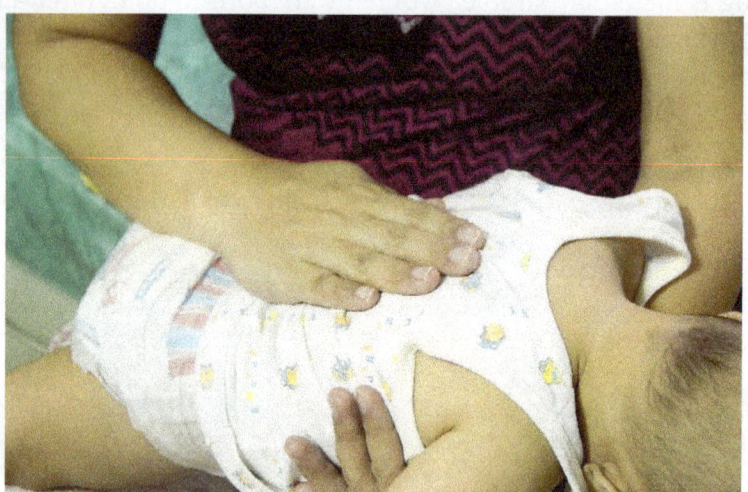

6. Watch out for gas. If your baby seems very unhappy and you cannot find any other cause, they are likely gassy. Help them to work the gas out of their system by laying them across your lap on their stomach and with their butt slightly elevated. Pat their back and draw your hand downward to help work the gas out; gravity will do most of the work.

Method 3

Ensuring Proper Hygiene

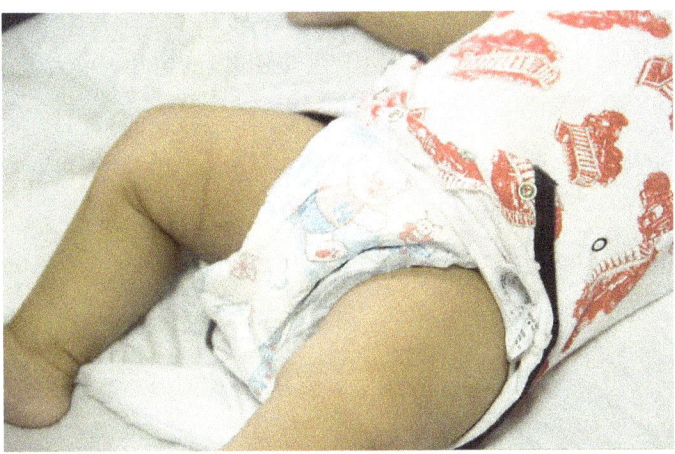

1. Know when to change your baby's diaper. This part won't be too hard. If your baby's diaper is filled, change it! If your baby's diaper is wet, change it! A soiled diaper will smell, so it won't be hard to tell when it's time for a change. Wet diapers can be a little more challenging. Set a timer and be sure to at least check their diaper every two hours. If you notice it is wet before then, however, change it then.

- A baby should never be left in a soiled diaper for long, as this can lead to a wide range of health problems. Plus, it isn't very sanitary for you! Very full diapers will leak and you probably don't want poop in your carpets.

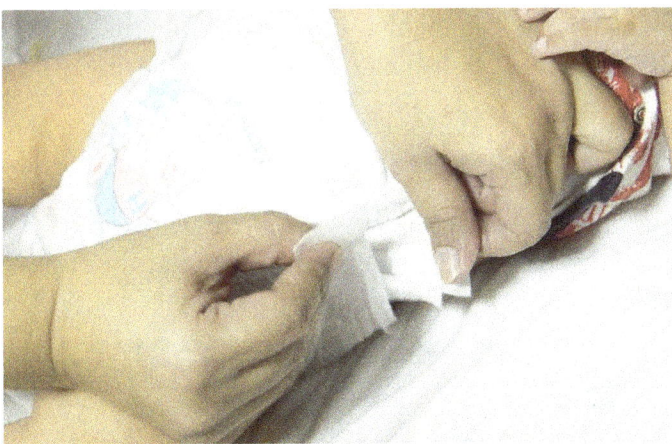

2. Understand how to change your baby's diaper. Diaper changing is very simple but if done incorrectly many problems can occur. Leaks, chafing, and pinching can result from an improperly placed diaper. Follow a few simple guidelines to be sure that you are keeping yourself clean and your baby happy.

- Place your baby on the changing area, flat on their back. Do not leave them unattended in this area for any period of time and try to always have at least one hand on them to keep them from rolling away.

- Open the soiled diaper but do not take it all the way off.

- Clean your baby thoroughly with the appropriate wet wipes. Do this similarly to how you would clean yourself.

- Place the dirty wipes in the diaper and then, lifting the baby's lower body up by the ankles, slide it out from under them. Roll it up and throw it away.

- Take out a fresh diaper, open it completely, and then slide it into position. Be sure that it is facing the correct direction.

- Close the diaper and check that the elastic around the legs is properly fit and is not too tight or pinching your baby.

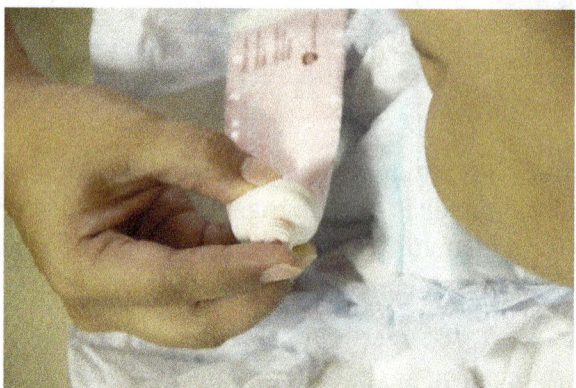

3. Combat diaper rash. Diaper rash is a common skin irritation that results when the baby's skin cannot get dry, is rubbed too hard by the diaper, or when your baby has other health problems. It is often a result of not being changed enough or wearing a diaper that is too small, though it is easy to get diaper rashes and you should not feel bad if your baby gets one.

- Combat diaper rash with the appropriate creams or powders when changing your baby's diaper and change their diaper as soon as it is soiled.

- Make sure that diapers and your baby's clothing fit, watch for dietary or product changes (as your baby may have an allergy), and be aware that antibiotics can make your baby susceptible to diaper rash. Seek help if the rash has not healed in a few days.

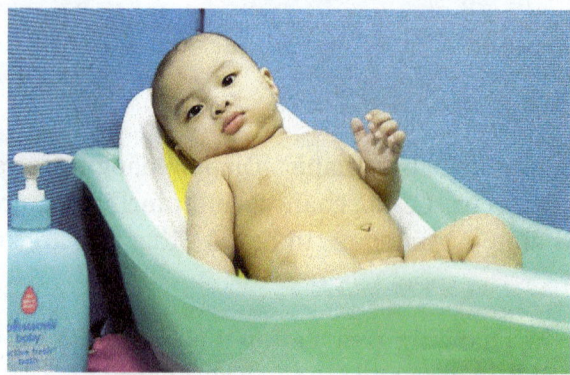

4. Bathe your baby. Babies do not sweat like adults and so will not have to be bathed as often.

Give them a bath once a week or after a particularly bad diaper. Use products that are labeled for babies and bathe them in a sink or baby bath. Never leave them unattended when they are in the water.

- Sponge bathe infants until their umbilical cord has fallen off and any circumcision is healed.

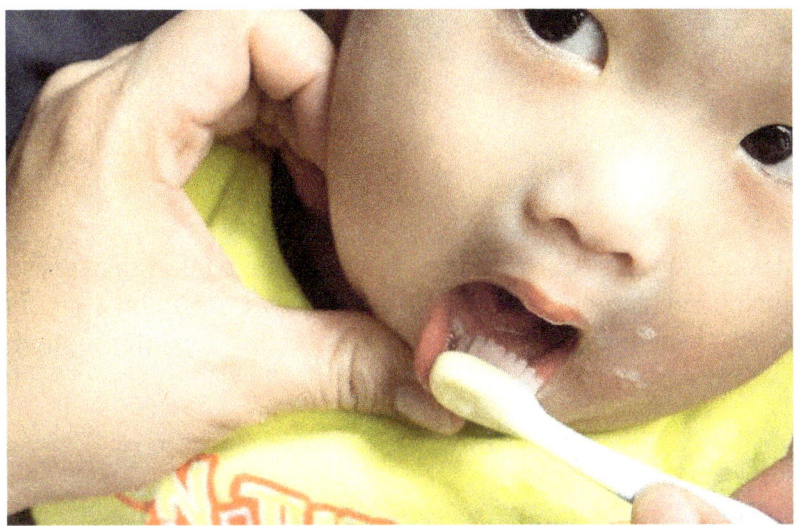

5. Don't forget to brush "teeth". Babies may not have teeth, but once they are a few months old you may want to start them brushing anyway. This will stimulate their gums and can help encourage teething. Get baby toothbrushes, which are basically rubber brushes, and gently brush their gums once every few days.

Method 4

Putting your Baby to Sleep

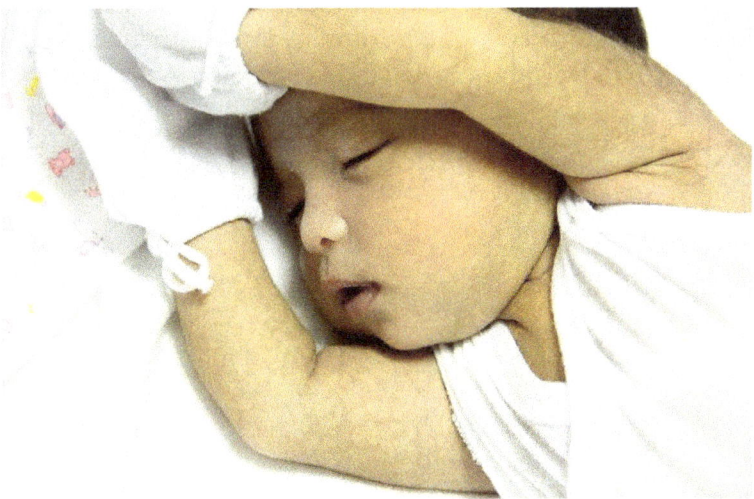

1. Be aware of when your baby sleeps. Babies do sleep a lot but not for very long periods of time. Each child will have it's own natural sleep rhythm which you will learn with time. Try to accommodate it and plan your own sleep schedule as much as you can.

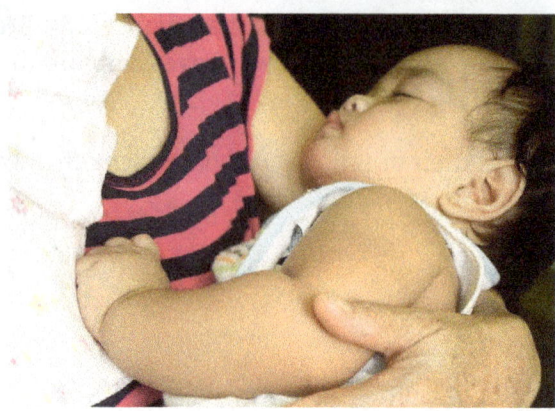

2. Know how to put your baby to sleep. Your baby may need help falling asleep, so know some basic ways to help your baby. You can hold your baby in your arms or up on your shoulder and either walk with them or rock them in a chair. Babies respond well to repetitive sounds, so make cooing sounds or you can sing them a lullaby.

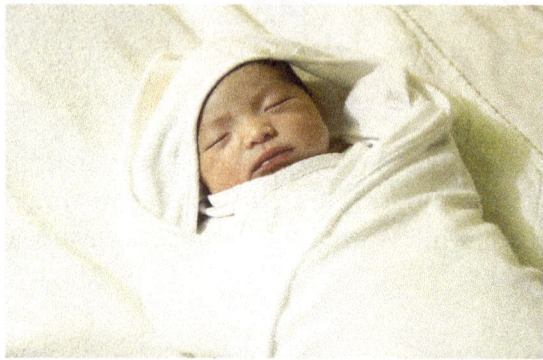

3. Understand swaddling. Swaddling is a method of wrapping up a baby in a blanket so that they don't move. While it might seem strange to an adult, it is extremely comforting for a baby as it makes them feel secure. It will also keep them from surprising themselves if they move in their sleep. Watch the video below to learn how to swaddle your baby.

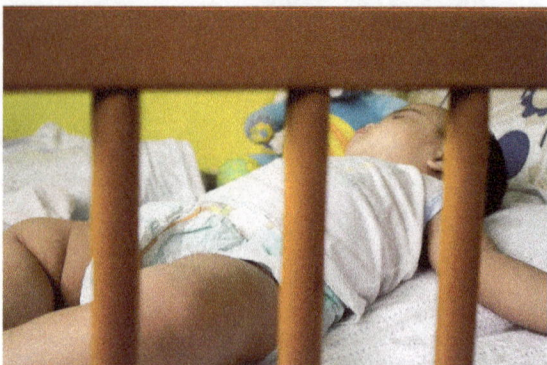

4. Avoiding SIDS. SIDS, or sudden infant death syndrome, is a very mysterious condition which you will want to protect against. No one particularly understands what causes it and some question whether it exists at all, but there are a few practices which seem to be related to the deaths. Avoid these and your baby should be fine:

- Protect your baby by always putting them to sleep on their back

- Don't put a pacifier into your baby's mouth

- Use a firm mattress in your baby's crib

- Remove soft or fluffy bedding and stuffed animals

Method 5

Playing with Him or Her

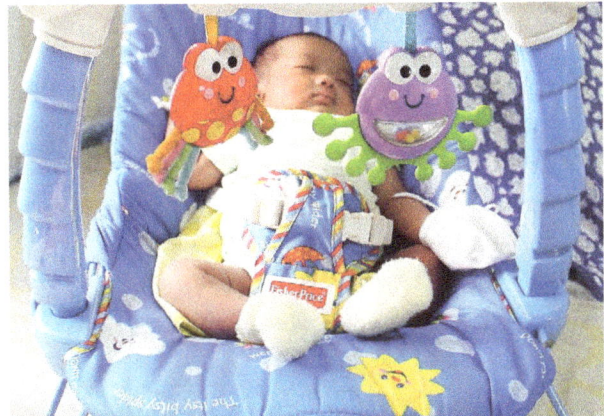

1. Sit your baby in infant swings and seats. These will allow your baby to see the action going on around them, as well as a comfortable place to fall asleep if they get tired during the day. Try to get seats which bounce in response to your child's movement and swings that can swing themselves. These will help keep baby entertained while you get things done. Just don't leave them unattended.

2. Let your baby play with toys. Once babies are old enough to hold objects, you can give them toys to play with. Get age appropriate toys that they can put in their mouths, as this is baby's favorite way to play! Toys that make sounds or have lights are particularly fun for your baby.

- It is easy to make many toys that your baby can play from objects you find around the house. You do not need to spend a lot of money. For example, you can tie a bunch of plastic bags into a clean sock so that you have a soft ball which crinkled when you squish it. Baby will be fascinated.

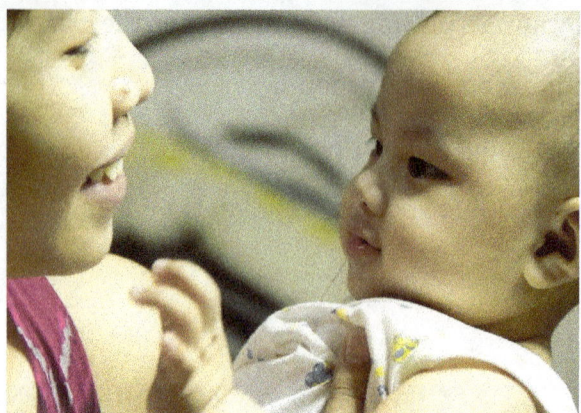

3. Sing to your baby. Sing your baby lots of songs. This will make them very happy, help the two of you bond, and will also help their brains develop. Sing songs that you like or children's songs that you know! You will create memories to last a lifetime if you choose a song that is just for the two of you.

4. Read with your baby. Read your baby lots of books. This will accommodate them to the idea of reading early on and will help their brains develop by exposing them to the rhythm and sounds of language. Make your reading entertaining by moving your hands across the page and using your "exciting" voice.

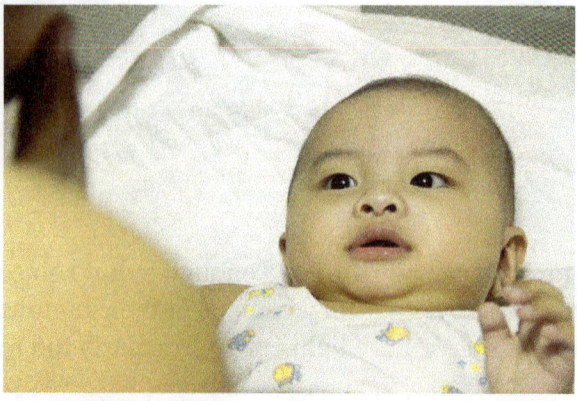

5. Socialize your baby. Your baby will need to spend time around other children of a similar and different age. This will help your child learn to interact and be around others. Set up play-dates so that your baby gets to spend playtime with a friend.

- Play with others in small groups. Your baby will become easily overwhelmed unless they are naturally very, very social so try to schedule play-dates with only one or two other children at a time.

- Let your baby watch you socialize. Your baby will learn a lot by watching you interact with your friends and other children. Relax while you are around other people, as your baby can pick up on your tension and may feel that other people should be feared. Be friendly and open and smile as you talk with other people. Hug them when it is appropriate. Your baby will learn that this is how we interact with others.

- Don't be too protective. Your baby should be allowed to get into arguments with their friends. Even a little physical fighting is not unexpected. Try to let your baby sort these things out on their own, as this is how they learn to interact with other people. If you pick them up at the slightest sign of trouble then they will never learn.

Method 6

Dealing with Illness

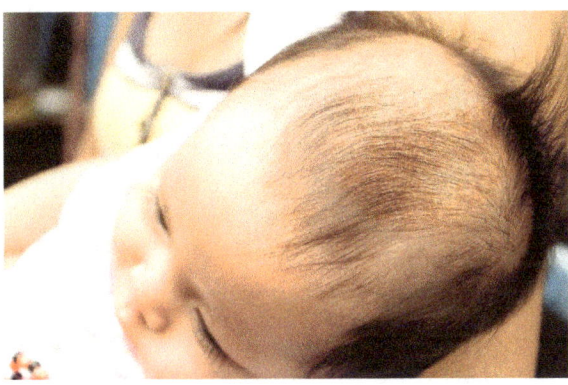

1. Don't stress about cradle cap. Cradle cap is a skin condition that is very normal for newborns. This will look like a scaly, yellow or white series of patches on their skin. It is not a serious condition and should resolve itself in a few months. If it seems overly severe, talk to your doctor.

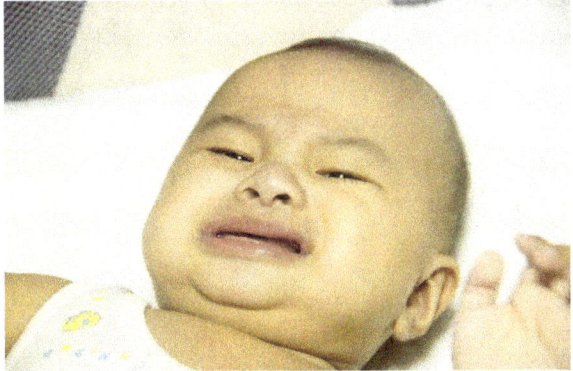

2. Look out for colds. Colds are normal in small children and should not be a cause for concern. Usually they will go away from two weeks. However, if your child is younger than 2-3 months, go to doctor as this can result in more serious health conditions.

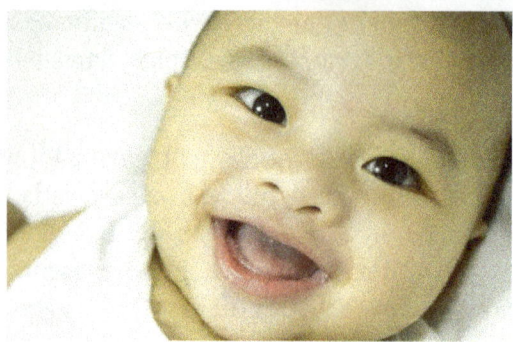

3. Deal with thrush. Thrush is an oral yeast infection, usually a result of taking antibiotics. It will appear as whitish patches in and around the mouth or cracks at the corners of the mouth. Prevent thrush by keeping bottles and pacifiers clean. Though it is not a terribly threatening illness, if your child contracts thrush you should talk to your doctor to get the appropriate creams to treat the problem.

Method 7

Caring for your Baby Outside

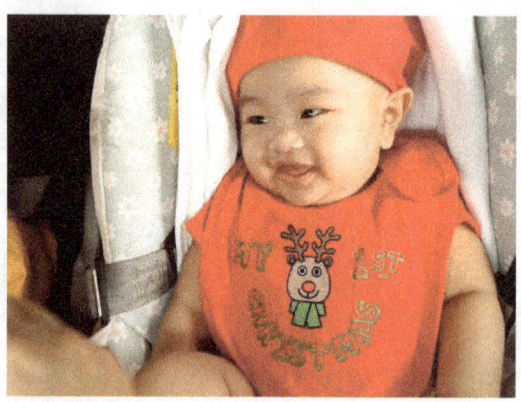

1. Get a car seat. You will need to get a car seat before your baby is born, as one will be necessary to take your new baby home. Be sure to always use a car seat which is appropriate for the age and weight of your child. Rear-facing car seats are the safest and should be used until your child is at least 1 year old.

2. Use a stroller or baby carrying wrap. You will want a method to carry your baby while you are shopping or out walking around. You can get a stroller and push them or, if you want to save space, carry your baby in a carrying wrap. These are perfectly comfortable for both of you and will also help you bond.

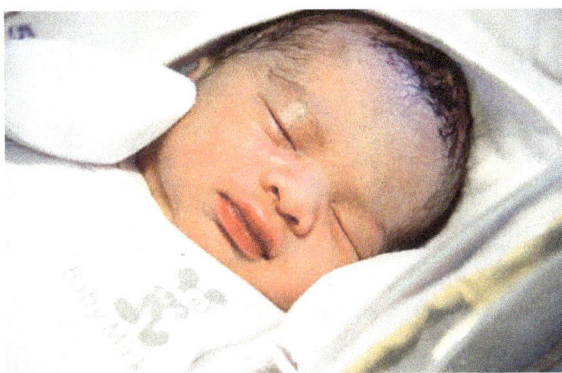

3. Be careful where you take your newborn. Newborns have very weak immune systems and should be exposed to as little illness as possible. Do not take them to very crowded or dirty places, avoid other children's birthday parties, and encourage others to touch the baby only on their feet (rather than the face or hands) to keep illness from spreading.

How to Swaddle a Newborn

Are you a tired new parent trying to get your newborn baby to sleep through the night? Wondering how to duplicate the swaddling technique demonstrated by the nurse in the hospital? An amazing swaddle could be your key to a good night's sleep. It may seem like a lot of complicated folding, but properly swaddling you baby is very easy.

Part 1

Folding the Swaddling Blanket

1. Obtain your swaddling blanket. Be sure to use a cotton blanket that is at least 24 x 24 inches.

- This is the standard size for swaddling a nearly newborn baby. As the baby grows, you may need to use a larger blanket, about 40 x 40 inches.

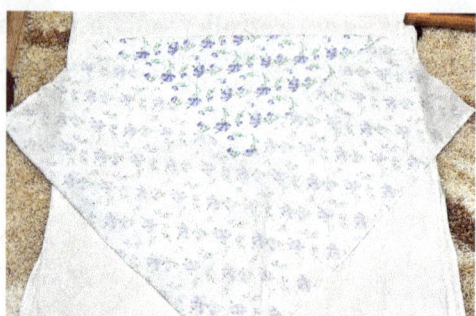

2. Fold the blanket for swaddling. Position the swaddling blanket on a flat surface such as carpeting or on a bed. Rotate the square blanket so the corners of the blanket are pointed up, down, and to the sides, or in a diamond shape, rather than being in the position of a normal square. Fold the top corner of the blanket down about eight inches.

- If the baby is bigger, you are going to fold less of the top corner down. If the baby is smaller, you are going to fold the top corner down further.

- If you wish you can fold the folded fabric down one more time to make an approximate 2 inch ridge. This offers more neck support, but it's not necessary.

- The blanket should now look like a diamond or the Superman symbol.

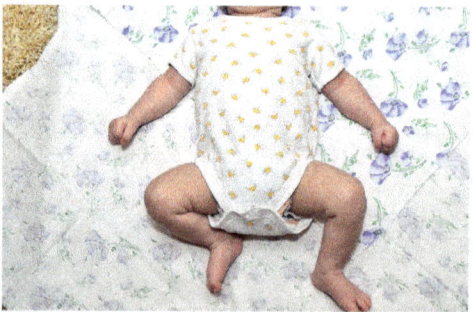

3. Place you baby on the blanket. Place your baby in the center of the blanket, with the top of the baby's shoulders right at the folded top.

Part 2

Swaddling the Baby

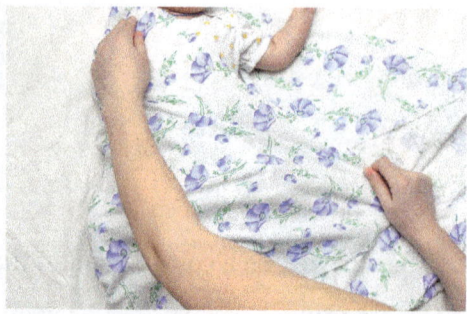

1. Make the first swaddle fold across the baby. Hold the baby's left hand and place it at his hip.

Allow the baby's elbow to be slightly bent. Take the left corner of the blanket, and bring it across the baby to his right side.

- Allow his right arm to be free once you bring the blanket across to his right side.

- Roll the baby to his left so you can tuck the blanket underneath his back.

2. Fold the bottom of the blanket. Grab the bottom corner of the swaddling blanket and bring it up toward the baby. The corner is going to be tucked behind the baby's back, near her right shoulder. Make sure that the baby's right arm is held down at her hip, again with her elbow slightly bent.

- Don't pull the bottom corner of the blanket too tight. You want the baby to have some mobility and freedom to kick her legs as they're swaddled. However, you do want the blanket taut enough so when the baby does kick, she feels a little bit of resistance.

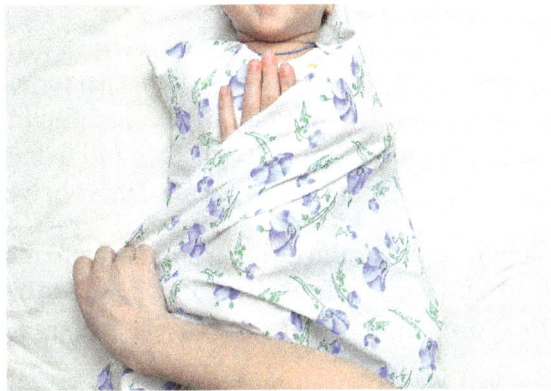

3. Make the last swaddle fold across the baby. Hold the blanket in place by lightly placing your hand on the baby's chest. Use your other hand to grab the folded piece of blanket approximately five inches away from your baby's neck. Bring this portion of the blanket over to the center of the baby's chest to make a slight V-neck. Hold this V in place with your thumb.

- Then pick up the last corner of the swaddling blanket (the right corner), and bring it across the baby and up to his left shoulder. Again, tuck the remaining blanket behind and underneath the baby's back.

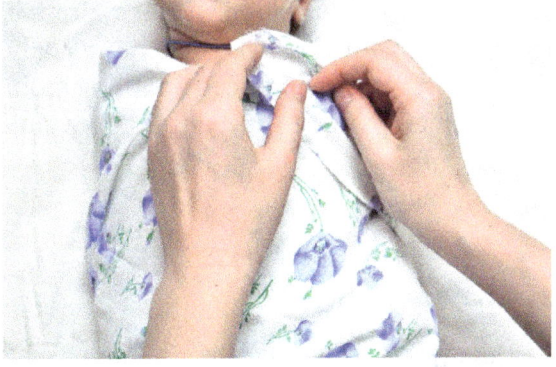

4. Tuck in the loose corner. With the last portion of the blanket wrapped around the baby, take the corner of the blanket, pull it horizontally across the baby's back, and bring it over to the front of the baby's right shoulder to tuck it into one of the blanket folds.

How to Clean a Circumcision

Though it is a routine procedure, a circumcision requires proper care and cleaning to heal properly. When caring for a newly circumcised newborn, clean the area after every diaper change, keep the area dry, wash the wound gently, let it air dry, dress the wound with gauze and vaseline, and do frequent diaper changes. When caring for an adult circumcision, soak the wound 48 hours after the procedure to remove the initial bandage, change the dressing every day or two, shower carefully, and keep it dry. Watch for possible signs of infection like persistent redness, swelling, bleeding, and yellow discharge, as well as sores or difficulty urinating.

Part 1

Caring for a Newborn's Circumcision

1. Clean the area after every diaper change. After every diaper change, make sure that no stool or urine remain on the circumcision area. Gently clean it with a soft cloth soaked with water and a mild baby soap, then dab it with a clean, wet cloth to rinse. Avoid using baby wipes on the area for at least the first 7-10 days as they may be abrasive and cause your baby pain.

2. Let the area air dry. After cleaning, allow the circumcision area to air dry on its own. Towel drying can cause irritation to the wound while it is healing. If you give your baby a sponge bath, gently dry the rest of their body with a towel and avoid the circumcision area.

3. Check and change your baby's diaper frequently. To prevent infection or irritation, check your baby's diaper frequently. Newborns may urinate 20 times a day, so check your baby's diaper every 2-3 hours (also when the baby cries, or you just sense a change is needed) to make sure it is not wet or soiled. Urine and stool may cause an infection to the circumcision wound if left for too long.

4. Opt for sponge baths. During the 7-10 days that your baby's circumcised penis is healing, avoid submerging it in water. Give your baby sponge baths with water and a mild baby soap. Wash your baby's head, face, and body separately, making sure to dry each area and cover your baby between parts to keep them warm.

5. Dress the wound. While your baby's circumcision is healing, dress it to keep your baby's diaper from rubbing against it. Follow your doctor's instructions, but usually after cleaning and air drying, gently cover the wound area with vaseline to keep anything from sticking to it. Your doctor may also recommend wrapping a small piece of gauze around the circumcision before putting on your baby's diaper.

Part 2

Looking After an Adult Circumcision

1. Avoid a bath or shower for the first 48 hours. During the first 48 hours after an adult circumcision, avoid getting the wound wet by skipping a bath or shower. Instead, clean up with a wet cloth or towel, avoiding the bandaged area. The circumcision wound should be watertight after 48 hours.

2. Remove the initial bandage. The bandage and gauze applied by the doctor after the circumcision should be removed 48 hours after the procedure by soaking the area in a shallow bath. Fill a bath or basin with warm water and salt (epsom salt or regular table salt) to promote healing. Let the water soak the bandage long enough to allow you to remove it without pieces of gauze sticking to the wound.

- Only soak the area long enough to remove all the dried blood and gauze fibers from the area, then pat it dry gently with clean gauze.

3. Apply clean bandages regularly. Change your bandages every 24-48 hours, or if they get wet. A few drops of urine can be overlooked, but liquid that saturates through the bandage will be cause for a new dressing. Apply a small amount of vaseline to the glans and shaft of the penis to prevent the bandage from sticking to the skin.

4. Wait at least 2 weeks before a bath. While a shower can be safe for the circumcised penis after 48 hours, the wound should not be submerged in a bath until it is healed (with the exception of removing the initial dressing). Taking a bath can wash bacteria into the wound, which may cause an infection. Initial healing normally takes 2-3 weeks, though healing time may vary depending on an individual's age, lifestyle, and medical history.

5. Shower carefully. When showering during the time the circumcised penis is healing, avoid letting the shower stream hit the wound directly. Shelter the wound site with your hand to prevent injury. Your hand will absorb the force of the water while still allowing the area to get wet.

Part 3

Monitoring the Wound

1. Check for redness, swelling or a fever. Check the wound site for signs of redness and swelling. Redness and swelling of the circumcision area are both normal during the 7-10 days it takes to heal. If the area grows redder or more swollen 5-10 days after the procedure, or if the area seems warm or more painful, contact your doctor since this could indicate an infection. Call your pediatrician right away if your baby has a fever (100.4° F or higher rectally), he will need to be seen immediately.

2. Look for blood. Check for signs of blood during the first few days after the circumcision. A few drops of blood (smaller than the size of a quarter) are normal during this period. Larger drops of blood, and more persistent bleeding, are signs for concern and warrant an immediate call to your doctor or child's pediatrician.

3. Watch for lasting yellow or green discharge. A small amount of scabbing and yellow discharge is normal during the healing process, but it is a cause for concern if it lasts longer than a week. Also note if the discharge is green, has a bad smell or is increasing in amount as this can be signs of an infection. Check the circumcision site carefully for discharge. If you see any 7 days after the procedure, contact your pediatrician.

4. Inspect the wound site for sores. While a small amount of scabbing is normal while the circumcision site heals, you should not see any sores around the area. Check the wound for sores, and contact your doctor immediately if you see any. Crusty, fluid-filled sores may be a sign of infection.

5. Keep track of urination. In the case of both newborn and adult circumcisions, a problem with urination is an important warning sign of complications or an infection. If your newborn does not urinate within 6-8 hours of the procedure, call your pediatrician immediately. If there is any pain or difficulty urinating following an adult circumcision, contact your doctor right away.

How to Burp a Sleeping Baby

When a baby burps, they release gas and feel more comfortable. Most young babies who like to nurse at night often fall asleep while they are eating, but still, need to be burped. So, it's important to find a burping position that allows your baby to burp properly but doesn't wake them up. If you create the right environment for a good burp and find the right method for burping your baby based on their eating and sleeping patterns, you should have no trouble getting your sleeping baby to burp.

Part 1

Choosing the Right Burping Method

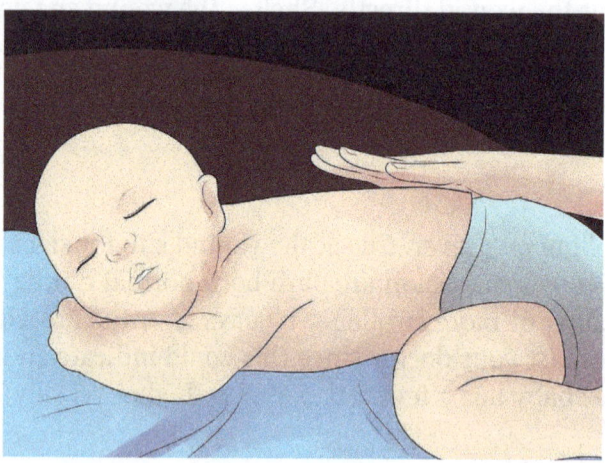

1. Hold your baby and burp them. This technique is good for babies who sleep on their stomach or who like to cuddle when they sleep.

- Slowly move your baby next to your body so you do not wake them up.

- Allow your baby's head or chin to rest on your shoulder and cup their bottom to support them so they don't slip as you hold them.

- Place your other hand on their back and gently pat it to help them burp.

- If your baby has developed control of their head and neck, you can try to hold your baby at a slight distance from your shoulder to burp them. Position your baby's tummy near your shoulder and gently press their tummy using your shoulder. Make sure your baby is still breathing comfortably and cup their bottom with one hand while placing the other hand on their back. Continue to gently press their tummy with your shoulder until they burp.

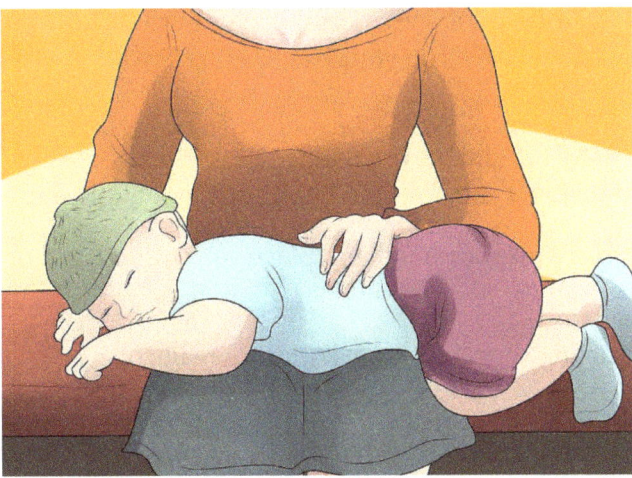

2. Lay your baby down and burp them. This method is great if you are already lying next to your baby and feeding them, as all you need to do is pull your baby close and prop their head and tummy against your lap.

- Place your baby on your lap, perpendicular to your body.

- Put their tummy on your leg and gently apply pressure to your baby's tummy with your leg. Make sure your baby's body is even across your legs so blood does not rush to their head.

- Tilt your baby's head to one side so they can breathe properly even when they are lying on their tummy.

- Use your hand to support their head by placing your thumb and index finger on their jaw or chin, just below their ear. Do not place your hand against their neck or near their throat as you don't want to choke your baby or constrict their breathing.

- Wait until your baby burps.

3. Lean your baby against your body. This technique works best for babies who like to sleep on their stomach and for heavy sleepers, as it can be difficult to get your baby into position without waking them up.

- First, lean back slightly against a comfortable chair or couch forming a 130 degrees angle. You can also use several pillows on your bed to elevate yourself instead of sitting on a chair or couch.

- Slowly lean your baby up against your body. Have them face down. Their head should be on your chest and their stomach should be against your stomach.

- Support their bottom with your hand and place your other hand on their back to gently pat them.

- Continue lightly patting your baby's back until they burp.

Part 2

Creating an Ideal Burping Environment

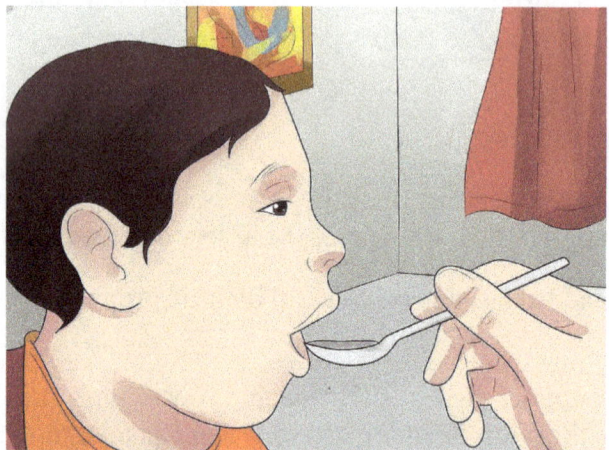

1. Feed your baby in a quiet, distraction-free room or area to cut down on their burps. Most babies are more likely to swallow air when they are distracted by loud noises or voices during feeding, which can cause them to become gassier and need to burp more often.

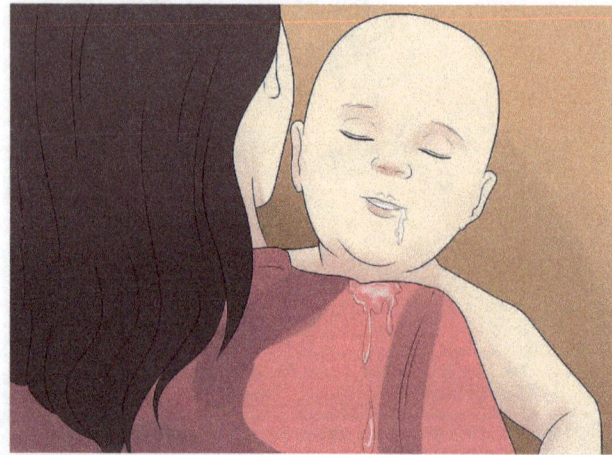

2. Don't be alarmed if your baby spits up as they burp. This is a common part of burping and occurs because the air in your baby's stomach is usually trapped in the milk they just ate, so when the air

comes out, the milk comes along with it. You may notice that milk also comes out of your baby's nose. Spit up from the mouth and nose is a normal thing for many babies to do as they burp so don't worry if this happens.

- Spit up can also be caused by reflux. Reflux occurs when milk and gastric juices flow back up from the baby's tummy and come out of their mouth, resulting in the baby spitting up. If your baby keeps spitting up a large amount of milk, you may want to try the upright position of burping by holding your baby or leaning your baby to avoid milk from flowing back to their mouth.

- Your baby should outgrow spitting up when they reach 12 to 24 months of age.

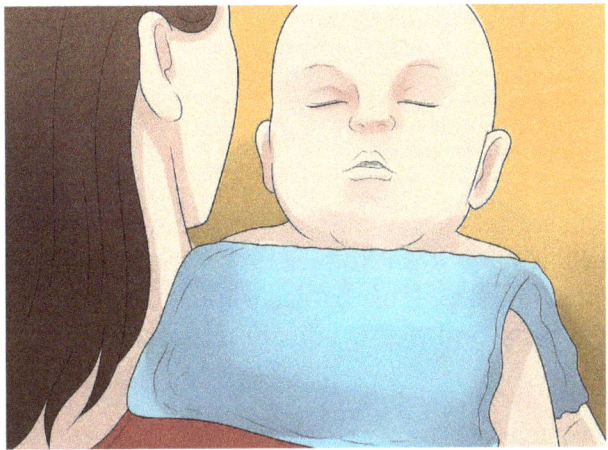

3. Put a clean cloth over your shoulder or chest as you burp your baby. This will help you avoid getting the baby's spit-up on your clothes. You can also use the clean cloth to wipe your baby's mouth and nose as you burp them.

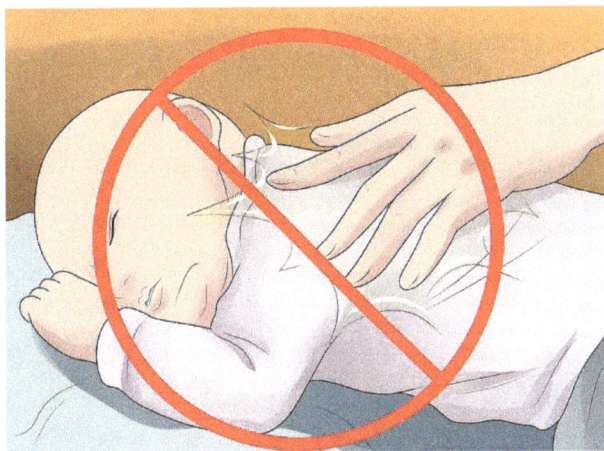

4. Avoid forcing your baby to burp if they seem comfortable after feeding. It's okay if your baby does not burp after every feeding, as long as they appear comfortable and not gassy. Your Baby may burp during their next feeding or burp more, which is fine.

- Always pat your baby gently on their back as your burp them as a hard or sharp pat does not encourage your baby to burp any faster or easier.

Part 3

Understanding your Baby's Burping Habits

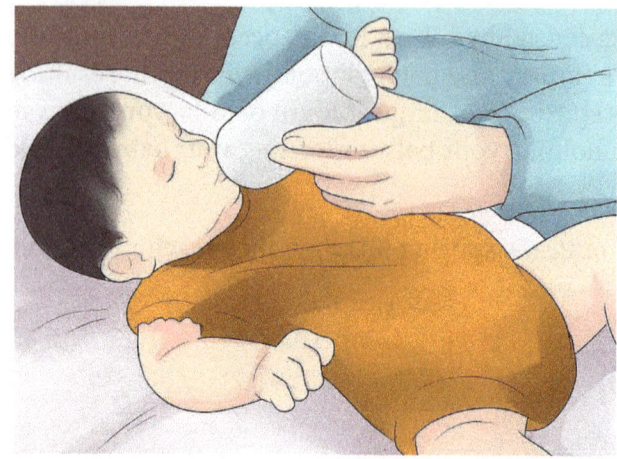

1. Notice if your baby squirms or gets fussy while you feed them. Because most babies can't just tell you when they need to burp, it's important to pick up on your baby's body language to recognize when they are gassy and need to burp. Most babies who need to be burped are typically squirmy during their feeding and get fussy, and visibly uncomfortable.

- Burping is essential for infants as they need to let go of the gas in their bodies due to drinking milk. So, it is especially important to encourage them to burp when they fall asleep during their feeding.

- Most babies burp on their own at around two months old and outgrow burping by around four to six months old, so you don't need to worry about burping them after that point.

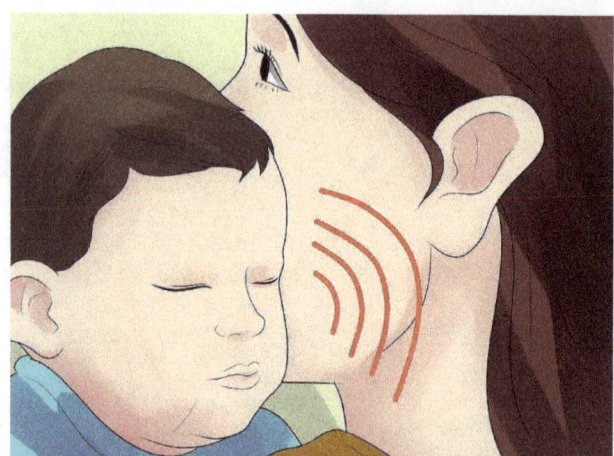

2. Keep track of your baby's burps after feeding. Notice how frequently they need to be burped after each feeding. If your baby doesn't burp much during they day, chances are you don't need to worry about burping them at night.

- Most babies who eat at night don't need to be burped because they nurse less anxiously at night and as a result, suck in less air.

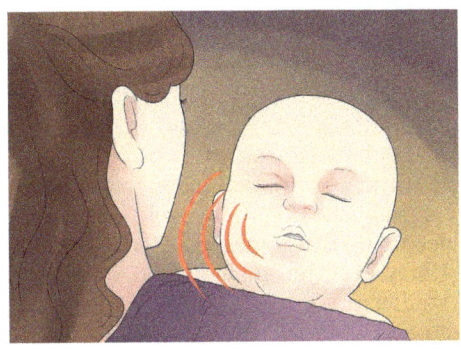

3. Remember that some infants may burp more often than others. This could be because of the way they are being fed, as bottle fed infants usually swallow more air than those that breastfed, and will have more gas.

- In general, most breastfed babies need to be burped when you switch breasts and when the feeding is complete. Bottle fed babies should generally be burped every two to three ounces of milk they drink.

- If you are bottle feeding your baby, look for specialist feeding bottles that eliminate air during feeding, thereby lessening the amount of air being trapped inside your baby's tummy.

Permissions

All chapters in this book are published with permission under the Creative Commons Attribution Share Alike License or equivalent. Every chapter published in this book has been scrutinized by our experts. Their significance has been extensively debated. The topics covered herein carry significant information for a comprehensive understanding. They may even be implemented as practical applications or may be referred to as a beginning point for further studies.

We would like to thank the editorial team for lending their expertise to make the book truly unique. They have played a crucial role in the development of this book. Without their invaluable contributions this book wouldn't have been possible. They have made vital efforts to compile up to date information on the varied aspects of this subject to make this book a valuable addition to the collection of many professionals and students.

This book was conceptualized with the vision of imparting up-to-date and integrated information in this field. To ensure the same, a matchless editorial board was set up. Every individual on the board went through rigorous rounds of assessment to prove their worth. After which they invested a large part of their time researching and compiling the most relevant data for our readers.

The editorial board has been involved in producing this book since its inception. They have spent rigorous hours researching and exploring the diverse topics which have resulted in the successful publishing of this book. They have passed on their knowledge of decades through this book. To expedite this challenging task, the publisher supported the team at every step. A small team of assistant editors was also appointed to further simplify the editing procedure and attain best results for the readers.

Apart from the editorial board, the designing team has also invested a significant amount of their time in understanding the subject and creating the most relevant covers. They scrutinized every image to scout for the most suitable representation of the subject and create an appropriate cover for the book.

The publishing team has been an ardent support to the editorial, designing and production team. Their endless efforts to recruit the best for this project, has resulted in the accomplishment of this book. They are a veteran in the field of academics and their pool of knowledge is as vast as their experience in printing. Their expertise and guidance has proved useful at every step. Their uncompromising quality standards have made this book an exceptional effort. Their encouragement from time to time has been an inspiration for everyone.

The publisher and the editorial board hope that this book will prove to be a valuable piece of knowledge for students, practitioners and scholars across the globe.

Index

CPSIA information can be obtained
at www.ICGtesting.com
Printed in the USA
BVHW061958260822
645617BV00004B/209